Effective Teaching Strategies That Accommodate Diverse Learners

Edward J. Kameenui
University of Oregon

Douglas W. Carnine
University of Oregon

Merrill,
an imprint of Prentice Hall
Upper Saddle River, New Jersey   Columbus, Ohio

Library of Congress Cataloging-in-Publication Data

Effective teaching strategies that accommodate diverse learners / [edited by] Edward J. Kameenui, Douglas W. Carnine.

      p. cm.

    Includes bibliographical references and index.

    ISBN 0-13-382185-4 (pbk.)

      1. Teaching—United States. 2. Multicultural education—United States. 3. Minorities—Education—United States. 4. Curriculum change—United States. I. Kameenui, Edward J. II. Carnine, Douglas.

    LB1025.3.E36   1998

    371.102—dc21   97-12048
                                                             CIP

Cover photo: Phyllis Picardi/International Stock
Editor: Ann Castel Davis
Production Editor: Louise N. Sette
Photo Researcher: Jason Brainard
Design Coordinator: Julia Zonneveld Van Hook
Text Designer: Pagination
Cover Designer: Raymond Hummons
Production Manager: Deidra M. Schwartz
Electronic Text Management: Marilyn Wilson Phelps, Matthew Williams, Karen L. Bretz, Tracey B. Ward
Illustrations: Barry Bell Graphics
Director of Marketing: Kevin Flanagan
Marketing Manager:,Suzanne Stanton
Advertising/Marketing Coordinator: Julie Shough

This book was set in Century Schoolbook by Prentice Hall and was printed and bound by R.R. Donnelley & Sons Company. The cover was printed by Phoenix Color Corp.

© 1998 by Prentice-Hall, Inc.
Simon & Schuster/A Viacom Company
Upper Saddle River, New Jersey 07458

Photo credits: Anne Vega/Merrill, pp. 1, 19, 45, 113, 161, 179; Scott Cunningham/Merrill, pp. 71, 93, 139.

Printed in the United States of America

10 9 8 7 6 5 4 3

ISBN: 0-13-382185-4

Prentice-Hall International (UK) Limited, *London*
Prentice-Hall of Australia Pty. Limited, *Sydney*
Prentice-Hall of Canada, Inc., *Toronto*
Prentice-Hall Hispanoamericana, S. A., *Mexico*
Prentice-Hall of India Private Limited, *New Delhi*
Prentice-Hall of Japan, Inc., *Tokyo*
Simon & Schuster Asia Pte. Ltd., *Singapore*
Editora Prentice-Hall do Brasil, Ltda., *Rio de Janeiro*

PREFACE

This book is about diverse learners—students who, by virtue of their instructional, experiential, cultural, socioeconomic, linguistic, and physiological backgrounds, bring different and oftentimes additional requirements to instruction and curriculum. What are these "different" and "additional" instructional and curricular requirements? Why are they different? Why are "additional" instructional and curricular requirements necessary for these learners? What is it about diverse learners that requires teachers, publishers, and developers of educational materials (e.g., textbooks, basal reading programs), as well as school administrators, legislators, and others, to consider these additional burdens? Will a teacher's effective response to these additional instructional and curricular requirements help the average and high-performing learners?

Although this book is about diverse learners, it would be of little value if it focused exclusively on them and their learning and behavioral characteristics, because as we see it, they are not the issue. Instead, they are the challenge, and they are *our challenge* and *our promise*. So, in the interest of full and accurate disclosure, this book is about the teaching, instruction, and curricula required to give diverse learners a fighting chance in today's classrooms as well as outside the classroom.

We offer in this text a synthesis of our critical examination over the past five years of pedagogical and curricular requirements in schools. What is demanded explicitly or implicitly of students with diverse learning and curricular needs by typical school tasks and materials in grades K–8? Based on these analyses, we have developed a core of six architectural principles for designing, modifying, or evaluating the instruction and curriculum for diverse learners. These six principles are the *core* of this text and serve to frame our analysis and recommendations in teaching beginning reading (Chapter 3), writing (Chapter 4), mathematics (Chapter 5), science (Chapter 6), and social studies (Chapter 7), and also in teaching language minority students (Chapter 8).

The text consists of nine chapters—an introductory chapter, a chapter on the characteristics of diverse learners, six content-specific chapters, and a chapter on the contextual issues (i.e., social, economic) that influence curriculum change and reform. But the heart of the text is the six principles—**Big Ideas, Conspicuous Strategies, Mediated Scaffolding, Primed Background Knowledge, Strategic Integration,** and **Judicious Review**—and the application of these principles across very different and sometimes unwieldy knowledge structures and skills in reading, science, social studies, and mathematics. We assert that these six principles serve as the organic basis if not the DNA for the design of instruction and curriculum for diverse learners.

We view these principles as stipulating the very "minimum" instructional and curricular elements necessary for the adequate design of school materials. However, architectural principles for designing instruction and principled curricular and instructional analyses are necessary but insufficient to ensure that diverse learners succeed in the classroom. As most practitioners know, the harsh reality is that the day-to-day success of teachers and children resides in the instructional and curricular details—in the examples teachers use to teach a concept such as *proportion* in mathematics; in the strategies used to make visible and clear how best to work with concepts efficiently, effectively, broadly, and deeply; in the integration of concepts across topics; and in the decisions made to schedule further review and practice that students may need to ensure that critical concepts or big ideas are not forgotten, or that these ideas are not confused with other highly similar concepts or ideas.

In this text, we offer guidelines for determining the curricular and instructional priorities in teaching diverse learners, who are typically behind their school-age peers in academic performance and content coverage. In addition, we describe concrete examples of how key concepts (big ideas) in reading, mathematics, science, social studies, and writing are taught, scaffolded, integrated, and supported. What the reader will discover is surprising conceptual and technical coherence and generality of the six principles as they are applied across the content areas. For students with diverse learning and curricular needs, there is no time to waste and little room for error and reckless experimentation. These students are deserving of our best thinking and our best instructional and curricular efforts.

Acknowledgments

We would like to thank the reviewers of this text: Jeanne M. Bauwens, Boise State University; Andrew R. Beigel, SUNY, New Paltz; Frederick Brigham, Bowling Green State University; Sandra B. Cohen, University of Virginia; Greg Conderman, University of Wisconsin at Eau Claire; and Gayle Hosak, University of Texas at El Paso.

CONTENTS

1

Introduction　　*1*

2

Characteristics of Students with Diverse Learning and Curricular Needs　　*19*

5

Effective Strategies for Teaching Mathematics   *93*

6

Effective Strategies for Teaching Science   *113*

7

Effective Strategies for Teaching Social Studies   *139*

8

Modulating Instruction for Language Minority Students   *161*

9

Contextual Issues and Their Influence on Curricular Change 179

Appendix

Big Ideas: Beginning Reading, Math, Science, Social Studies 193

Index 213

C H A P T E R

1

Introduction

Edward J. Kameenui, Douglas W. Carnine, and Robert C. Dixon
University of Oregon

STUDENTS WITH DIVERSE learning and curricular needs, primarily children of poverty, children with disabilities, and children with limited English-speaking skills, are being buffeted by numerous forces—cultural, familial, sociological, and educational—which place them at increasing social and educational risk. For example, the cultural, familial, and sociological forces that influence the lives of children *outside* of school appear to affect in subtle but profound ways how children learn about their world and themselves when *inside* school. According to Hodgkinson (1991), these forces are responsible for the "spectacular changes that have occurred in the nature of the children who come to school" (p. 10). Children from homeless shelters and preschool children are "destined for school failure because of poverty, neglect, sickness-handicapping condition, and lack of adult protection and nurturance" (p. 10).

Concurrent with the cultural, familial, and sociological changes that place diverse learners at risk, educational leaders are demanding more from *all* students. Students and teachers alike are asked to move beyond the mere acquisition of basic knowledge and skills and to integrate thinking and content-area knowledge in authentic problem-solving activities that involve "mental representations of problem situations and of relevant knowledge" (Davis & Maher, 1996, p. 5). In the early 1900s, the challenge of integrating thinking and content area knowledge was formidable, even in the education of the elite. As Resnick (1987) stated, "Although it is not new to include thinking, problem solving, and reasoning in *someone's* school curriculum, it is new to include it in *everyone's* curriculum" (p. 7).

The increased expectations of educational leaders for diverse learners are manifested in *curriculum standards*—that is, goals that indicate what students should have learned upon completion of their public school education. These standards have been developed and promoted by a range of professional organizations, each calling for curriculum changes for *all* children.

- ▼ Standards of The National Council of Teachers of Mathematics (1989): "We believe that *all* students can benefit from an opportunity to study the core curriculum specified in the *Standards*" (p. 259).
- ▼ The National Center for History in the Schools (Crabtree, Nash, Gagnon, & Waugh, 1992): "A reformed social studies curriculum should be required of *all* students in common, regardless of their 'track' or further vocational and educational plans" (p. 9).
- ▼ The National Committee on Science Education Standards and Assessment (1993): "The commitment to *science for all* implies inclusion not only of those who traditionally have received encouragement and opportunity to pursue science, but of women and girls, all racial and ethnic groups, students with disabilities, and those with limited proficiency in English" (p. 1).
- ▼ The Standards Projects for English Language Arts of the International Reading Association and National Council of Teachers of English (1996): "promote equality of educational opportunity and higher academic achievement for *all* students" (p. 2).

Research into Practice

Educational reform efforts have focused primarily on the *goals* of teaching and instruction and less on *how* the proposed curriculum standards will be attained (Cuban, 1990). Unless careful attention is given to selecting, modifying, developing, and publishing validated and effective instructional tools and approaches, the higher expectations of the curriculum outcome standards may actually increase learning failure among diverse learners. Giving careful attention to validated and effective approaches has implications for educators, as well as for publishers who create, design, develop, and publish the tools used by classroom teachers. Table 1–1 provides a framework for evaluating how and by whom the information in this book can be used.

Selecting Instructional Tools

Teachers select materials to provide the students with a beneficial instructional milieu. A critical aspect of an instructional program is its approach to big ideas and strategies, especially in preparing students for higher-order thinking. An educational tool that does not deal with big ideas but does use time efficiently to present individual concepts and strategies in a clear manner, with appropriate scaffolding and practice and review, can provide students with a benign educational milieu and thereby increase their probability of success. However, as students approach the middle-school level with its more difficult content, the lack of big ideas may result in less success, particularly for diverse learners. Furthermore, tools organized around big ideas also enrich the learning of higher-performing students.

Persons entrusted with the responsibility of selecting materials should examine how big ideas are developed throughout grade levels. For example, big ideas might be apparent in grades 3 and 4 as the foundation for more complex

TABLE 1–1
Information Use

How This Information Can Be Used	Who Can Most Realistically Use This Information
Developing New Instructional Tools	• School/District Curriculum Committees • Publishers/Developers
Supplementing or Modifying Existing Tools	• Curriculum Specialists • School/District Curriculum Committees • Teachers • Publishers/Developers
Evaluating and Selecting Instructional Tools	• School Administrators • Adoption Committees • Teachers

concepts is established. One could note how the teaching of lower-order concepts prepares students for more complex tasks. Whenever possible, new strategies should build on what has been taught earlier. After noting the overall structure of how concepts are taught, one would examine the other aspects of the program: the presentation of strategies, scaffolding, sensitivity to differences in prior knowledge, and the effectiveness of judicious review.

Modifying Instructional Tools

Teachers confront the reality of selecting available instructional tools and using them in a manner that provides effective and efficient instruction. Teachers can modify programs, for example, by supplementing existing lessons with more practice and with clear strategies and scaffolds. The modification process, though, depends on the organization of the content around big ideas. If a tool is not organized around big ideas, the modifications may support higher levels of success, but will not provide a vehicle for helping all students develop deeper understanding and problem-solving proficiency.

Identifying and Promoting Effective Instructional Tools

Ideally, developers and publishers would construct tools that enable the teacher to accommodate the entire range of students for whom a program is appropriate. It would not be realistic to expect an instructional tool for sixth-graders to be appropriate for students performing at a third-grade level. However, it would be fair to say that the tool should be appropriate for all students who pass a pretest for the sixth-grade level program. The tool should contribute to a supportive instructional environment for diverse learners while not holding back the development of higher-performing students. A key element in meeting this difficult objective is to organize the tool around big ideas. When incorporated with the other aspects of curriculum design (i.e., the conspicuous strategies, mediated scaffolding, sensitivity to differences in prior knowledge, and the effectiveness of review), teaching big ideas gives the teacher a means of establishing a strong knowledge base for all students.

We must strongly emphasize, however, that while the inclusion of the six instructional features discussed throughout this book in instructional tools would quite likely improve the effectiveness of those tools, a set of validated instructional practices does not necessarily add up to a validated instructional *program* (Slavin, 1989). This implies that publishers and developers should create "beta versions" of their tools, as software developers often do, and should field-test them prior to publication. On the one hand, we recognize that this practice imposes a burden upon publishers and developers in terms of both cost and time. We empathize with the pressures publishers face to get their product out into a quickly changing and often fickle market. On the other hand, the costs of publishing untested instructional tools are high and varied, with the highest cost exacted upon the learner who cannot easily recapture a school year or two lost to fashionable but unsuccessful experimentation. A reasonable middle ground might be to design validated instructional features into the beta version of an instructional tool, in order to dramatically improve the odds of ending up with an effective tool, and then to test that tool. Such an approach promises publishers and developers a relatively quick and successful field test, while offering teachers the promise of an effective tool that can be used for all learners.

As the expectations for student performance increase, the number of diverse learners grows larger. Meeting these new expectations in today's classrooms is a formidable challenge, one that will not be met without acknowledging that teachers of diverse learners need and deserve high-quality educational tools. Even as the specific recommendations presented in this book might be debated, effective tools must be made available to teachers. Moreover, teachers deserve ample staff development support to ensure that they will be able to use these tools successfully.

BEYOND THE DESIGN OF HIGH-QUALITY TOOLS

Validated and effective instructional approaches are characterized by the six curriculum design features that serve as the conceptual framework for the majority of the chapters in this book. However, the social, cultural, economic, and educational contexts in which such curricular and instructional strategies and tools are used are also critical. The six features identified herein are critical to the design of effective strategies and tools for students with diverse learning and curricular needs, especially when one considers the pervasive academic failure of these learners, and the typical lack of attention to this knowledge base in the development of educational tools and standards. Most of the chapters in this book apply the six features to content areas: reading, language arts, mathematics, science, and social studies. This analysis is incomplete for one large segment of our student population: students who are limited- and non-English-speaking. Consequently, a chapter is devoted to this important population. Finally, the context in which quality instructional tools are selected and used has a pervasive influence on what students learn. The next chapter examines these contexts and describes the changing demographics of students with diverse learning and curricular needs.

REFERENCES

ADAMS, M. J. (1990). *Beginning to read: Thinking and learning about print.* Cambridge, MA: MIT Press.

BROPHY, J. (1990). Teaching social studies for understanding and higher-order applications. *The Elementary School Journal, 90*(4), 367–417.

CORNO, L., & SNOW, R. E. (1986). Adapting teaching to individual differences among learners. In M. E. Wittrock (Ed.), *Handbook of research on teaching* (3rd ed., pp. 605–629). Upper Saddle River, NJ: Merrill/Prentice Hall.

COWLE, I. M. (1974). Is the "new math" really better? *The Arithmetic Teacher, 21*(1), 68–73.

CRABTREE, C., NASH, G. B., GAGNON, P., & WAUGH, S. (Eds.) (1992). *Lessons from history: Essential understandings and historical perspectives students should acquire.* Los Angeles: The National Center for History in the Schools, University of California.

CRONBACH, L. J., & SNOW, R. E. (Eds.) (1977). *Aptitudes and instructional methods.* New York: Irvington/Naiburg.

CUBAN, L. (1990). Reforming again, again, and again. *Educational Researcher, 19*(1), 3–13.

DAVIS, R. B., & MAHER, C. A. (1996). A new view of the goals and means for school mathematics. In C. Wagner & M. Pugach (Eds.), *What's worth knowing: How curriculum trends affect special education.* New York: TC Press.

DIXON, R. (1994). *Research synthesis in language arts: Curriculum guidelines for diverse learners.* Monograph for National Center to Improve the Tools of Educators. Eugene, OR: University of Oregon.

DIXON, R., CARNINE, D. W., & KAMEENUI, E. J. (1992). *Research synthesis in mathematics: Curriculum guidelines for diverse learners.* Monograph for National Center to Improve the Tools of Educators. Eugene, OR: University of Oregon.

FLESCH, R. (1955). *Why Johnny can't read.* New York: Harper and Row.

GROSSEN, B., & LEE, C. (1994). *Research synthesis in science: Curriculum guidelines for diverse learners.* Monograph for National Center to Improve the Tools of Educators. Eugene, OR: University of Oregon.

HODGKINSON, H. (1991). Reform versus reality. *Phi Delta Kappan, 73,* 9–16.

INTERNATIONAL READING ASSOCIATION AND NATIONAL COUNCIL OF TEACHERS OF ENGLISH. (1996). *The standards projects for English language arts.*

KAMEENUI, E. J. (1993). Diverse learners and the tyranny of time: Don't fix blame; fix the leaky roof. *The Reading Teacher, 46*(5), 376–383.

KAMEENUI, E. J., SIMMONS, D., BAKER, S., CHARD, D., DICKSON, S., GUNN, B., LIN, S.-J., SMITH, S., & SPRICK, M. (1994). *Research synthesis in beginning reading and literacy: Curriculum guidelines for diverse learners.* Monograph for National Center to Improve the Tools of Educators. Eugene, OR: University of Oregon.

MACAROW, L. (1970). New math. *School Science and Mathematics. 70*(5), 395–397.

MILLER, S., CRAWFORD D., HARNISS, M., & HOLLENBECK, K. (1994). *Research synthesis in social studies: Curriculum guidelines for diverse learners.* Monograph for National Center to Improve the Tools of Educators. Eugene, OR: University of Oregon.

MUTHUKRISHNA, A., CARNINE, D., GROSSEN, B., & MILLER, S. (1993). Children's alternative framework: Should they be directly addressed in science instruction? *Journal of Research in Science Teaching, 30*(3), 233–248.

NATIONAL COUNCIL OF TEACHERS OF MATHEMATICS. (1989). *Curriculum and evaluation standards for school mathematics.* Reston, VA: Author.

NATIONAL COMMITTEE ON SCIENCE EDUCATION STANDARDS AND ASSESSMENT. *Science Education Standards: A sampler.* Washington, DC: National Research Council.

OFFNER, C. D. (1978, March). Back to basics in mathematics: An educational fraud. *The Mathematics Teacher, 71*(3), 211–217.

PARMAR, R. S., & CAWLEY, J. F. (1993). Analysis of science textbook recommendations provided for students with disabilities. *Exceptional Children, 59*(6), 518–531.

RAPPAPORT, D. (1976). The new math and its aftermath. *School Science and Mathematics, 76*(7), 563–570.

RAVITCH, D., & FINN, C. (1987). *What do our 17-year-olds know?* New York: Harper & Row.

RESNICK, L. B. (1987). *Education and learning to think.* Report of the Committee on Mathematics, Science, and Technology Education, Commission on Behavioral and Social Sciences and Education, National Research Council. Washington, DC: National Academy Press.

SHYMANSKY, J., KYLE, W., & ALPORT, J. (1983). The effects of new science curricula on student performance. *Journal of Research in Science Teaching, 20*(5), 387–404.

SLAVIN, R. (1989). PET and the pendulum: Faddism in education and how to stop it. *Phi Delta Kappan, 90,* 750–758.

SMYLIE, M. A. (1988). The enhancement function of staff development: Organizational and psychological antecedents to individual teacher change. *American Educational Research Journal, 25,* 1–30.

SNOW, R. E. [in collaboration with E. Yalow] (1982). Education and intelligence. In R. J. Sternberg (Ed.), *Handbook of human intelligence* (pp. 493–586). London: Cambridge University Press.

STAVY, R., & BERKOVITZ, B. (1980). Cognitive conflict as a basis for teaching quantitative aspects of the concept of temperature. *Science Education, 64*(5), 679–692.

AUTHOR NOTE

Preparation of this chapter manuscript was supported in part by The National Center to Improve the Tools of Educators (H180M10006) funded by the U.S. Department of Education, Office of Special Education Programs.

Correspondence concerning this chapter should be addressed to Edward J. Kameenui, Institute for the Development of Educational Achievement, College of Education, University of Oregon, Eugene, OR 97403-1211. Electronic mail may be sent via Internet to Edward_Kameenui@ccmail.uoregon.edu.

C H A P T E R

2

Characteristics of Students with Diverse Learning and Curricular Needs

Scott K. Baker, Edward J. Kameenui, and Deborah C. Simmons
University of Oregon

FEW WOULD ARGUE that, for many of its students, American education is in crisis. In response to that crisis, the U.S. Department of Education has called for a "dramatic overhaul of our nation's public school system" (U. S. Department of Education, p. 1). This program for change, spearheaded in the publication entitled *Goals 2000: Educate America Act*, is designed to "dramatically reform our schools by establishing high academic and occupational standards and providing support to states and communities to help them reach those standards" (p. 1). National education goals to be reached by the year 2000 include:

> All children will begin school ready to learn.
>
> High school graduation rates will be at least 90 percent.
>
> Students will demonstrate competency in all core academic subject areas.
>
> American students will be first in the world in science and mathematics.
>
> Every adult American will be literate and possess the skills necessary to compete in a global economy.
>
> Every school will be safe, disciplined, and drug free. (p. 5)

A number of key points highlight the immensity of this challenge. First, the attainment of each goal would represent a significant improvement over current conditions in American education. For example, a recent study by the Department of Education indicated that almost half of the 191 million adults in America are either illiterate or can perform only simple literacy tasks such as finding an intersection on a street map or calculating postage for certified mail. Perhaps one of the most alarming findings was that of the 44 million Americans who have the poorest literacy skills, a full 20 percent had received their high school diplomas. While one could argue about precisely what constitutes "literacy," even for high school graduates, the national education goals would seem to represent a significant challenge.

Second, an upward trend toward the attainment of these goals is not occurring, and the forces necessary to infuse change are not readily apparent. The only statistic on trend in the Department of Education's report indicates that the number of illiterate young adults increased significantly from 1983. More ominous, perhaps, is that the number of children living in poverty has also steadily increased (Hodgkinson (1993). Poverty is associated with numerous debilitating social outcomes, including low levels of educational achievement. During the 1980s, the poverty rate for children increased 11 percent, reaching 17.9% of all children by 1989. By 1993, the level had increased to 23 percent, which according to Hodgkinson, "is one of the highest youth poverty rates in the 'developed' world and has shown little inclination to decline" (p. 620).

Finally, *Goals 2000* is meant to apply to *all* students. National goals are to be established that reflect "challenging national performance standards that define what *all students* [emphasis added] should know and be able to do in core subject areas such as science, math, history, geography, language and the arts, and support local reform efforts to make those standards a reality in every classroom" (p. 2). *All* students include the 3,000 who currently drop out of school each day, students with disabilities whose acquisition of basic competency skills can be especially challenging, students from non-English language backgrounds whose command of English is frequently rudimentary, students who have recently migrated to this country and may have very little experience with formal education, and students from extremely impoverished environments who are far from prepared to begin school ready to learn. If *all* truly refers to "all students," then the challenges we face are indeed profound.

The focus of this chapter is on students with diverse learning and curricular needs, who, by virtue of their instructional, experiential, cultural, socioeconomic, linguistic, and physiological backgrounds, bring different and oftentimes additional requirements to instruction and curriculum. The first part of this chapter highlights how changing demographic conditions in the United States are resulting in large increases in the number of students who potentially have diverse learning and curricular needs. The second part of this chapter describes important characteristics of students with diverse learning and curricular needs, to help clarify the challenge educators face in designing and delivering high-quality educational programs that work for *all* students (Carnine & Kameenui, 1992).

A DEMOGRAPHIC PORTRAIT OF DIVERSITY

Part of the impetus for *Goals 2000* has been the sweeping changes that have occurred throughout the world during the last ten years. With the movement toward a global, market-oriented economy, business and government leaders have emphasized the crucial role schools play in producing a work force capable of meeting the demands of global competition. Not only will the bulk of this work force need strong skills in traditional academic subjects like reading and math, but they also will require a level of knowledge and skill in the sciences and technology that have traditionally been expected only of students with advanced degrees. In attempting to educate all American students to a higher level than ever before, the strongest challenge facing educators is how to accomplish this task with a student population that is becoming increasingly diverse.

Hodgkinson's (1992) report for the Center of Demographic Policy of the Institute for Educational Leadership clearly highlights the increasing diversity of American society. For example, while the number of individuals in the nation increased by 9.8 percent during the 1980s, the increase in White Americans, who represent 75 percent of the population, showed the smallest increase (6.0 percent) of any group. The second largest population group in the nation, Black Americans (12.1 percent), grew by 13.2 percent, and the number of Hispanic Americans grew by an astounding 53.0 percent. Three states—California, Texas, and Florida—accounted for over half of the nation's growth during the 1980s; by 2010, over 50 percent of the youth population in each of these states will be minorities (Hodgkinson, 1992). Minorities now constitute the majority in many areas, and rapidly are becoming an increasingly large percentage of the total population. The pattern of these changes is expected to continue throughout the Twenty-first Century.

The fastest growing demographic group in the country from 1980 to 1990 was the prison population, which increased 139 percent (Hodgkinson, 1992). With over one million individuals incarcerated, the United States has the highest prison population in the world. At the time of Hodgkinson's report, seven times as many Black men were in the U.S. prisons as there were Black men imprisoned in South Africa before the end of apartheid. The relationship between incarceration and education is unambiguous: 82 percent of America's prisoners are high school dropouts. Policy implications, strictly in terms of cost-effectiveness, are also unambiguous: At a typical cost of between $20,000 to $30,000 per prisoner per year, taxpayers spend roughly five times as much money to house a prisoner as they do to educate a child.

The composition of the American family also changed dramatically during the 1980s. As Hodgkinson (1992) states, "the 'Norman Rockwell' family—a working father, housewife mother and two children of public school age—was SIX percent of all households for most of the decade" (p. 3). Dramatic increases during the decade were seen in single-parent families; those headed by women increased 21.2 percent and those headed by men increased 87.2 percent. Although single-parent families do not cause poor educational achievement, they are associated with numerous educational risk factors, including family poverty, low parental education, and domestic stress.

Poverty is perhaps the greatest risk associated with increases in the number of students with diverse learning and curricular needs. The increase in the number of individuals living in poverty, especially children, is among the most alarming demographic statistics of the 1980s. Nearly one child in four (23 percent) currently lives in poverty. The millions of children are poor but do not meet the official government definition of poverty also are exposed to the multitude of educational risks associated with poverty.

The relationship between poverty and children's educational achievement seems to be mediated by parents' level of education. In general, the more educated parents are, the more likely it is they will raise children who do well in school. The connection is relatively straightforward. Educated parents actively prepare their children for the kinds of experiences that will help them do well in school. Less educated parents are frequently unaware of the connection between home experiences and school success, and even when parents are aware of the connection, they frequently lack the knowledge and opportunities to provide positive school-related experiences to their children. Also, well educated parents are better able to help their children overcome the effects of poor or insufficient instruction than less well educated parents (Feitelson, reported in Samuels, 1995).

Understanding the connection between home experiences and school success seems to have little to do with developing effective policies to help students most in need. We have known for a long time that school achievement could be explained more by home conditions and social class than by school factors (Coleman et al., 1966). However, the complexity of variables involved in developing stronger public policy initiatives to systematically provide more

Keep ''''
👁s
open for
green disk!

tudents in the home seems slim, given the current
ment involvement in domestic programs.
, continue to face schools. A report issued recently by
rvice (ETS) (cited in Hodgkinson, 1993) highlights the
and parents' education played in the performance of 9-
specific academic areas. When tested for reading skills,
ldren could search for specific information, relate ideas,
. White children performed better than Hispanic chil-
ned slightly better than Black children. The most dra-
, were related to parents' level of education. Twenty-two
arents had some college experience read at the interme-
diate level versus 6 percent of children whose parents were high school dropouts.

The performance of children in relation to issues of ethnicity and race were strongly mediated by parents' level of education (Hodgkinson, 1993). That is, when parents' education was controlled for, White, Hispanic, and Black children performed similarly on the reading test. The same kind of results in the ETS study were found in math and science. In math, 29 percent of children whose parents had a college degree performed at the intermediate level, compared to 6 percent of children whose parents were high school dropouts. In science, 36 percent of children whose parents graduated from college could apply basic scientific information, compared to only 9 percent of children whose parents were high school dropouts.

It is important to reiterate that poverty does not play a direct causal role in achievement. Rather, factors associated with differences between home and school "cultures" are critical (Bloom, 1982). In other words, a child growing up in an impoverished environment typically does well in school if the culture of the child's home closely matches the culture of the child's school.

Nonetheless, the implications from Hodgkinson's (1992) report are clear. The number of children in the country who can be classified as diverse learners because of the special circumstances they bring to public education is growing at a pace that currently outstrips educators' abilities to keep up. Unless significant educational changes are made in response to the dramatic changes occurring in classrooms throughout the country, including the development and utilization of instructional strategies that address the needs of diverse learners, the number of children who "fall through the cracks" in public education will continue to rise.

High-Quality Instructional Strategies to Teach Increasingly Diverse Students

More than thirty years ago, the educator John Carroll (1963) proposed a model of school learning that still serves as an excellent guide for thinking about the importance of designing high-quality instructional strategies for diverse learners. Carroll premised his model on the observation that learning was a function of the time it took a student to learn or complete a particular objective. Carroll identified three factors related to the time it takes to learn an objective: characteristics inherent in the learner, the time allocated for learning, and the quality of instruction. The only characteristic inherent in the learner that educators have much influence over is perseverance, which, according to Carroll, is best addressed by focusing on the quality of instruction. Of the remaining factors, the most difficult to impact is quality of instruction. Yet quality of instruction is a crucial focus if increased standards of performance are to be reached by diverse learners.

Providing high-quality instruction may become even more difficult in the future because of diminishing educational resources and increased student diversity. As learner diversity increases, teachers are faced with the task of preparing for, and responding to, an increasingly heterogeneous group of students. One cost-effective way to help teachers provide high-quality instruction to *all* students is to ensure teachers have sufficient opportunities to *access* and *use* high-quality instructional strategies. Developing effective strategies that help teachers organize and present information to students efficiently and meaningfully requires a careful analysis of what we want students to know and understand, which requires, at a minimum, an organizational structure of knowledge.

Knowledge is organized and constructed in a way not unlike the design and construction of a building. Just as numerous raw materials are used in the construction of a building, information exists in various and multiple forms. However, just as a collection of raw materials is not a building, a bank of information is not knowledge. Building materials are joined by nails, screws, solder, plus a host of bonding agents, and then assembled to create a structure that has both form and function. Similarly, disjointed pieces of information are connected through a complex web of relationships to create knowledge—knowledge that can be used to solve problems, used to organize and structure new incoming information, and reorganized and re-assembled in endless ways to create new knowledge.

Builders rely on blueprints to guide them in assembling materials to construct buildings. For teachers, the blueprints are the instructional strategies and curriculum programs they use to help students acquire information. Students in turn use that information to construct their own individualized webs of knowledge. Instructional strategies and curriculum programs need to be flexible and robust if teachers are to have a realistic opportunity to meet the needs of *all* students in their classrooms—a truly daunting challenge given the increasing diversity of the student population.

Blueprints are complicated documents. It takes a skilled builder to use a blueprint to make a building out of a loose assemblage of raw materials. Similarly, it takes a skilled teacher to effectively use instructional strategies to help learners transform disjointed pieces of information into the webs of knowledge that define educational success.

LEARNER CHARACTERISTICS

Effective instructional strategies for diverse learners must be constructed with relevant learner characteristics in mind. In the remainder of this chapter, four important characteristics of diverse learners are discussed: *memory skills, learning strategies, vocabulary knowledge,* and *language coding,* especially as it is related to early literacy development. Important differences between diverse learners and average achievers are presented, as well as a brief description of the implication each characteristic has for the instructional design principles highlighted throughout this book. The relationship among these characteristics is emphasized.

Many other characteristics could be described that represent well established differences between diverse learners and average achievers. Some of these characteristics represent large, multi-component constructs such as intelligence or achievement motivation. Important elements of constructs such as intelligence are partly subsumed in the four characteristics of diverse learners. For example, vocabulary knowledge is typically the subtest on measures of intelligence that most closely predicts an individual's overall IQ score. Constructs such as achievement motivation are highly influenced by previous achievement success. The effective implementation of instructional strategies to help students achieve greater academic success should have a noticeable effect on students' motivation to do well in school.

Other learning differences between diverse learners and average achievers seem to be the clear result of more fundamental underlying differences. The area of reading contains several well known examples. Eye-movement differences between good and poor readers have led to interventions to address reading difficulties. However, these eye-movement differences appear to be caused *by* reading skill differences rather than being the cause *of* reading skill differences. Therefore, the remediation of reading problems through eye-movement training has been misguided (Stanovich, 1986).

It is also clear that good and poor readers use context cues differently during reading. In contrast to initial expectations, however, researchers found that poor readers use context *more* than good readers, not less. This unexpected finding was attributed to a more fundamental underlying difference: Poor readers use context cues as a word-recognition strategy, whereas good readers use context cues as a reading-comprehension strategy.

The four characteristics presented in this chapter are important in fundamental ways. First, the characteristics represent some aspect of language use which most researchers agree is the most crucial area differentiating diverse learners from average achievers. Second, the characteristics seem to play a causal role in the differences in language use between diverse learners and average achievers. Third, the characteristics represent alterable rather than unalterable variables. In other words, diverse learners can improve on these characteristics, and educators can facilitate improvement by using high-quality instructional strategies. An empirically validated framework of effective strategies is described throughout this book.

Memory Skills

Memory skills are used to receive, organize, and retrieve information to which individuals have been exposed (Swanson & Cooney, 1991). Important learning and instructional considerations related to the memory skills of diverse learn-ers are presented in Table 2–1.

For the vast majority of diverse learners, memory skills seem to be intact at the point of receiving information from the environment (i.e., the sensory input stage). Some problems at this stage may be attributable to deficits in attention, but these do not appear to seriously impair performance on memory tasks (Swanson & Cooney, 1991). Numerous differences between diverse learn-ers and average achievers have been found in how information is organized in working memory and retrieved from storage in long-term memory (Mann & Brady, 1988; Torgesen, 1985).

Working memory functions in two important ways. First, it organizes information by integrating new information with existing information (e.g., when sorting items into categories or updating the details and meaning of a story as new information is presented). Second, it temporarily stores informa-tion for the learner's use (e.g., when repeating a list of items or summarizing the story line of a television show just seen). The degree to which diverse learners' problems with working memory can be attributed to difficulties at the organizational and storage levels is unclear (Swanson & Cooney, 1991).

Learners organize information in working memory primarily through rehearsal and categorization strategies. According to Swanson and Cooney (1991), rehearsal "refers to the conscious repetition of information, either sub-vocally or orally, to recall information at a later date" (p. 108). Categorization

TABLE 2–1

Learning and Instructional Considerations in Addressing Memory Skills of Diverse Learners

Important Considerations for Diverse Learners	Instructional Implications for Diverse Learners
• Normal reception of information from the environment	• Engage in explicit instruction in effective use of rehearsal and categorization strategies.
• Problems with working memory skills (rehearsing and categorizing information)	• Emphasize long-term retention of underlying meaning of important content.
• Problems with long-term memory (storing information on permanent basis)	• Have learners actively use new information.
• Differences compared to average achievers in naming common objects, recalling or recognizing items, and repeating sentences	• Emphasize connections between pieces of information.
• Perform as well as average achievers on tasks with non-verbal components, such as recognizing and recalling abstract figures	• Connect new learning to learner's experiences.
	• Systematically monitor retention of information and knowledge over time.

involves organizing incoming information (e.g., ordering and classifying) in a way that is meaningful for the learner. Significant differences in how learners rehearse information (e.g., memorizing a phone number) and categorize information (e.g., arranging things by group membership—animals, furniture, foods, etc.) in working memory have been found between diverse learners and average achievers (Swanson & Cooney, 1991; Torgesen, 1985).

Long-term memory is where information is stored on a permanent basis. Information in working memory is transferred to long-term memory if it is used sufficiently. One's name, date of birth, state capitals, and other such knowledge is stored in long-term memory. Information is stored in long-term memory through a complex series of linkages, associations, and organizational patterns (Swanson & Cooney, 1991). The reason some information in long-term memory seems to be accessible one day and not the next stems from the strength of the connections to a particular piece of information. Individual differences on tasks related to long-term memory can be attributed to the way information is connected in memory and the strategies learners use to retrieve information.

Performance on tasks that tap working memory and long-term memory skills has been the primary means of identifying memory problems in diverse learners (Mann & Brady, 1988). For example, one of the most pervasive long-term memory tasks requires learners to name common objects (e.g., dog, house, car, flower) as quickly as possible. On these kinds of tasks, diverse learners consistently name objects less quickly than average achievers (Torgesen, 1985; Wagner & Torgesen, 1987). On related tasks requiring the verbal recall or visual recognition of recently presented items—tasks that tap working memory skills—diverse learners consistently respond less quickly and accurately than average achievers (Mann & Brady, 1988). Other working memory tasks on which diverse learners perform more poorly than average achievers include the repetition of sentences (Mann & Brady, 1988) and the recall of strings of digits or objects (Torgesen, Wagner, Simmons, & Laughon, 1990).

Diverse learners do not do poorly on all memory tasks. Numerous studies have documented that the memory problems associated with diverse learners are related specifically to tasks with a verbal component. When memory tasks involve nonverbal information, differences between diverse learners and average achievers are not readily apparent (Mann & Brady, 1988; Liberman & Liberman, 1990; Torgesen, 1985; Wagner & Torgesen, 1987). For example, tasks employing stimuli that cannot easily be named, such as abstract visual figures, typically do not produce reliable differences between diverse learners and average achievers (Torgesen, 1985). Likewise, diverse learners demonstrate performance equal to that of average achievers on tasks that require memory for nonsense shapes or photographs of unfamiliar faces (Liberman & Liberman, 1990). Torgesen and Houck (1980) gave diverse learners and average achievers a recall task in which items were either nonsense syllables or familiar patterns such as words and digits. These researchers found that diverse learners could recall the sequences of nonsense syllables almost as well as average achievers, although their recall of words and digits was severely impaired.

Designing Instruction to Improve Memory Skills   The ubiquitous demands placed on memory skills in school settings create natural opportunities to use instructional design features to address the memory problems of diverse learners. In addition, because the memory problems of diverse learners seem to be linked to language-based tasks rather than being the product of organic deficiencies, memory differences between diverse learners and average achievers may be reduced significantly given the right approach. Of the six design features addressed in this book—big ideas, conspicuous strategies, mediated scaffolding, strategic integration, primed background knowledge, and judicious review—*conspicuous strategies* is perhaps the most important feature teachers can incorporate into their classroom routines to help facilitate memory skills (i.e., the retention of information). The two strategies used most frequently to facilitate the efficient organization of working memory—rehearsal and categorization—serve as natural big ideas to enhance memory performance.

Teachers can help make rehearsal and categorization conspicuous by incorporating these skills into larger instructional issues. For example, Graham and Harris (1989) helped students with learning disabilities improve their narrative writing by teaching them to memorize the mnemonic "W-W-W, What = 2, How = 2" for seven story grammar questions:

- ▼ <u>Who</u> is the main character and who else is in the story?
- ▼ <u>When</u> does the story take place?
- ▼ <u>Where</u> does the story take place?
- ▼ <u>What</u> does the main character want to do?
- ▼ <u>What</u> happens when he or she tries to do it?
- ▼ <u>How</u> does the story end?
- ▼ <u>How</u> does the main character feel?

Teachers then modeled a five-step learning strategy which incorporated the story grammar mnemonic in writing stories in response to very descriptive pictures. Teachers used a think-aloud strategy to rehearse and complete the five-step sequence. Students completed the extended instructional sequence by using the five-step strategy to write their own stories.

It is important that teachers systematically reduce the support or *scaffolding* they provide, so that students will gradually assume responsibility for using memory strategies on their own. The sequence in the Graham and Harris (1989) example incorporated a natural reduction in scaffolding as students learned to write narrative stories. The sequence also provided abundant additional opportunities for the effective utilization of scaffolding. For example, after students demonstrate a certain degree of narrative writing proficiency using the "W-W-W, What = 2, How = 2" mnemonic and the five-step writing strategy, teachers might reduce the degree to which they concretize the steps in the writing process to teach students ways to remember a different set of strategies for expository writing.

In applying the *primed background knowledge* and *strategic integration* principles of instructional design, teachers can help students establish the important connections among units of information stored in memory. For example, teachers can help students gain an understanding of convection cells (a big idea in science) by building knowledge of density, temperature, air movement, high and low pressure, and the interrelationships among these concepts (see Chapter 6 on teaching science). The stronger the connections, the more efficiently students should be able to access information.

Teachers also can structure opportunities for students to practice making explicit the ways they are connecting new information with old. For example, students can use foundational skills in writing (e.g., main idea, active voice, subject-verb agreement) as the building blocks for learning to write within different text structures (e.g., narrative, compare-contrast, descriptive, explanatory). Finally, *judicious review* helps teachers ensure that students have maintained their conceptual and procedural grasp of important big ideas. For example, students may not recall as easily the specifics of the story grammar mnemonic and the five-step writing sequence if they have not used them recently, but it is more important that they have internalized the critical, underlying writing concepts, such as the structure of story grammar and the stages of the writing process.

Strategy Knowledge and Use

Daneman (1991) noted that learners can absorb new information only in relation to what they already know. For example, an individual who knows nothing about baseball would have trouble understanding a "sacrifice bunt." However, an individual who understands chess and the strategy of sacrificing a pawn to improve board position could gain an understanding of a sacrifice bunt as a strategy for improving the chances of scoring a run. To make this analogy, the learner engages in some type of strategy to compare the two situations. A strategy can be thought of as a reasonably efficient and intentional routine that leads to the acquisition and utilization of knowledge (Prawat, 1989). It is possible that two people with the same advanced knowledge of chess but minimal knowledge of baseball might acquire knowledge about a "sacrifice bunt" differentially because of differences in how they use knowledge.

Important learning and instructional considerations regarding diverse learners' knowledge and use of strategies are presented in Table 2–2.

The use of learning strategies occurs in many different school-related contexts, including solving math verbal problems by creating diagrams of known and unknown quantities; grouping items into discrete categories (e.g., food, clothing, furniture); writing stories by integrating awareness of story grammar, background knowledge, and the intended audience; and studying for a test using a combination of note taking, rehearsal, and summarization techniques. In general, research has found that diverse learners do not use these and other types of learning strategies as effectively as average achievers (Wong, 1991).

Strategy use in the classroom is critical to educational success. Palincsar and Klenk (1992) provided a framework for understanding the importance of

TABLE 2–2
Learning and Instructional Considerations in Addressing Diverse Learners'
Knowledge and Use of Strategies

Important Considerations for Diverse Learners	Instructional Implications for Diverse Learners
• Has difficulty monitoring learning and adjusting to task demands and learning outcomes (inactive learner).	• Ensure that necessary skills underlying efficient use of target strategy are firm.
• Has difficulty adjusting to structure of intentional learning environments—i.e., being focused and goal directed.	• Provide multiple examples of when to use and not use particular strategy.
• Uses similar strategies as average achievers, but uses them less efficiently.	• Make each step in new strategy explicit. Have learners demonstrate proficiency using each step as well as combining steps to use whole strategy.
• May use different strategies than average achievers to compensate for difficulties with fundamental aspects of problem.	
• Has difficulty giving up basic, successful strategies for more powerful ones.	

learning strategies. They suggested that learning demands placed on students in the home are fundamentally different than the learning demands placed on students in school. Home experiences provide multiple opportunities for incidental learning to occur. In incidental learning, knowledge is a natural byproduct of everyday experiences. Learning environments are unstructured, and it is generally assumed that a child's natural curiosity is the only condition necessary for important outcomes to occur. In school, however, learning opportunities are organized so that intentional learning occurs. In contrast to incidental learning, intentional learning opportunities are characterized by structure, stated expectations, and time constraints. Learners are encouraged to be purposeful, goal directed, self-regulated, and actively engaged.

According to Palincsar, David, Winn, and Stevens (1991), learners who most effectively respond to the intentional learning demands of school classrooms are those students who use conspicuous learning strategies, actively monitor task demands in relation to their own learning, and adjust their learning strategies on the basis of their own learning outcomes. A similar model is provided by Johnston and Winograd (1985), who referred to students who monitor their own learning outcomes as "active learners." Active learners use strategic, goal-directed behaviors to plan, monitor, and evaluate their learning. Palincsar and Klenk (1992) observed that these active or intentional learning behaviors are problematic for diverse learners across a number of academic domains.

Researchers have attempted to determine whether the use of different strategies or the less efficient use of similar strategies distinguishes diverse learners from average achievers. Although it appears that both instances do occur, the general finding is that diverse learners and average achievers use similar strategies but differ in how efficiently they use them. For example, Griswold, Gelzheiser, and Shepherd (1987) investigated whether diverse learners and average achievers used the same strategies for memorizing the definitions of vocabulary terms. They found that although average achievers learned more unknown words than diverse learners, the groups did not differ in the kind of strategies they used, nor in the time they spent studying the vocabulary words.

There appear to be understandable reasons for diverse learners' use of different strategies than average achievers. Wong and Wong (1986) conducted a study in which low, average, and high achievers were asked how well hypothetical students would remember passages that varied in vocabulary difficulty (easy or difficult) and organizational structure (organized or disorganized) if they were to study the passages for either 15 or 30 minutes. Both low and average achievers had difficulty explaining that it takes more time to study difficult material than it does to study easy material. Only high achievers verbalized this concept.

Wong and Wong (1986) then gave passages of easy or difficult vocabulary and organized or disorganized structure to low and high achievers and observed their study habits. Two important findings emerged: The low and high achievers spent the same amount of time studying the passages, but their study patterns differed. Low achievers studied the passages with difficult vocabulary longer than they studied the disorganized passages. High achievers, on the other hand, studied the disorganized passages longer than they studied the passages with difficult vocabulary. This pattern may have indicated that the two groups used different study strategies when presented with the same task. However, an alternate explanation is that, given the well known vocabulary difficulties of diverse learners compared to average achievers, the low achievers in this study used an optimum study strategy given the task requirements. It is plausible that the high achievers found the passages with disorganized content more challenging than the passages with difficult vocabulary.

Diverse learners also may be reluctant to give up strategies that are useful in the initial stages of learning, but which over time should be replaced with more efficient strategies. For example, a high level of automaticity in basic fact math problems is needed to solve higher-level math problems (Silbert, Carnine, & Stein, 1990). Initially, most students learn to solve basic fact problems by invoking some type of counting strategy. Not only do diverse learners take more time than average achievers to master counting strategies, but they also take longer to master automaticity of basic facts. For example, students may learn initially to solve division problem "50/5" the long way. After some practice, students should not need a paper and pencil to work the problem out, but should know the answer "automatically." An overreliance on counting strategies to solve basic fact problems prohibits a student from being able to successfully perform more complex operations. Problems at this level tend to persist even for diverse learners in the higher grades (Dixon, 1990).

Kirby and Becker (1988) indicated that lack of automaticity in basic operations and strategy use—either the use of an inefficient strategy or the use of the right strategy at the wrong time—were responsible for the majority of math problems that children experience. As they stated, the results of their studies "do not suggest that children with learning problems in arithmetic have any major structural defect in their information processing systems or that they are qualitatively different from normally achieving children in any enduring sense. Instead, the results are consistent with the interpretation that such children may not be carrying out even simple arithmetic in the correct manner, and that they require extensive practice in the correct strategies" (p. 15).

Similarly in reading, apparent differences in effective strategy use between diverse learners and average achievers may be partly attributable to problems with more fundamental learning strategies. For example, the finding that diverse learners use passage context less efficiently than average achievers to learn the meaning of new vocabulary words may be the result of strategy difficulties in reading comprehension. Both Spear and Sternberg (1986), who investigated the literature on the reading problems of diverse learners, and Weisberg (1988), who reviewed the research on reading comprehension, arrived at a similar conclusion: Diverse learners do not use reading comprehension strategies effectively. Weisberg noted that diverse learners have difficulty using strategies to integrate their background knowledge with the text material to better increase comprehension. Spear and Sternberg indicated there was strong evidence that diverse learners are less efficient at scanning text, more passive in their approach to reading, and less flexible in adjusting their reading strategies to suit varying purposes.

Spear and Sternberg (1986) made a critical point, however, in noting that even the apparent reading comprehension strategy deficiencies of diverse learners may be mediated by a more fundamental problem: generalized low reading skills. Part of what is interpreted as inherent strategy problems may be the result of reading failure itself. As Spear and Sternberg suggested, "because of their prolonged difficulty learning to read, these youngsters do not profit sufficiently from the experiences with text through which normal children seem to induce and practice strategies" (p. 9). Thus, in coming full circle, it may be that apparent strategy deficiencies on the part of some diverse learners have root causes in basic skill deficiencies. In reading, lack of strategy use in determining vocabulary meaning from context may stem from deficient reading comprehension strategies. Deficient reading comprehension strategies, in turn, may stem from more fundamental problems with basic reading skills and the consequences of prolonged reading failure.

Designing Instruction to Improve Strategy Use   It is important to emphasize that differences between diverse learners and average achievers in their use of learning strategies do not stem from organic, "inside-the-head" problems. There seem to be understandable reasons why diverse learners sometimes use different learning strategies than average achievers. They may be focusing on more fundamental aspects of a particular learning task than other students, and thus using different strategies to solve the task. In some cases they may be more reluctant than average achievers to give up strategies they have learned for strategies with which they are unfamiliar but which are necessary to solve complex problems efficiently.

Instructional design principles for strategy use focus on at least three important points. First, teachers should be prepared to address seriously the basic skill problems that frequently underlie students' poor use of strategies to solve complex problems. When diverse learners are struggling to use strategies to solve complex problems, it may be that the component tasks involving basic skills are demanding attentional resources that would otherwise be available to address the more complex components of the problem (Stanovich, 1986; 1994). In this case, more automaticity with basic skills may be needed for students to solve complex problems. From a design perspective, this has implications for initial instruction and judicious review.

Second, if diverse learners have the necessary skills to solve complex problems, then teachers should make the use of important strategies *conspicuous*. Strong *scaffolding* or support should be provided initially to ensure that diverse learners use the specific strategy correctly. Third, the *judicious review* of strategies that are not a frequent part of ongoing tasks should be incorporated into the instructional programs. In this case, it is important to distinguish strategies that are given up permanently for new strategies (e.g., using a number line for adding and subtracting, which leads directly to learning basic math facts automatically), from strategies that are still important but are not a regular part of daily tasks (e.g., how to set up a compare-and-contrast structure for expository writing).

Vocabulary Knowledge

The problems diverse learners have with memory tasks and using strategies to learn efficiently and meaningfully have learning consequences beyond the boundaries of each characteristic. For example, poor memory skills have implications for the efficient use of strategies to summarize a text. More profoundly, the learner characteristics discussed thus far have implications for skills not easily addressed by specific instructional design principles, nor easily implemented during specific instructional sessions. Rather, some skills require an instructional focus that extends across all curricular activities, in nearly all contexts. Vocabulary knowledge is perhaps the best example. Vocabulary development must occur in multiple curricular areas and in the context of multiple instructional techniques if the vocabulary gap between diverse learners and average achievers is to be substantially reduced. Important learning and instructional considerations regarding vocabulary knowledge and use among diverse learners are presented in Table 2–3.

Given the numerous factors that affect the vocabulary development of diverse learners, it is not surprising that vocabulary researchers (Anderson & Nagy, 1991; Baumann & Kameenui, 1991; Beck, McCaslin, & McKeown, 1980;

TABLE 2–3
Learning and Instructional Considerations in Addressing Diverse Learners'
Vocabulary Knowledge and Use

Important Considerations for Diverse Learners	Instructional Implications for Diverse Learners
• Vocabulary difficulties are apparent early and get worse over time, both in the number of words known and depth of knowledge.	• Address vocabulary problems early and comprehensively.
	• Match vocabulary goals with instruction.
• Word learning is partly attributable to exposure quantity. Diverse learners are exposed to unknown words less frequently than average achievers.	• Combine direct instruction in word meanings with techniques to help students become independent word learners.
	• Set goals for students to learn many words at basic levels of meaning and fewer, critical words at deeper levels.
• Reading is important vehicle for vocabulary growth. Diverse learners read much less than average achievers, primarily because reading is a frustrating and failure-prone experience.	• Have students tie new vocabulary to their own experiences.
	• Institute a strong beginning reading program as the primary vehicle for helping students become independent word learners.

Beck & McKeown, 1991; Kameenui, Dixon, & Carnine, 1987; Stahl, 1983, 1985; Stahl & Fairbanks, 1986) agree on the following points:

1. Large vocabulary differences exist between diverse learners and average achievers in terms of the number of words known and depth of word knowledge.
2. Vocabulary differences between diverse learners and average achievers are apparent early and increase over time.
3. Vocabulary knowledge of diverse learners needs to be addressed strategically and comprehensively if debilitating educational effects are to be avoided.

Research on vocabulary knowledge and instruction has begun to emphasize the importance of accurately defining "vocabulary knowledge," and implementing instructional strategies that closely match the goals of vocabulary knowledge (Baumann & Kameenui, 1991).

Baumann and Kameenui (1991) proposed that words are known at three successively deeper levels of knowledge: association, comprehension, and generation. A child with associative knowledge is able to link a new word with a specific definition or a single context. A child with comprehension knowledge either demonstrates a broad understanding of a word in a sentence or is able to use definitional information to find an antonym, classify words into categories, and so forth. A child with generative knowledge has the ability to produce a novel response to a word, such as an original sentence or a restatement of the definition in his or her own words.

In addition, Baumann and Kameenui (1991) provided a framework for thinking about the influence learning contexts have on vocabulary acquisition. When a word is embedded in a rich context of supportive and redundant information, the learner is more likely to acquire its meaning than when the same word is found in a lean context, as, for example, when the word is surrounded by other equally difficult and unfamiliar words. These researchers suggested that it also is important to understand the task conditions under which the meaning of the word is being assessed. For example, it is misleading to conclude that a student does not have partial knowledge of a word because that student fails to provide a verbal definition of the word in an unprompted context. Similarly, if a student is required to demonstrate full knowledge, but instruction is limited to providing opportunities to acquire only partial word knowledge, the problem is not necessarily that the student has difficulty learning new vocabulary. It may be that instruction does not match the outcome goals.

The number of words students learn per year is extremely large. Early estimates of new words learned per year varied from 1,000 (Clifford, 1978) to 7,000 (Miller, 1985). More recently, Beck and McKeown (1991) and Baumann and Kameenui (1991) reviewed the literature and suggested that 3,000 new words is probably the most accurate estimate of yearly vocabulary growth. Researchers have found consistently that, in addition to important differences in vocabulary size between diverse learners and average achievers, diverse learners also acquire significantly fewer new words per year than average achievers (White, Graves, & Slater, 1990).

As Nagy and Anderson (1984) pointed out, the number of words diverse learners need to learn to catch up to their average-achieving peers is too great to expect direct instruction alone to make a serious impact. These researchers suggested that "any approach to vocabulary instruction must include some methods or activities that will increase children's ability to learn words on their own" (p. 325), and that "for enhancement of children's vocabulary growth and development, there can be no substitute for voluminous experience with rich, natural language" (Anderson & Nagy, 1991, p. 722). Anderson and Nagy recommend that the primary way for diverse learners to be exposed to "rich, natural language" is through structured reading opportunities.

Unfortunately, but not surprisingly, diverse learners do much less reading than average achievers. Nagy and Anderson (1984) estimated that students in grades 3 through 9 read between 500,000 and 1,000,000 words of text a year and that "the least motivated children in the middle grades might read 100,000 words a year while the average children at this level might read 1,000,000. The figure for the voracious middle grade reader might be 10,000,000 or even as high as 50,000,000. If these guesses are anywhere near the mark, there are staggering individual differences in the volume of language experience, and therefore, opportunity to learn new words" (p. 328).

The reasons why diverse learners read less than average achievers are not surprising, but the consequences may be far more debilitating than even educators who recognize the importance of reading might assume (Beck & McKeown, 1991; Stanovich, 1986). Because diverse learners do not read as well, they are exposed to fewer words in print than average achievers, and given an equal amount of reading time, they naturally do not cover as much text. In addition, because diverse learners frequently find reading a frustrating experience, they typically engage in just about any activity other than reading if given the option (Stanovich, 1986). When Juel (1988) talked to beginning readers about activities they would rather do than read, 40 percent of diverse readers said they would rather clean their room than read, compared to 5 percent of average achievers. As one child put it, "I'd rather clean the mold around the bathtub than read" (p. 442).

Designing Instruction to Improve Vocabulary Knowledge   Directly teaching word meanings cannot be the *sole* instructional strategy to assist diverse learners in developing adequate vocabulary knowledge; there are simply too many words to learn and too little time for instruction. Adequate vocabulary growth occurs primarily through narrative reading and secondarily through content area reading. Thus, to develop effective vocabularies, diverse learners must become proficient readers at an early age and must read extensively outside of school. Design considerations, discussed in the next chapter, come into play in developing reading proficiency early.

Vocabulary deficiencies may have a doubling detrimental influence on learning in the content areas. We can illustrate this point with the following passage from a high school psychology text:

> If you think that a person deliberately tried to hurt you, you would say that the behavior was dispositional. This means that it is attributed to the personality of the individual. As a result, you might get angry.
>
> However, you might blame the behavior on the situation. The bus stop was crowded and the person may have lost balance. In this case the behavior was situational. This means that it is attributed to the situation or environment. Your reaction, then, might be to forget the whole incident.
>
> By attributing people's behavior to different causes, we assign meaning to various events. This meaning, in turn, helps determine our reactions and attitudes.

The intent of this passage is to teach students two new concepts deemed important by the authors: dispositional attribution and situational attribution. The most difficult category of vocabulary knowledge is new concept knowledge. At the very least, diverse learners would have to have prior knowledge of the *other* vocabulary words in the passage—behavior, attributed, situation, environment, causes, assign, reactions, attitudes—to have even a slim chance at acquiring the new concept knowledge. Students who lack knowledge of the other vocabulary words are unlikely to learn the new concepts, which at some point may become (unknown) descriptive terms for other new concepts. Vicious circles of vocabulary deficits such as this present additional challenges for diverse learners in content area subjects.

In a sense, solving verbal mathematics problems is a specialized reading comprehension issue within which vocabulary plays a crucial role. Assume, for example, that students are studying graphs of performance on a physical fitness test taken by all classes in the school. Here are two problems that could be associated with the graphs:

1. How many average students are in the school?
2. What is the average of students in the school?

Although part of the difference in the questions is syntactic, that difference is largely a result of two related but different concepts being represented by one label: average. Even simpler vocabulary words in mathematics, such as "less," can create difficulties for diverse learners who have not learned multiple meanings.

Nagy and Anderson's views on vocabulary acquisition (Anderson & Nagy, 1991; Nagy & Anderson, 1984) raise an interesting question: How is it that average-achieving students seem to acquire both deep and broad vocabulary knowledge better through the haphazard process of reading than through the controlled and purposeful process of direct instruction? Our speculation is that a clear trade-off exists between volume of reading and efficiency. That is, deep vocabulary knowledge does develop, albeit inefficiently, as students do more and more reading. Students might have to read great volumes of material to learn a concept such as *gregarious*, for instance, because they are unlikely to experience the concept frequently enough through only limited reading.

We cannot simply recommend that diverse learners be exposed to more rich language as the principal means of helping them improve their vocabularies, because their vocabulary deficits are a major impediment to doing such reading. Therefore, *in addition to more rich language exposure,* diverse learners are likely to benefit from planned vocabulary instruction that:

- ▼ focuses upon the most important concepts within a content area. In the passage above, are situational and dispositional attribution among the *most* important concepts in psychology?
- ▼ emphasizes explicit strategies for learning words and concepts from context.
- ▼ purposefully scaffolds students through the gradual deepening of vocabulary knowledge that otherwise occurs incidentally and inefficiently.
- ▼ relates new knowledge to existing knowledge. The psychology passage seems to overlook the rather straightforward association of situational attribution with the concept of "accidents," and of dispositional attribution with "on purpose" or even "intentionally."
- ▼ reviews the most important conceptual knowledge judiciously, in a way that deepens understanding as efficiently as possible.

Language Coding

The final characteristic is an important aspect of the language-based memory problems of diverse learners that has particularly strong implications for the development of reading proficiency. These language-based problems may be attributable, in part, to the way diverse learners store verbal information for use. For example, someone who hears an individual say, "the balance of power is an important concept in our democracy," is able to store and retrieve that phrase beyond the instance in which it was spoken. Research has shown that retrieving information stored in both long-term memory (Liberman & Liberman, 1990; Liberman & Shankweiler, 1985; Mann & Brady, 1988; Snowling, 1991; Torgesen, 1985; Torgesen et al., 1990; Wagner, 1988) and working memory (Liberman & Shankweiler, 1985; Mann & Brady, 1988; Stanovich, 1985; Wagner, 1988; Wagner & Torgesen, 1987) depends, in part, on how the information is stored. Important learning and instructional considerations related to the way language is coded by diverse learners are presented in Table 2–4.

It is likely that the problems diverse learners have retrieving verbal information stored in memory emanates from weakly established phonological codes. Phonological codes represent the sounds constituted in words and aid in efficiently storing verbal information (Liberman & Liberman, 1990). Average achievers store information primarily in terms of its phonological codes—that is, on the basis of the *sounds* in words. Diverse learners, on the other hand, store information primarily in terms of its semantic features—that is, on the basis of the *meaning* of words (Liberman & Shankweiler, 1985; Snowling, 1991; Torgesen, 1985; Torgesen et al., 1990; Wagner, 1988).

Studies investigating the verbal errors committed by different groups of students provide evidence that linguistic information is stored differently by diverse learners and average achievers. Torgesen (1985) reported that when

TABLE 2–4
Learning and Instructional Considerations in Addressing Language Coding of Diverse Learners

Important Considerations for Diverse Learners	Instructional Implications for Diverse Learners
• Language coding has critical implications for reading development. • Diverse learners rely primarily on semantic features to code language. Average achievers rely primarily on phonological features. • The way language is coded is strongly influenced by early literacy experiences involving the "nature" of words.	• Provide rich and varied experiences involving the meaning and sounds of words. • Provide abundant explicit experiences in making the connection between sounds in words and alphabetic counterparts.

diverse learners and average achievers were given word-recognition tasks, diverse learners committed more errors when the distracter words were similar in meaning to the target words (e.g., dog, puppy), whereas average readers made more errors when the distracter words were similar phonologically to the target words (e.g., dog, log). Numerous studies using both auditory and visual presentations of letters, words, and sentences found large differences in recall between diverse learners and average achievers when the items are phonologically distinct (e.g., *a, f, r, z; hat, dog, fun, time*), because average achievers do not encounter phonological interference when storing the different-sounding items. Recall differences between diverse learners and average achievers decrease when the items are less distinct (e.g., *b, c, e, z; hat, fat, sat, rat*), because average achievers encounter more confusion when storing the similar-sounding items (Torgesen, 1985). Other studies have established that when diverse learners and average achievers store verbal information similarly, differences in accessing information in working memory are greatly reduced (Wagner & Torgesen, 1987).

The way children temporarily or permanently store language in memory is a difficult characteristic to address directly through instructional design because the process of storing language is not easily observed, inferred, or described. In essence, learners exert little control over whether information is stored on the basis of its semantic or phonological features. Thus, it is difficult for teachers to determine the extent of storage problems, receive feedback on how students store information, and evaluate the effectiveness of approaches to enhance learners' phonological coding.

One hypothesis as to why average achievers tend to store information on the basis of its phonological codes more naturally than diverse learners is that, prior to beginning school, the average achievers have been exposed to environments that foster knowledge about the composition of words, including awareness that words can be mapped onto symbols (i.e., print), and that words are composed of discrete sounds (Adams, 1990). Phonological coding, therefore, becomes a natural and effective storage tool. On the other hand, many diverse learners do not naturally acquire facility with the phonological code and thus rely more heavily on semantic strategies, with which they are more familiar, to store information.

Designing Instruction to Improve Language Coding   One feature of instructional design that can help learners store information in working memory on the basis of its phonological codes is to strengthen the connection between phonological coding and reading acquisition. Because storing information phonologically is especially crucial in beginning reading, effective instruction may be enhanced if phonological coding is introduced early in reading instruction so as to equip diverse learners with an effective storage strategy. To date, there is little evidence that instructional strategies used with diverse learners in kindergarten and first grade include a strong focus on direct activities to improve phonological awareness (Baker, Kameenui, Simmons, & Stahl, 1994). The effectiveness of these instructional strategies can be gauged, in part, through the ease with which students acquire beginning reading skills (see Chapter 3 on beginning reading).

SUMMARY

Diverse learners and average achievers can be differentiated on many other learning characteristics besides those presented in this chapter. However, it is necessary to distinguish between characteristics that are merely consequences of other, more primary characteristics and characteristics that play a causal role in contributing to academic learning problems. For example, Stanovich (1986) has shown that characteristics such as eye movements during reading and the use of context in word recognition distinguish diverse learners from average achievers. Differences between diverse learners and average achievers on these characteristics resulted in numerous misguided intervention efforts. In fact, eye movement and context use have been shown to *result from* individual differences in reading skill, not cause them.

The learning characteristics that have the strongest causal connection to academic failure are rooted in the area of language. The connectedness among four of these characteristics were stressed in this chapter. In isolation, each characteristic would present a significant challenge for students to overcome in acquiring academic proficiency. In combination, they represent too great a challenge for students to overcome given the instructional strategies currently in use. Important points to remember about the learning characteristics of diverse learners in relation to language processing, memory, learning strategies, and vocabulary include the following.

- ▼ Diverse learners and average achievers seem to store verbal language in memory differently. Average achievers rely much more on the phonological codes of language than diverse learners. Diverse learners focus more on the semantic features of language, perhaps to compensate for their poor phonological coding skills.
- ▼ Diverse learners do not use verbal information in working memory as efficiently as average achievers. Differences in memory performance between diverse learners and average achievers are not readily apparent with nonverbal information, such as abstract shapes and figures.
- ▼ Diverse learners do not access information in long-term memory as well as average achievers. They extract information more slowly, less accurately, and in less detail. Moreover, diverse learners may have less information in long-term memory available for access.
- ▼ Diverse learners do not use learning strategies as effectively as average achievers. Diverse learners are not devoid of strategies. In fact, they tend to use similar strategies as average achievers, but they use them less efficiently.

▼ Poor strategy use by diverse learners when solving complex problems may stem from difficulties they have with more fundamental aspects of the problems, which may require different strategies to solve.

▼ Diverse learners have vocabularies that are considerably smaller than the vocabularies of average achievers. Diverse learners have more difficulty than average achievers processing word meanings to deeper levels of understanding.

▼ Deficits in the vocabulary knowledge of diverse learners exist as early as the first grade and grow increasingly large each year. The consequences of vocabulary deficits are extreme. Vocabulary knowledge plays a causal role in successful reading throughout an individual's lifetime, and greatly impacts performance in many academic subject areas.

Differences between diverse learners and average achievers in these and other learning characteristics result in deficiencies in performing basic skills and more complex, higher-level problems. Basic skill deficiencies are apparent as early as the first grade (obvious language differences are apparent before students are in kindergarten) and the gap increases steadily over time (Juel, 1988; Stanovich, 1986). It is not at all surprising that when the focus shifts to content area material, diverse learners soon demonstrate difficulties. As the content becomes more unfamiliar and learners are expected to assume greater control over their own learning and draw more heavily on their previous learning, the academic gap between diverse learners and average achievers grows increasingly wider.

These factors are alarming considering that by the year 2000, all American students are to be competent in all subject areas, highly literate, and world leaders in science and mathematics. Current trends in education and the changing demographic landscape of American society provide numerous reasons to appreciate the ambitiousness of *Goals 2000*, and the resolve necessary to meet the goals. However, the power of the data—declining test scores, breakdowns in the family structure, greater numbers of children living in poverty, increases in violence, crime, drug addiction, school dropouts, and so forth—are vivid reminders of the enormity of the challenges educators face.

Educators can assert little control over most of these factors. They can, however, assert a great deal of control over what occurs in the classroom, and they will need to if students are to acquire the knowledge needed to meet *Goals 2000*. Carroll's (1963) economical model of learning identifies student characteristics, opportunities to learn, and quality of instruction as the factors responsible for student learning.

One of a teacher's primary responsibilities is to teach students how to transform massive amounts of information into knowledge that can be used to solve increasingly complex academic problems. One of the most likely ways to ensure high-quality instruction is to provide teachers with effective strategies to assist their students. Instructional strategies should provide the plans for teachers to structure opportunities for students to turn information into knowledge, just as blueprints provide builders with the plans for transforming raw materials into buildings. Just as a builder is responsible for integrating the blueprint plans with the raw materials to construct the building, teachers are responsible for integrating strategies with information to help students assemble meaningful knowledge. The chances of success are greatly enhanced if builders begin construction with high-quality blueprints. Likewise, teachers must begin instruction with high-quality strategies.

REFERENCES

ADAMS, M. J. (1990). *Beginning to read: Thinking and learning about print.* Cambridge, MA: The MIT press.

ANDERSON, R. C., & NAGY, W. E. (1991). Word meanings. In R. Barr, M. L. Kamil, P. B. Mosenthal, & P. D. Pearson (Eds.), *Handbook of reading research* (pp. 690–724). New York: Longman.

BAKER, S. K., KAMEENUI, E. J., SIMMONS, D. C., & STAHL, S. (1994). Beginning reading: Educational tools for diverse learners. *School Psychology Review, 23,* 372–391.

BAUMANN, J. F., & KAMEENUI, E. J. (1991). Research on vocabulary instruction: Ode to Voltaire. In J. Flood, D. Lapp, & J. R. Squire (Eds.), *Handbook of research on teaching the English language arts* (pp. 604–632). Upper Saddle River, NJ: Merrill/Prentice-Hall.

BECK, I. L., McCASLIN, E. S., & McKEOWN, M. G. (1980). *The rationale and design of a program to teach vocabulary to fourth-grade students.* Pittsburgh, PA: University of Pittsburgh, Learning Research and Development Center.

BECK, I., & McKEOWN, M. (1991). Conditions of vocabulary acquisition. In R. Barr, M. Kamil, P. Mosenthal, & P. D. Pearson (Eds.), *Handbook of reading research* (Vol. 2, pp. 789–814). New York: Longman.

BLOOM, B. (1982). *Human characteristics and school learning.* New York: McGraw-Hill.

CARNINE, D. W., & KAMEENUI, E. J. (Eds.). (1992). *Higher order thinking: Designing curriculum for mainstreamed students.* Austin, TX: Pro-Ed.

CARROLL, J. B. (1963). A model of school learning. *Teachers College Record, 64,* 723–733.

CLIFFORD, G. J. (1978). Words for schools: The applications in education of the vocabulary researchers of Edward L Thorndike. In P. Suppes (Ed.), *Impact of research on education: Some case studies* (pp. 107–198). Washington, DC: National Academy of Education.

COLEMAN, J. S., CAMPBELL, E. Q., HOBSON, C. J., McPARTLAND, J., MOOD, A. M., WEINFELD, F. D., & YORK, R. L. (1966). *Equality of educational opportunity.* Washington, DC: U.S. Government Printing Office.

DANEMAN, M. (1991). Individual differences in reading skills. In R. Barr, M. L. Kamil, P. B. Mosenthal, & P. D. Pearson (Eds.), *Handbook of reading research* (Vol. 2, pp. 512–538). New York: Longman.

DIXON, B. (1990). *Research review of mathematics instruction.* Eugene, OR: Technical Report for the National Center to Improve the Tools of Educators.

GRAHAM, S., & HARRIS, K. R. (1989). A components analysis of cognitive strategy instruction: Effects on learning disabled students' compositions and self-efficacy. *Journal of Educational Psychology, 81*(3), 353–361.

GRISWOLD, P. C., GELZHEISER, L. M., & SHEPHERD, M. J. (1987). Does a production deficiency hypothesis account for vocabulary learning among adolescents with learning disabilities? *Journal of Learning Disabilities, 20*(10), 620–626.

HODGKINSON, H. L. (1992). *A demographic look at tomorrow*. Institute for Educational Leadership, Center for Demographic Policy.

HODGKINSON, H. (1993). American education: The good, the bad, and the task. *Phi Delta Kappan, 74*(8), 619–623.

JOHNSTON, P. H., & WINOGRAD, P. N. (1985). Passive failure in reading. *Journal of Reading Behavior, 17*(4), 279–301.

JUEL, C. (1988). Learning to read and write: A longitudinal study of fifty-four children from first through fourth grade. *Journal of Educational Psychology, 80*(4), 437–447.

KAMEENUI, E. J., DIXON, R., & CARNINE, D. W. (1987). Issues in the design of vocabulary instruction. In M. G. McKeown & M. B. Curtis (Eds.), *The nature of vocabulary acquisition* (pp. 129–145). Hillsdale, NJ: Lawrence Erlbaum.

KIRBY, J. R., & BECKER, L. D. (1988). Cognitive components of learning problems in arithmetic. *Remedial and Special Education, 9*(5), 7–16.

LIBERMAN, I. Y., & LIBERMAN, A. M. (1990). Whole language vs. code emphasis: Underlying assumptions and their implications for reading instruction. *Annals of Dyslexia, 40,* 51–76.

LIBERMAN, I. Y., & SHANKWEILER, D. (1985). Phonology and the problems of learning to read and write. *Remedial and Special Education, 6*(6), 8–17.

MANN, V. A., & BRADY, S. (1988). Reading disability: The role of language deficiencies. *Journal of Consulting and Clinical Psychology, 56*(6), 811–816.

MILLER, P. H. (1985). Metacognition and attention. In D. L. Forrest-Pressely, G. E. MacKinnon, & T. G. Waller (Eds.), *Metacognition, cognition and human performance* (pp. 181–218). New York: Academic Press.

NAGY, W., & ANDERSON, R. C. (1984). How many words are there in printed school English? *Reading Research Quarterly, 19,* 304–330.

PALINCSAR, A. S., DAVID, Y. M., WINN, J. A., & STEVENS, D. D. (1991). Examining the context of strategy instruction. *Remedial and Special Education, 12*(3), 43–53.

PALINCSAR, A. S., & KLENK, L. (1992). Fostering literacy learning in supportive contexts. *Journal of Learning Disabilities, 25*(4), 211–225, 229.

PRAWAT, R. S. (1989). Promoting access to knowledge, strategy and disposition in students: A research synthesis. *Review of Educational Research, 59*(1), 1–41.

SAMUELS, S. J. (1995). Home factors and success in school: A response to Allington [Letter to the editor]. *The Reading Teacher, 48,* 647–648.

SILBERT, J., CARNINE, D., & STEIN, M. (1990). *Direct instruction mathematics* (2nd ed.). Upper Saddle River, NJ: Merrill/Prentice Hall.

SNOWLING, M. J. (1991). Developmental reading disorders. *Journal of Child Psychology Psychiatry, 32*(1), 49–77.

SPEAR, L. D., & STERNBERG, R. J. (1986). An information processing framework for understanding reading disability. In S. Ceci (Ed.), *Handbook of cognitive, social, and neuropsychological aspects of learning disabilities* (Vol. 1, pp. 3–31). Hillsdale, NJ: Lawrence Erlbaum.

STAHL, S. A. (1983). Differential word knowledge and reading comprehension. *Journal of Reading Behavior, 15*(4), 33–50.

STAHL, S. A. (1985). To teach a word well: A framework for vocabulary instruction. *Reading World, 24,* 16–27.

STAHL, S. A., & FAIRBANKS, M. M. (1986). The effects of vocabulary instruction: A model-based meta-analysis. *Review of Educational Research, 56*(1), 72–110.

STANOVICH, K. E. (1985). Explaining the variance in reading ability in terms of psychological processes: What have we learned? *Annals of Dyslexia, 35,* 67–96.

STANOVICH, K. E. (1986). Matthew effects in reading: Some consequences of individual differences in the acquisition of literacy. *Reading Research Quarterly, 21*(4), 360–407.

STANOVICH, K. E. (1994). Romance and reality. *The Reaching Teacher, 47*(4), 280–291.

SWANSON, H. L., & COONEY, J. B. (1991). Learning disabilities and memory. In B. Y. L. Wong (Ed.), *Learning about learning disabilities* (pp. 104–127). San Diego, CA: Academic Press.

TORGESEN, J. K. (1985). Memory processes in reading disabled children. *Journal of Learning Disabilities, 18*(6), 350–357.

TORGESEN, J. K., & HOUCK, G. (1980). Processing deficiencies in learning disabled children who perform poorly on the digit span task. *Journal of Educational Psychology, 72,* 141–160.

TORGESEN, J. K., WAGNER, R. K., SIMMONS, K., & LAUGHON, P. (1990). Identifying phonological coding problems in disabled readers: Naming, counting, or span measures. *Learning Disability Quarterly, 13,* 236–243.

U. S. DEPARTMENT OF EDUCATION. (1991). *America 2000: An education strategy.* Washington, DC: Author.

WAGNER, R. K. (1988). Causal relations between the development of phonological processing abilities and the acquisition of reading skills: A meta-analysis. *Merrill-Palmer Quarterly, 34*(2), 261–279.

WAGNER, R., & TORGESEN, J. (1987). The nature of phonological processing and its causal role in the acquisition of reading skills. *Psychological Bulletin, 101,* 192–212.

WEISBERG, R. (1988). 1980s: A change in focus of reading comprehension research: A review of reading/learning disabilities research based on an interactive model of reading. *Learning Disability Quarterly, 11*(2), 149–159.

WHITE, T. G., GRAVES, M. F., & SLATER, W. H. (1990). Growth of reading vocabulary in diverse elementary schools: Decoding and word meaning. *Journal of Educational Psychology, 82*(2), 281–290.

WONG, B. Y. (1991). The relevance of metacognition to learning disabilities. In B. Y. Wong (Ed.), *Learning about learning disabilities* (pp. 232–258). San Diego, CA: Academic Press.

WONG, B. Y. L., & WONG, R. (1986). Study behavior as a function of metacognitive knowledge about critical task variables: An investigation of above average, average, and learning disabled readers. *Learning Disabilities Research, 1*(2), 101–111.

AUTHOR NOTE

Preparation of this chapter manuscript was supported in part by The National Center to Improve the Tools of Educators (H180M10006), funded by the U. S. Department of Education, Office of Special Education Programs.

Correspondence concerning this chapter should be addressed Scott K. Baker, Institute for the Development of Educational Achievement, College of Education, University of Oregon, Eugene, OR 97403-1211. Electronic mail may be sent via Internet to Scott_Baker@ccmail.uoregon.edu.

C H A P T E R

3

Effective Strategies for Teaching Beginning Reading

Edward J. Kameenui, Deborah C. Simmons, Scott Baker
University of Oregon

David J. Chard
Boston University

Shirley V. Dickson
University of Northern Illinois

Barbara Gunn
Oregon Research Institute

Sylvia B. Smith, Marilyn Sprick
University of Oregon

Su-Jan Lin
National Changhua University of Education, Taiwan

INTRODUCTION

THE PURPOSE OF this chapter is to apply the findings of current research on beginning reading to the development of effective instructional strategies for children with diverse learning needs. The demographic and instructional contexts of beginning reading instruction are first described to frame the often controversial but nonetheless highly consequential outcomes of beginning reading instruction for children with diverse learning needs. Next, the extant research on beginning reading is reviewed as a basis for the three big ideas that undergird effective beginning reading instruction: phonemic awareness, alphabetic understanding, and automaticity with the code. Applying the six-principle framework detailed in Chapter 1, each big idea is described and examples illustrating the application of the principles are provided. Finally, criteria for evaluating strategies for teaching beginning reading are presented.

We define beginning reading as the period when readers first learn and apply strategies to recognize words, to the time when they are able to identify words with ease and fluency. Fluent word recognition is a hallmark of skilled readers (Juel, 1991; Stanovich, 1986). In focusing word recognition in beginning reading, our intent is not to disregard the importance of comprehension but to underscore the importance of word recognition and its relation to comprehension.

Many experts agree there is no single point in time when a learner progresses from an emerging reader to one who can use and access information from print automatically. Rather, this transformation is more likely a continuum along which the emergent reader learns to link and associate oral and written language reliably and fluently. For many children, this period begins prior to kindergarten and culminates by the end of second grade, a period when many children read 100 or more words per minute. For diverse learners, difficulty at becoming proficient at word recognition may persist throughout the elementary grades. In fact, Daneman (1991) noted that the individual differences in reading fluency increase over time and are evident even among college students. Rather than designate parameters as grade levels or ages that define beginning reading, we refer to the processes and abilities that characterize beginning readers.

Much of the knowledge we have relating to reading development comes from investigations of skilled readers. From these studies, researchers have identified skills and strategies that distinguish successful from less successful readers. Our objectives in this chapter are to make explicit those processes that underlie successful beginning readers, and to propose design principles to enhance the likelihood that diverse learners will profit from beginning reading instruction. To fulfill these objectives, we have relied heavily upon an extensive review of the research on beginning reading completed by Simmons and Kameenui (in press).

Current Issues

National Education Goals designate, that "By the year 2000, all children will start school ready to learn" (*America 2000,* 1991, p. 1). The challenge to meet this goal is clear. An increasing number of children continue to enter school *not* ready to learn, and the likelihood that they will ever catch up with their average-achieving peers is not very promising (Juel, 1988). Research suggests consistently that learning to read early in life is fundamental to later school success (Stanovich, 1986; 1994). Moreover, there is consistent evidence that children with low reading achievement in early grades have greater likelihood of school dropout, pregnancy, and unemployment (McGill-Franzen & Allington, 1991; Slavin, 1989), and that they consequently face great risks of negative academic, social, and economic outcomes.

Kozol (1985) estimated that approximately one-third of Americans lack basic literacy skills. To suggest that effective beginning reading strategies will eradicate illiteracy in America would be extraordinarily myopic. Nevertheless, we would be equally shortsighted if we failed to allow the emerging body of scientific evidence on beginning reading to shape the strategies we use.

PRINCIPLES FOR IMPROVING INSTRUCTIONAL STRATEGIES IN BEGINNING READING

Instructional Context

The logic of beginning reading is both simple and elusive. It is simple because in order to read, a beginning reader must confront some basic elements of the spoken and printed English language: sounds, letters, words, and sentences (Ehri, 1991). A reader, however advanced, cannot gain "meaning" or even "misunderstanding" from a text without somehow encountering these elements (Kameenui, 1996). As Adams (1990) pointed out, "If we could release children from letterwise processing of text, we could expedite their graduation into efficient, skillful readers. Yet the single immutable and nonoptional fact about skillful reading is that it involves relatively complete processing of the individual letters of print" (p. 105). In spite of this unequivocal and widely shared observation, consensus about whether or when to actually teach any, some, or all of these elements—sounds, letters, words, sentences—and at what stage of the reading process to teach them, is nonetheless elusive (Adams, 1990; Juel, 1991; Stanovich, 1994).

The debates about the role of instruction (explicit, implicit, incidental) in beginning reading are not new. As Stanovich has noted, the "reading wars" have exacted their rage on the field for more than 100 years (Kameenui, 1994). However, these longstanding debates should not suggest that little is known about beginning reading. In fact, we know much about how to design reading activities that promote a solid and successful start in reading and literacy for every child in America. For example, we know that word identification is the central subprocess of the complex act of reading (Stanovich, 1991). This does not deny or diminish the fact that constructing meaning from textual material is the most important goal of reading. It only serves to emphasize that skill at recognizing words is the major determinant of reading ability in the early grades and contributes substantially to differences among good and poor readers.

Research on Beginning Reading

Despite the debate over beginning reading instruction, there is ample evidence of the strong relation between word recognition and higher-order comprehension processes. Across researchers and research investigations, findings converge to the same conclusion: word-recognition skills facilitate comprehension rather than the reverse (Daneman, 1991; Juel, 1991; Stanovich, 1991). The relation between fluent word recognition and comprehension has been the subject of extensive investigation. Across this body of beginning reading research, there is pervasive, if not conclusive, evidence of the need and benefit of word-identification instruction, and more specifically instruction that emphasizes the phonological basis of words.

Phonological Bases of Reading Acquisition

In the not-too-distant past, researchers investigating the causes of reading problems focused their efforts not on reading words, but on "seeing" them (Mann & Brady, 1988; Vellutino, 1991; Vellutino & Denckla, 1991; Vellutino & Scanlon, 1987a; Wagner & Torgesen, 1987). Research from this period focused largely on visual-perceptual and perceptual-motor abilities as the cause of reading difficulties. For example, studies examined children's abilities to trace visual patterns, to discriminate between visual figures, or follow mazes and stay within the lines. Findings consistently failed to confirm that these nonlinguistic facilities—visual perceptual and perceptual motor abilities—caused reading delay (Spear & Sternberg, 1985; Vellutino, 1991). In reality, training students in visual or perceptual-motor processes simply did not improve reading ability. Nevertheless, results of this line of inquiry forced researchers to examine language-based deficits of reading (Mann & Brady, 1988). In particular, in the late 1970s and throughout the 1980s, researchers paid significant attention to the linguistic basis of reading delay (Spear & Sternberg, 1986; Stanovich, 1986; Vellutino & Scanlon, 1987).

Such emphasis on language-based explanations of reading acquisition revealed that good and poor readers differ on virtually every dimension of language: phonology, morphology, semantics, and syntax. Yet, there emerged from this body of research a remarkably lucid and coherent theme: The basis of early reading delay resides largely in phonological processing ability (Felton, 1993; Liberman & Liberman, 1990; Stanovich, 1985, 1986; Wagner & Torgesen, 1987; Vellutino, 1991). What does this really mean? According to Wagner and Torgesen (1987), "phonological processing refers to the use of phonological information (i.e., the sounds of one's language) in processing written and oral language" (p. 192). Specifically, the essence of reading delay can be largely attributed to children's inability to detect, access, manipulate, and relate the sounds and codes (i.e., letters and words) of language.

BEGINNING READING: DESIGNING INSTRUCTION AROUND BIG IDEAS

In a recent synthesis of research on beginning reading (Chard, Simmons, & Kameenui, 1995), numerous sources identified the phonological causes and correlates of beginning reading. Some authors represented these factors in terms of stage models through which beginning readers progress (Ehri, 1991; Juel, 1991), while others proposed possible interactive and reciprocal dimensions and phases of beginning reading acquisition (Stanovich, 1986; Vellutino, 1991; Wagner & Torgesen, 1987). Across the proposed models and dimensions, the critical features were quite apparent. The determining influences and dimensions of successful beginning reading were described using varied vocabulary and were constructed with differing numbers of elements. Nevertheless, the framework of the various models revealed foundational concepts, or big ideas, common to all models and to the architecture of beginning reading instruction (Ehri, 1991, Juel, 1991, Stanovich, 1986, Vellutino, 1991, Wagner & Torgesen, 1987). Not only did the literature review reveal common unifying principles, it further suggested a specific sequence of phonologically based big ideas that promote beginning reading.

In content reading areas such as science (see Chapter 6) and social studies (see Chapter 7), efficient and effective teaching is gained by designing instruction around a limited number of important concepts, principles, facts, laws, and theories called "big ideas." By understanding a few big ideas, such as convection and scientific inquiry (e.g., identifying variables to control and test), students are equipped with a governing principle, concept, or pattern for organizing, unifying, and understanding other ideas, principles, concepts, and patterns. For example, understanding the workings of a convection cell in the context of a pot of boiling water should help naive learners understand the same circular patterns of movement in the atmosphere and the earth's mantle (see Woodward & Noell, 1992, and Chapter 6 of this text). Moreover, the convection cell is intentionally designed and used to represent the same processes that occur in very different contexts.

In beginning reading instruction, "big ideas" don't come in the form of a unifying concept such as the convection cell. In this chapter, we use big ideas in beginning reading to refer to *a set of unifying curriculum activities* necessary for successful beginning reading. Such curricular activities are instructional anchors that, when accomplished and routinized, provide learners enormous capacity to identify printed words and translate alphabetic codes into meaningful language. In the next section, we describe three big ideas: phonemic awareness, alphabetic understanding, and automaticity with the code. We present these big ideas from simple to more complex, with phonemic awareness a prerequisite to the alphabetic understanding and alphabetic understanding fundamental to automaticity with the code.

Phonemic Awareness

One of the most compelling and well established findings in the research on beginning reading is the important relation between phonemic awareness and reading acquisition (see reviews by Adams, 1990; Ehri, 1991; Golinkoff, 1978; Juel, 1991; Wagner & Torgesen, 1987; Spector, 1995; and Stanovich, 1994). As Spector (1995) pointed out, phonemic awareness is known by many different names, such as phonetic analysis, phonological awareness, auditory analysis, phonologic reading, phonological processing, and linguistic awareness. Phonemic awareness also holds several different definitions, such as the ability to perceive spoken words as a sequence of sounds (Spector, 1992), the awareness of and access to the sounds of language (Wagner & Torgesen, 1987), and "the ability to deal explicitly and segmentally with sound units smaller than the syllable" (Stanovich, 1994, p. 283). Phonemic awareness refers to the process of working with language at the phoneme level, whereas phonological awareness is more encompassing and deals with the range of activities in which learners hear and manipulate sounds either at the sentence, word, onset-rime, or phoneme level.

Juel (1991) defined phonemic awareness as "unnatural" and "the realization that oral words are sequences of meaningless sounds (i.e., phonemes) which occur in many different words the child hears and says every day" (p. 778). Interest and research in phonemic awareness spans emergent literacy and beginning reading, and whether it is prerequisite to reading ability or interactive and augmented is subject to debate. This debate does not appear to diminish the interest or importance of phonemic awareness.

For all practical purposes, phonemic awareness is the child's awareness of *sounds* in letters and words. Central to phonemic awareness, as Spector (1995) noted, is the "ability to analyze and synthesize . . . the sound structure of words" (p. 39). In other words, children must be made aware of phonemes; that is, they must come to know that words are made up of individual sounds (phonemes). In addition, beginning readers must also come to know that individual sounds combine to make up a word. Moreover, they must recognize that the same sounds are found in many different words (e.g., the *s* in *sit* has the same sound as the *s* in *miss*).

Recent path analyses by Torgesen, Wagner, and Rashotte (1994) indicated that phonological awareness is a construct comprised of multiple dimensions (e.g., rhyming, blending, segmenting) that relate differentially to reading acquisition. More specifically, the difficulty of phonological awareness components and their relation to reading acquisition could be considered to exist on a continuum. Components such as rhyming are considered easier and less directly related to reading, while those requiring analysis (e.g., segmenting) and synthesis (e.g., blending) are considered more difficult and more directly associated with reading achievement. These advances in phonological awareness research carry significant instructional implications. Therefore, to suggest that students need phonological awareness training is useful but overly simplistic.

Many children seem to develop phonemic awareness intuitively. Considerable evidence suggests that children who enter school with a facility for hearing sounds in words are the same children who come from language-rich environments in which oral language, word play, reading, and print experiences are commonplace. For some learners, this immersion in the sounds and meaning of language forms the rudiments for early reading acquisition. For other learners, this incidental and indirect approach is simply insufficient to address the phonological deficits they bring to the literacy environment (Stanovich, 1986).

For pedagogical purposes, the evidence appears convincingly clear: Students who enter first grade with little phonemic awareness experience less success in reading than students who enter school with the ability to analyze and synthesize the sound structure of words. While it would be overly simplistic to point to a single cause of reading failure, the research reviewed suggests that poor readers have difficulty using the sounds of the language in processing written and oral information. Adams (1990) made the strongest case for teaching phonemic awareness when she stated, "This is not hard to do, and it is just too risky not to" (p. 71). Moreover, it appears that phonemic awareness is "too risky" to do as part of formal reading instruction (Adams, 1990; Ehri, 1991; Juel, 1991; O'Connor, Jenkins, Leicester, & Slocum, 1993). Rather, phonemic awareness should be in place before formal reading instruction begins.

What does the absence of phonemic awareness look like to a classroom teacher? According to Stanovich (1994, pp. 283–84), children lacking phonemic awareness *cannot*:

1. segment words into sounds (e.g., "What sounds do you hear in the word *hot*?")
2. retain sounds in short-term memory and combine them to form a word (e.g., "What word would we have if you put these sounds together: /s/, /a/, /t/?")
3. detect and manipulate sounds within words (e.g., "Is there a /k/ in *bike*?")
4. perceive a word as a sequence of sounds (e.g., How many sounds do you hear in the word *fish*? /f/, /i/, /sh/)
5. isolate beginning, medial, and ending sounds (e.g., "What is the first sound in *rose*?")
6. say words with selected sounds deleted (e.g., "What word would be left if the /k/ sound were taken away from *cat*?")

The contribution and role of phonological awareness to beginning reading acquisition cannot be overestimated. Nevertheless, recent research indicates that merely including phonological awareness activities is unlikely to address the needs that some diverse learners bring to classrooms. Torgesen, Wagner, and Rashotte's recent longitudinal investigation of phonological processing indicated that approximately 30 percent of their at-risk sample showed "no measurable growth in phonological awareness following an 8-week training program that produced significant growth in the majority of children" (1994, p. 284). Moreover, O'Connor's investigations of phonological awareness of 4- to 6-year-old children with disabilities indicated little transfer to novel words and limited generalization between types of phonological awareness (O'Connor et al., 1993).

Spector (1995) reported that activities such as memorization of nursery rhymes, alliteration games, and trade books that play with language by emphasizing the sounds of words may enhance sensitivity to sounds. Such activities can be promoted by parents at home and by teachers at school. However, it is important to note that for diverse learners, the intensity and systematicity of instruction necessary to develop solid phonological awareness skills and to intercept early reading difficulties will require carefully designed sequences of instruction.

Alphabetic Understanding

Another big idea in beginning reading is alphabetic understanding, which is a necessary requirement for operating in an alphabetic writing system. According to Perfetti (1985), "acquisition of the alphabetic code is a critical component—indeed, the definitive component—of reading in an alphabetic language" (p. 501). Alphabetic understanding refers to a child's understanding that words are composed of individual letters (graphemes) and "the use of grapheme-phoneme relations to read words" (Ehri, 1991, p. 387). As Adams (1990) stated, "Very early in the course of instruction, one wants the students to understand that all twenty-six of those strange little symbols that comprise the alphabet are worth learning and discriminating one from the other because each stands for one of the sounds that occur in spoken words" (p. 245).

Alphabetic understanding is concerned with the "mapping of print to speech" and establishing a clear link between a letter and a sound. A beginning reader must come to know each letter as a "discrete, self-contained" visual pattern that can be printed or pointed to "one by one" (Adams, 1990, p. 247). Ehri and Wilce (1987, cited in Ehri, 1991) argued that as soon as children master letters and exhibit the ability to read a few words in isolation, they are capable of operating alphabetically and of using letter-sound relations to read sight words. Relatedly, Liberman and Liberman (1990) noted that readers must become explicitly aware "that each word is formed by consonants and vowels that an alphabet represents . . . and this awareness must be taught explicitly if the child is to grasp the alphabetic principle" (p. 51). Moreover, they concluded that preliterate children do not have much of this awareness of the relation between sound and print, and those who have more perform predictably superior to those who have less.

During the alphabetic stage, readers learn unfamiliar spellings by drawing on their emerging knowledge of letter-sound correspondences. According to Ehri (1991), rudimentary alphabetic readers have begun to read words by processing letter-sound relations. Although their vocabularies are limited by the letter-sound relations they know, they are developing an ability to use letters to connect words in memory by associating them with sounds in their pronunciations.

The importance of developing an awareness and facility with mapping sounds to letters is furthered by the apparent limitation of whole-word identification strategies (Liberman & Liberman, 1990; Mann & Brady, 1988; Vellutino, 1991; Vellutino & Scanlon, 1987b). In learning to identify printed words represented by an alphabet, facility in whole-word naming will rapidly reach its limit unless accompanied by a facility in segmenting (e.g., "What sounds do you hear in the word *hot*?" [Stanovich, 1994, p. 283]) and blending (e.g., putting individual sounds together [Mann & Brady, 1988]). Such facilities are not easily or simply acquired. A code-emphasis approach to beginning reading "makes intellectual demands of the child" (Liberman & Liberman, 1990). Juel (1991) noted that "learning the rules that underlie alphabetic writing systems is deemed neither easy nor natural" (p. 775). Nevertheless, there is convincing evidence that early attainment of decoding skill strongly and accurately predicts later reading comprehension.

Our research review accented three realities that would be reckless to ignore:

1. A primary difference between good and poor readers is the ability to use letter-sound correspondences to identify words (Juel, 1991).
2. Students who acquire and apply alphabetic understanding early in their reading careers reap long-term benefits (Stanovich, 1986).
3. Teaching students to listen, remember, and process the sounds in words is a difficult, demanding, yet achievable goal with long-lasting effects (Liberman & Liberman, 1990).

Given the converging evidence of the importance of understanding the alphabet (Juel, 1988, 1991; Liberman & Shankweiler, 1985), the role of instructional strategies should be to reduce the intellectual demands of this complex activity. Strategies can promote alphabetic understanding by identifying requisite components and designing instruction to communicate their effective and efficient acquisition. Accordingly, students with diverse learning needs who lack alphabetic understanding will *not* be able to:

1. associate an alphabetic character (i.e., a letter) with its corresponding phoneme or sound (e.g., What is the sound this letter? [show letter *b*])
2. identify a word based on a sequence of letter-sound correspondences (e.g., *Mat* is made up of three letter/sound correspondences: /m/, /a/, /t/.)
3. blend letter-sound correspondences to identify decodable words (e.g., "Blend the sounds of these letters to make a word: /mmmmaaannn/.")
4. segment words into their component sounds (e.g., "The word is *plan*. What sounds do you hear in the word?")
5. use letter-sound correspondences to identify words in which letters do not represent their most common sound (e.g., "Blend the sounds of the letters to help you figure out a word that makes sense: *was*.")

6. identify and manipulate letter-sound correspondences within words (e.g., "What word would you have if you changed the *n* in *nap* to an *l*."
7. read pseudowords/nonsense words that follow common consonant/vowel patterns (e.g., *tup*) with reasonable speed.
8. apply knowledge of the alphabetic code to identify words in isolation and in connected text.

Automaticity with the Code

A third big idea is automaticity with the phonological/alphabetic code or the ability to translate fluently letters to sounds and sounds to words. LaBerge and Samuels (1974) described the fluent reader as "one whose decoding processes are automatic, requiring no conscious attention" (cited in Juel, 1991, p. 760). There is considerable and converging evidence that many students with reading delay lack the ability to decode words automatically. Consequently, they have less capacity to allocate toward comprehension (Juel, 1991; Sawyer, 1992; Stanovich, 1986, 1994). Poor readers do not code the sounds of words as fully or efficiently as good readers; thus, their ability to remember and recall needed information is impaired (Mann & Brady, 1988; Torgesen, 1985).

Directly stated, a lack of decoding fluency places increasing demands on a reader's ability to remember and process information. Unless readers become automatic with the alphabetic code, the time and attention required to identify a "word" directly limits the cognitive resources available to process the meaning of the sentence in which the word appeared. Stanovich (1994) explained this relation by indicating that comprehension fails "not because of overreliance on decoding, but because decoding skill is not developed enough" (p. 283). Apparently, word decoding automatically activates a word's meaning in the learner's vocabulary. Thus, the third big idea underscores the importance of readers moving beyond the ability to relate sounds and symbols to the ability to use the alphabetic code automatically and with little or no conscious effort.

Researchers have linked this word identification automaticity with the progression from the alphabetic phase of reading to an orthographic phase. In the alphabetic phase, readers focus largely on individual letters and sounds; in the orthographic phase, emphasis is on the awareness of patterns in which letters frequently appear (e.g., spelling patterns). According to Ehri (1991), the orthographic phase of word reading emerges after competence is gained in the alphabetic phase of reading. In the orthographic phase of reading (Ehri, 1991), readers begin to process the familiar sequence of letters as units and use such sequences to speed up word reading.

Ehri (1991) further noted that an effective strategy for teaching students to read unfamiliar words is by detecting known words and word parts. Noting that older readers are more likely to read words by identifying the sameness in them, there is value in teaching students to read unfamiliar words by looking for familiar parts. Finally, she concluded that regardless of how students are taught to read (by a phonics approach or by a whole word approach), those who make progress in learning to read require the ability to translate sounds into words and to read words as whole units by sight.

Cunningham and Stanovich (1991, cited in Haskell, Foorman, & Swank, 1992) determined that the ability to use patterns of letters was highly related to word identification skills and that individual differences in this ability were largely explained by differences in exposure to print. They concluded that "the more readers are exposed to print, the better they ar~ ~+ ~+~~~+i~~ ~ ~~~~~~~~ of letters from familiar words" (p. 41). Additionally, I *levelled books* "the child must be exposed to words (decodable wor words become automatically accessible. . . . For son *importance of* automaticity requires tremendous amounts of practi *controlled vocab.*

It is important to note that exposing children suggest that words must always be decontextualized lists. Rather, words containing familiar letter-sound part of text and stories containing controlled vocab recognize early the importance of deriving meaning f.~... ~~~. ~..~..~..~~., ~~~~.

At the risk of oversimplifying this important stage of reading, automaticity of the code appears to result from prerequisite ability with phonemic awareness and alphabetic understanding combined with repeated opportunities to practice and apply these capacities to the point of overlearning (Adams, 1990; Felton, 1993). Therefore, instructional strategies should focus on steps that will allow students to:

1. identify letter-sound correspondences accurately and efficiently.
2. identify familiar sequences of letters (i.e., spelling patterns) to increase decoding efficiency.
3. efficiently identify and translate letters into sounds to identify words accurately.
4. apply maximum resources to the difficult task of blending isolated phonemes to make words because of undeveloped phonemic awareness or facility with the alphabetic code.

No standard operational definition of automaticity exits. However, normative data on oral reading fluency reported by Hasbrouck and Tindal (1992) can be used to assess children's reading automaticity relative to other readers of comparable grade levels. These normative data are based on a nine-year period using standardized and validated curriculum-based measurement procedures. The authors report 25th, 50th, and 75th percentile norms for fall, winter, and spring for grades 2 through 5. For example, in the fall, children in grade 2 scoring at the 75th percentile read 82 correct words per minute, while children scoring at the 25th percentile read 23 correct words per minute. In the spring of grade 2, the median scores ranged from 65 to 124, with a 50th percentile norm of 94 words per minute. Such data provide reasonable parameters for gauging whether children are reading with sufficient automaticity to facilitate comprehension.

Clearly, automaticity of word reading is not the end goal of reading instruction. However, according to stage models of reading acquisition, automaticity marks the end of the beginning reading period and the transition to more advanced stages of literacy learning.

Implications for Instructional Design

To the beginning reader with diverse learning needs, the world of print must seem enormously complex and uninviting. Whereas some readers are able to unravel the intricate processes of translating print to meaning, many readers with diverse learning needs require explicit and systematic instruction. The conclusion that can be drawn from our review is that reversing and intercepting reading failure requires solutions that attend to a complex array of factors. Nevertheless, three big ideas permeate the research on beginning reading research and justly serve as an organizational framework for the design of beginning reading instruction. Focusing on phonemic awareness, alphabetic understanding, and automaticity with the code will allow instructional designers to focus on what is instructionally important and empirically validated. In the following section we illustrate how the principles of instructional design (e.g., conspicuous strategies, mediated scaffolding, strategic integration, and judicious review) can be applied to achieve more efficient and effective outcomes for beginning readers with diverse learning needs.

DESIGNING CONSPICUOUS STRATEGIES

Big ideas by themselves are not enough. For beginning readers to understand and use the big ideas of phonemic awareness, alphabetic understanding, and automaticity with the code, strategies are needed to make the meanings of these big ideas clear and understandable.

Strategies are a series of steps that can be purposefully employed to achieve a particular outcome. As stated in Chapter 7 of this book, "The strategies are literally the application of a big idea." To apply a big idea such as phonemic awareness requires a strategy or plan of action for making students aware that words are made of individual sounds or phonemes. Such a strategy involves multiple steps and a sequence of teaching events and systematic teacher actions. According to Felton (1993), the strategy for teaching children with phonological problems should be clear and unambiguous: "Children who do not have age-appropriate phonological awareness skills must be taught such skills directly. . . . Instruction should be explicit with no aspects of the process (including blending) left to intuition" (p. 587).

Phonemic Awareness

Phonemic awareness training strategies and programs are plentiful and varied (Adams, 1990; Ball & Blachman, 1991; Blachman, 1987; Byrne & Fielding-Barnsley, 1989; Calfee, Lindamood, & Lindamood, 1973; Carnine & Silbert, 1979; Cunningham, 1990; Liberman, Shankweiler, Camp, Blachman, & Werfelman, 1980; Spector, 1992, 1995). For many children, gaining an awareness of the sounds of our language is not easy, because, as Ball and Blachman (1991) pointed out, the individual sounds in words are "coarticulated"—that is, merged and not pronounced as separate, discrete parts—and require more "abstraction than discrimination" (p. 52). They stated: "Although we may teach children to 'hear' three sounds in *cat*, the three sounds are not separated in the acoustic stimulus itself" (p. 51). As Adams (1990) stated, "despite our working knowledge of phonemes, we are not naturally set up to be consciously aware of them" (p. 66). Clearly, a strategy for teaching phonemic awareness must, therefore, teach children to "attend to that which we have learned not to attend to" (Adams, 1990, p. 66). Because words are pronounced as whole units in conversational language, some learners do not naturally recognize the importance or purpose of the discrete sounds of language. A strategy must make this purpose and process conspicuous.

A strategy for developing phonemic awareness involves the steps of learning to segment and blend sounds in words. In an auditory blending task, the learner is told the parts of a word (subdivided into a series of isolated sounds, sound combinations, syllables, or other phonological components) and expected to produce the word from these auditory parts. At the phonemic awareness stage, the strategy involves auditory presentation of words without printed letters. The purpose of this design feature is to allow students to focus on the sound structure of language, thereby minimizing competing variables (i.e., the presence of letters).

Carnine, Silbert, and Kameenui (1990) developed a sequence of auditory tasks that emphasized listening to the individual sounds of words and blending the sounds to form words. Students learn through auditory blending to pronounce a series of sounds without pausing between sounds, and to follow the teacher's direction as to when to switch from sound to sound. No letters are used; the tasks are simply auditory. The teacher repeats the steps until students are able to blend the parts of each word without error. The following steps would comprise the instructional strategy for auditory blending that students eventually learn to perform independently.

1. The teacher models sounds in words: "Listen carefully as I say the sounds in run. I will say each sound, but I will not stop between sounds: /rrrrruuuuunnnn/; *run.*"
2. The children practice the sounds: "Let's try one together. Let's say the sounds in *sat.*"
3. Several more examples are modeled and practiced, and then students practice the auditory blending task independently.

We reiterate the importance of differentiating instruction according to learner needs. All children do not enter school with phonological awareness deficits. Some children already have mastered the phonologic basis of language. For these children, it would be a disservice to break down and synthesize the sounds of words. However, teachers have become increasingly aware of the number of diverse learners whose experiential, physiological, linguistic, or socioeconomic histories have hampered phonological awareness development and will benefit from systematic strategies in beginning reading (Smith, 1995).

Alphabetic Understanding

In the alphabetic phase of beginning reading, letters are added to the auditory blending strategy described earlier. What may appear to be a simple process of translating letters into sounds has been found particularly troublesome for students with diverse learning needs (Adams, 1990; Felton, 1993). More importantly, analyses of prominent beginning reading programs have revealed the absence of systematic procedures to teach students to translate letters to sounds and blend them into words (Stein, 1993). Therefore, it is not surprising that students fail to make the connections between learning the code and reading.

The first step in a strategy for teaching students the alphabetic characters is to teach individual letter-sound correspondences, such as /r/, /s/, or /a/. In teaching letter-sound correspondences, it is important to teach those letter-sound correspondences that occur frequently in common words (e.g., *ran, sat*) and also to limit the number of correspondences introduced per lesson. Once students have mastered two to three correspondences, the next step is for students to blend isolated sounds into meaningful words. In this step, the goal is to establish the connection between sounds and letters. Because students have practiced the process of blending at the phonemic awareness stage, they are prepared to apply this process to printed letters and words.

In a strategy for sounding-out words, Carnine, Silbert, and Kameenui (1990) illustrated how the blending strategy learned in the phonemic awareness stage can facilitate word identification. Students have learned in the auditory blending task to pronounce a series of sounds without pausing between each sound, and to follow the teacher's direction as to when to switch from sound to sound. In the alphabetic blending task, the students say the sounds when teacher points to the letters. This process is illustrated in the following sequence.

1. Teacher writes on board: *am, fit.*
2. Teacher states instruction: "Watch. When I touch a letter, I'll say its sound. I'll keep saying the sound until I touch the next letter. I won't stop between sounds."
3. Teacher models sounding out the first word: "My turn to sound out this word." Teacher touches under each letter of the first word, saying, "/aaaammm/."
4. Teacher leads students in sounding out the word: Teacher points to left of word and says, "Sound out this word with me. Get ready." Teacher touches under each letter and says "/aaaammm/" along with students.
5. Teacher tests students on the first word. Teacher points to left of word. "Your turn. Sound out this word by yourselves. Get ready." Teacher touches under each letter while students respond: "/aaaammm/."

6. Teacher has several students sound out the word individually.
7. Teacher repeats steps with other decodable words.

Automaticity with the Code

In his study of automaticity, Stanovich (1991) concluded that word identification demands less cognitive capacity as experience with words increases. Therefore, the more readers are exposed to and experience words, the more likely they are to develop automaticity with the patterns. Carrying through with the blending strategy, students would be given frequent opportunities to blend words with patterns that have been practiced in auditory blending exercises and to sound-blend words containing letter-sound correspondences and sequences that have been systematically taught.

As Adams (1990) noted, the purpose of strategy instruction is to make explicit those processes to which we do not typically attend. The strategies previously described make explicit the implicit strategies that good readers use to recognize sounds in words, relate sounds to letters, and blend sounds into words. In the following section we describe design procedures used to ensure that such strategies are achieved by students with diverse learning needs.

 ## DESIGNING MEDIATED SCAFFOLDING

Mediated scaffolding is particularly important for students who may not profit fully from traditionally sequenced and structured curricula. Scaffolds provide the learner with personal guidance or support during the initial phases of learning new and difficult information.

When scaffolding instruction, an important guideline is to align the amount of structure and support with the needs of the learner. Another recommendation is to scaffold instruction through prompts and support that can be easily and authentically embedded in instructional materials. Finally, it is important to withdraw scaffolds gradually once learners demonstrate mastery of a skill or strategy, so that they do not become overly dependent on a prop.

In beginning reading, scaffolds may be provided in two ways: through assistance by teachers or peers, and through the sequence and selection of tasks. During initial learning, teachers may scaffold instruction by modeling the precise process students will need to perform. For example, Carnine, Silbert, and Kameenui (1990) developed a format for teaching students to translate a series of blended sounds into a word:

1. The teacher models the individual sounds or word: "Listen, we're going to play a say-the-word game. I'll say a word slowly, then you say the word fast. Listen: /iiiiiiiffffff/. What word?"
2. The teacher leads students who are have difficulty by responding with them: "Let's try this one together."

3. The teacher assesses the students' ability to blend the sounds independently: "Now, it's your turn to blend the sounds by yourselves."
4. The teacher provides individual students with opportunities to practice blending the sounds into a word: "Now, I want to listen to each of you blend the sounds."

Teacher-mediated scaffolding is especially important for correcting students' errors, which at this stage of learning to read requires careful consideration and strategic teacher responses. Moreover, because phonemic awareness tasks are entirely auditory and do not involve the reading of actual words, the attention and processing requirements placed on diverse learners may be demanding. Carnine, Silbert, and Kameenui (1990) provided an extensive analysis and set of strategies for preventing and responding to students' errors involving phonemic awareness and the alphabetic code.

Teacher-mediated scaffolding may be followed by peer-mediated activities, depending on the age of the learners and the nature of the task. Finally, readers perform tasks independently with no scaffolding. As is the case with scaffolding in general, teacher and peer assistance is withdrawn gradually but systematically to relinquish responsibility to the individual learner.

Task scaffolds are embedded in the tasks themselves and designed to allow students to focus on the reading process and strategy by reducing the information they must generate independently. For example, an initial phonemic awareness task requires students to listen to the individual sounds of simple words (e.g., /m/, /a/, /n/) without referring to the printed representation of the word (*man*). A later task may require students to place a blank token in a series of squares corresponding to the number of sounds in a word. A more advanced task involving the alphabetic code is substituting letters for the blank tokens (i.e., physical marker without print) and requiring students to place the letters that correspond to the sounds in the series of squares (Spector, 1995). This progression of tasks gradually approximates the end goal, which is to associate sounds with letters in words.

DESIGNING STRATEGIC INTEGRATION

Identifying words from text requires that a reader integrate phonemic awareness, alphabetic understanding, and automaticity with the code. Students with diverse learning needs often fail to induce the connection between strategies; thus, it is imperative that instructional strategies are designed to communicate these relations.

As illustrated in the auditory blending strategy with phonemic awareness, and in the alphabetic blending strategy with alphabetic understanding, beginning reading strategies are not discrete but are integrally related. Students must not only understand these strategies as separate entities, but also learn the relations among strategies that lead to a complete and integrated strategy for decoding words.

One of the most consistent conclusions of research on beginning reading and strategic points of integration concerns phonemic awareness and letter-sound correspondence training. Repeatedly, experimental investigations have documented the insufficiency of either phonemic awareness or letter-sound correspondence training (Byrne & Fielding-Barnsley, 1989; Spector, 1995), unless combined with direct instruction in reading (Snowling, 1991). Relatedly, Ball and Blachman (1991) found that letter-name and letter-sound training without phoneme awareness training is not enough to improve early reading skills. The combination of instruction in phonemic awareness and letter-sound correspondences appears to be most favorable for successful early reading (Byrne & Fielding-Barnsley, 1989; Haskell, Foorman, & Swank, 1992; Rack, Snowling, & Olson, 1992).

The following steps should be considered in the strategic integration of phonemic awareness, letter-sound correspondence, and sound-blending strategies:

1. Select examples of words in which the most common sounds are represented (e.g., /n/ in *man* and *nut*).
2. Teach component parts prior to introducing the whole (e.g., all letter-sound correspondences that occur in a word should be taught to mastery prior to introducing the word).
3. Make explicit the connection between the strategies through instruction (e.g., "Do you remember how we heard the sounds in words and put those sounds together to make words? Today, we will blend the sounds of letters to make words").

A frequent criticism of code-emphasis approaches to beginning reading instruction is the lack of integration of code-based activities with other activities, such as story reading and spelling. It has been argued that children too often receive a phonics lesson that has limited application to the other activities in language arts. As Juel reported, "It is unfortunate that many basal series treat phonics lessons as if they had no relation to story reading (Beck, 1981, cited in Juel, 1991). An absolutely crucial element of strategic integration is that the words taught in phonemic awareness and sound-blending exercises are words that children actually see in stories they read.

Despite the perceived advantage of integrating code and connected text, in reality, creating stories in which the language is controlled is quite difficult. One strategy is to teach the letter-sound correspondences that have the greatest generality and use in words. This is similar to the "Wheel of Fortune" strategy, in which contestants select consonants that appear frequently in words (e.g., *s, r, t, l, m*) to assist them in identifying the word puzzle. In addition to teaching the most frequently used letter-sound correspondences, Juel (1991) recommended teaching those correspondences in which the same sound is represented by multiple patterns (e.g., /e/ as in *me, sea, see, neat, green,* and

Pete). A goal is to teach generalizable letter-sound correspondences and the blending process, and then to move quickly but judiciously into meaningful contexts such as stories.

DESIGNING PRIMED BACKGROUND KNOWLEDGE

Perhaps in no other facet of reading does background knowledge exact such consequences as in beginning reading. Successful reading acquisition depends largely on (a) the knowledge the learner brings to the reading task, (b) the accuracy of that information, and (c) the degree to which the learner accesses and uses that information. For diverse learners, priming background knowledge is critical to success, as it is designed to foster success on tasks by addressing the memory and strategy deficits many such students bring to beginning reading tasks.

For example, if learners are facile in hearing and manipulating sounds in words and can reliably identify letter-sound correspondences, they are prepared to learn how to apply that information to identify words. However, diverse learners may not access information in memory as efficiently and effectively, or may not consistently rely on effective strategies to identify unknown words. In such cases, the task of priming background knowledge is paramount to subsequent reading success. In the following discussion we identify and discuss three facets to guide the design of primed background knowledge.

First, identify essential preskills or background knowledge most proximal to the new task. This step may seem obvious; however, for beginning reading, a thorough understanding of the components of phonological awareness, alphabetic understanding, and automaticity, and of the relations among them, is pivotal to efficient and effective instruction and learning. Because diverse learners are often playing catch-up with their peers, priming the knowledge most proximal to the task will increase instructional efficiency. For instance, there are multiple dimensions to phonological awareness that are related differentially to reading acquisition. Specifically, while rhyming is a common phonological awareness task, other tasks, such as segmenting, are more highly related and therefore proximal to beginning word identification. Effective priming of background knowledge requires a careful analysis of the intricate components of beginning reading and the selection of information most relevant to the instructional objective.

Second, once proximal tasks are identified, one must determine whether the background knowledge needs to be primed or taught. Priming is a brief reminder or exercise that requires the learner to retrieve known information. For example, practicing a few examples of isolating initial sounds in words before teaching how to segment whole words primes or readies the learner for the more complex task. On some occasions, teachers may assume that learners have background knowledge such as knowledge of letter-sound correspondences or how to match words with the same beginning sounds. If, in actuality, learners never mastered the letter-sound correspondences, then a brief "reminder" that the letter *r* makes the /r/ sound will not suffice. Therefore, a second step is to determine whether priming will allow the learner to retrieve and use the information accurately and reliably. If so, then priming is the appropriate instructional strategy; if not, then a more thorough instructional sequence must be designed.

Third, priming is a prompt that elicits the correct information or readies the learner by focusing attention on a difficult task or component of a task. For example, prior to reading a short passage to improve automaticity, learners may be prompted to pay attention to words that have not been recently reviewed or words that may have been problematic in word lists. This may involve modeling how to segment a word or merely pointing to a previously problematic letter and reminding students to pay careful attention when they come to that letter.

The functions of priming background knowledge are to increase the likelihood that students will be successful on tasks by making explicit the critical features of tasks, and to motivate learners to access information they already know. Therefore, in most cases the level of priming should be brief and strategic. Prolonged priming that fosters dependence on teacher-provided information should be discouraged.

DESIGNING JUDICIOUS REVIEW

Successful beginning reading also depends on a review process to reinforce the essential building blocks of phonemic awareness, alphabetic understanding, and automaticity with the code. According to Dempster (1991), the pedagogical axiom "practice makes perfect" is simply not a reliable standard for ensuring successful learning. Simple repetition of information will not ensure efficient learning. We have derived several principles from the research to inform us on how best to provide a judicious review of information taught in beginning reading.

Carnine, Dixon, and Kameenui (1994) identify four critical dimensions of judicious review:

1. The review must be sufficient to enable a student to perform the task without hesitation.
2. It must be distributed over time.
3. It must be cumulative, with information integrated into more complex tasks.
4. It must be varied, so as to illustrate the wide application of a student's understanding of the information.

So how does a teacher select information for review, schedule review to ensure retention, and design activities to extend beginning readers' understanding of the skills, concepts, and strategies? These issues are discussed in the sections that follow.

Determining What To Review

Judicious review requires that the teacher select information that is useful and essential to further reading success. For example, Carnine, Silbert, & Kameenui, 1990) suggested that review include high-utility, frequently occurring letter-sounds, spelling patterns, and exercises. The requirements of judicious review will vary from learner to learner. In order to ensure judicious review for diverse learners, students' progress must be monitored carefully to ensure that the information reviewed is the information in need of review. Informal methods of documenting learner performance (e.g., collecting data on difficult words during oral reading practice) can serve to provide the information that should be included in review activities.

Scheduling Review

According to Dempster (1991), "spaced repetitions" in which a learner is asked to recall a learning experience is more effective than "massed repetitions," provided that "spacing between occurrences is relatively short" (p. 73). As early as 1917, Edwards (cited in Dempster, 1991) observed that elementary school children who studied academic information once for four minutes and again for two-and-one-half minutes several days later retained about 30 percent more information than students who received one continuous six-and-one-half minute session. Therefore, repeated presentations during shorter time increments distributed over time should be considered when scheduling instruction.

Such distributed activities lend themselves particularly well to the range of skills and strategies in beginning reading. For example, when developing automaticity with the code, words could be clustered into sets and reviewed over time. The amount of spacing between review sets must be determined by the facility of the reader. Initially, frequent review sessions would be scheduled, and as fluency develops, greater amounts of time would be interjected between review sessions. It is important to avoid the common but fatal practice of removing items (e.g., words, letter-sounds, phonemic activities) from review sets completely once a learner attains a high level of initial learning. Judicious review involves spacing review opportunities over time and reexamining important information to enhance retention. This suggests that teachers must retain a cumulative list of essential and high-utility information, and must present this information in spaced reviews and in different activities. Fortunately, in beginning reading spaced review will take care of itself if students read often and extensively.

Designing Review Activities

A common misconception is that review must be through rote rehearsal. The purpose of a judicious review is to provide learners with more opportunities to demonstrate what they know. The means and methods for having students demonstrate this knowledge can be as flexible and creative as teachers desire.

Decisions as to what to review, how often, and when depend to a large extent on exactly what has been taught, how often, and when, and on the particular outcome the teacher desires. For example, auditory blending tasks to develop phonemic awareness will require a different kind and schedule of review than letter-sound correspondence tasks to develop alphabetic understanding. Because auditory skills require no visual materials, they can be reviewed more spontaneously and for brief periods of time. Letter-sound correspondence review requires systematic analysis of visual and auditory information that may predispose students to failure, and therefore requires more deliberate planning. Of course, review activities will also depend on the learner's performance; that is, which phonemic awareness or alphabetic understanding activities were unsuccessful and why. In general, developing full automaticity with the code requires careful scheduling of review activities (Carnine, Silbert, & Kameenui, 1990).

The following guidelines should be considered in designing review activities for developing phonemic awareness, alphabetic understanding, and automaticity with the code:

1. Examine the types of errors (e.g., omission errors, substitution errors, no responses, slow responses) students made during reading activities for recognizing patterns.
2. Create "review sets" for a particular beginning reading activity. For example, for phonemic awareness/auditory blending, include in the review set those sounds or word types that were particularly difficult (i.e., sounds missed consistently and frequently) for the learner, as well as sounds *not* reviewed recently.
3. Schedule review activities for brief periods on multiple occasions within a lesson. For example, a review activity for auditory blending of one word would require approximately 15 seconds and should be presented periodically (3 to 4 times) throughout a 10–15 minute reading lesson.
4. Schedule review activities for brief periods (30 seconds to 1–2 minutes) on multiple occasions throughout a school day; that is, space the activities across the full range of teaching lessons in a day.
5. Devote more review time to new reading tasks than to familiar tasks.

SUMMARY

Simply stated, a primary purpose of educational research is to identify the things that matter. More than two decades of research validate that we know a great deal about what matters in beginning reading instruction. However, it is perplexing that this converging body of knowledge on prerequisites and requisites of beginning reading acquisition fails to find its way into the instructional strategies of classrooms and schools. Our synthesis of the literature leads us to conclude that beginning readers must develop an awareness of the phonemic properties of language, and insight, utility, and automaticity with the alphabetic code. To accomplish this, instructional strategies for beginning reading should be designed and selected according to the following criteria:

1. Effective instruction should provide a conspicuous strategy for teaching segmenting, blending, rhyming, sound substitution, and other phonemic awareness skills, as well as strategies for identifying letter-sound correspondences, common parts or spelling patterns in words, and sound-blending of words.
2. It should scaffold early phonemic awareness development by presenting auditory tasks without visual counterparts (i.e., letters); scaffold alphabetic tasks through selected letter-sound correspondences and words that minimize visually and auditorily confusing information; and scaffold irregular word identification by providing practice on predictable words.
3. It should scaffold new tasks through teacher modeling and selection of more easily blended words (e.g., those beginning with continuous sounds).
4. It should provide for mediation of difficult tasks through carefully designed sequences of exercises determined by what the learner already knows.
5. It should include judicious review which is structured to ensure mastery, automaticity, and retention of phonemic awareness and alphabetic understanding.
6. It should sustain and extend phonemic awareness by strategically integrating with alphabetic understanding to provide a more complete portrait of beginning reading.
7. It should integrate new and more complex tasks, increasing the complexity of phonemic awareness and alphabetic understanding tasks as learners demonstrate proficiency (e.g., blending, segmenting, and sound substitution).

CONCLUSION

As expectations for students increase, accountability for achievement grows. As classrooms become more complex environments and the needs of learners become more diverse, teachers must rely on effective strategies for developing beginning reading instruction. Educational research has brought us closer to identifying which factors determine effective beginning reading instruction. Now, our task is to ensure that this information is translated into strategies that we can use successfully. In addition, we must continue research into feasible mechanisms by which teachers can provide the differential instruction required for students with diverse learning needs. Models of instructional delivery such as cooperative teaching, grouping strategies, and peer tutoring, although beyond the scope of this chapter, must be considered as means to augment the effectiveness of instructional strategies.

REFERENCES

ADAMS, M. J. (1990). *Beginning to read: Thinking and learning about print.* Cambridge, MA: MIT Press.

BALL, E. W., & BLACHMAN, B. A. (1991). Does phoneme awareness training in kindergarten make a difference in early word recognition and developmental spelling? *Reading Research Quarterly, 24,* 49–66.

BECK, I. L. (1981). Reading problems and instructional practices. In G. E. MacKinnon & T. G. Waller (Eds.), *Reading research: Advances in theory and practice* (Vol. 2, pp. 53–95). New York: Academic Press.

BLACHMAN, B. A. (1987). An alternative classroom reading program for learning disabled and other low-achieving children. In W. Ellis (Ed.), *Intimacy with language: A forgotten basic in teacher education.* Baltimore, MD: The Orton Dyslexia Society.

BYRNE, B., & FIELDING-BARNSLEY, R. (1989). Phonemic awareness and letter knowledge in the child's acquisition of the alphabetic principle. *Journal of Educational Psychology, 81,* 313–321.

CALFEE, R., LINDAMOOD, P., & LINDAMOOD, C. (1973). Acoustic-phonetic skills and reading: Kindergarten through twelfth grade. *Journal of Educational Psychology, 64,* 293–298.

CARNINE, D. W., DIXON, R., & KAMEENUI, E. J. (1994). Math curriculum guidelines for diverse learners. *Curriculum Technology Quarterly, 3*(3), 1–3.

CARNINE, D. W., & SILBERT, J. (1979). Direct instruction reading. Upper Saddle River, NJ: Merrill/Prentice Hall.

CARNINE, D. W., SILBERT, J., & KAMEENUI, E. J. (1990). *Direct instruction reading* (2nd ed.). Upper Saddle River, NJ: Merrill/Prentice Hall.

CHARD, D. J., SIMMONS, D. C., & KAMEENUI, E. J. (1995). *Understanding the primary role of word recognition in the reading process: Synthesis of research on beginning reading.* (Tech. Rep. No. 15). Eugene, OR: University of Oregon, National Center to Improve the Tools of Educators.

CUNNINGHAM, A. E. (1990). Explicit versus implicit instruction in phonemic awareness. *Journal of Experimental Child Psychology, 50,* 429–444.

CUNNINGHAM, A. E., & STANOVICH, K. E. (1991). Tracking the unique effects of print exposure in children: Associations with vocabulary, general knowledge, and spelling. *Journal of Educational Psychology, 83,* 264–274.

DANEMAN, M. (1991). Individual differences in reading skills. In R. Barr, M. L. Kamil, P. B. Mosenthal, & P. D. Pearson (Eds.), *Handbook of reading research* (Vol. 2, pp. 512–538). New York: Longman.

DEMPSTER, F. N. (1991, April). Synthesis of research on reviews and tests. *Educational Leadership, 48,* 71–76.

EHRI, L. C. (1991). Development of the ability to read words. In R. Barr, M. L. Kamil, P. B. Mosenthal, & P. D. Pearson (Eds.), *Handbook of reading research* (Vol. 2, pp. 383–417). New York: Longman.

EHRI, L. C., & WILCE, L. S. (1987). Does learning to spell help beginners learn to read words? *Reading Research Quarterly, 18,* 47–65.

FELTON, R. H. (1992). Early identification of children at risk for reading disabilities. *Topics in Early Childhood Special Education, 12,* 212–229.

FELTON, R. H. (1993). Effects of instruction on the decoding skills of children with phonological-processing problems. *Journal of Learning Disabilities, 26,* 583–589.

GOLINKOFF, R. M. (1978). Critique: Phonemic awareness skills and reading achievement. In F. B. Murray & J. J. Pikulski (Eds.), *The acquisition of reading: Cognitive, linguistic, and perceptual prerequisites.* Baltimore, MD: University Park Press.

HASBROUCK, J. E., & TINDAL, G. (1992). Curriculum-based oral reading fluency norms for students in grades 2 through 5. *Teaching Exceptional Children, 24,* 41–44.

HASKELL, D. W., FOORMAN, B. R., & SWANK, P. R. (1992). Effects of three orthographic/phonological units on first-grade reading. *Remedial and Special Education, 13,* 40–49.

JUEL, C. (1988). Learning to read and write: A longitudinal study of fifty-four children from first through fourth grade. *Journal of Educational Psychology, 80*(4), 437–447.

JUEL, C. (1991). Beginning reading. In R. Barr, M. L. Kamil, P. B. Mosenthal, & P. D. Pearson (Eds.), *Handbook of reading research* (Vol. 2, pp. 759–788). New York: Longman.

KAMEENUI, E. J. (1994). Measurably superior instructional practices in measurably inferior times: Reflections on Twain and Pauli. In J. C. Cooper, T. Heron, J. Eshleman, & W. Heward (Eds.). *Behavior analyses in education: Focus on measurably superior instruction* (pp. 149–159). Pacific Grove, CA: Brookes/Cole.

KAMEENUI, E. J. (1996). Shakespeare and beginning reading: "The readiness is all." *Teaching Exceptional Children, 28*(2), 77–81.

KOZOL, J. (1985). *Illiterate America.* Garden City, N.Y.: Anchor Press/Doubleday.

LABERGE, D., & SAMUELS, S. J. (1974). Toward a theory of automatic information processing in reading. *Cognitive Psychology, 6,* 293–323.

LIBERMAN, I. Y., & LIBERMAN, A. M. (1990). Whole language vs. code emphasis: Underlying assumptions and their implications for reading instruction. *Annals of Dyslexia, 40,* 51–76.

LIBERMAN, I. Y., & SHANKWEILER, D. (1985). Phonology and the problems of learning to read and write. *Remedial and Special Education, 6,* 8–17.

LIBERMAN, I. Y., SHANKWEILER, D., CAMP, L., BLACHMAN, B., & WERFELMAN, M. (1980). Steps toward literacy. In P. Levinson & C. Sloan (Eds.), *Auditory processing and language: Clinical and research perspectives* (pp. 189–215). New York: Grune & Stratton.

MANN, V. A., & BRADY, S. (1988). Reading disability: The role of language deficiencies. *Journal of Consulting and Clinical Psychology, 56,* 811–816.

MANNING, J. C. (1995). Ariston metron. *The Reading Teacher, 48,* 650–659.

McGILL-FRANZEN, A., & ALLINGTON, R. L. (1991). Every child's right: Literacy. *The Reading Teacher, 45,* 86–90.

O'CONNOR, R. E., JENKINS, J. R., LEICESTER, N., & SLOCUM, T. A. (1993). Teaching phonological awareness to young children with learning disabilities. *Exceptional Children, 59,* 532–546.

PERFETTI, C. A. (1985). Reading ability. New York: Oxford University Press.

RACK, J. P., SNOWLING, M. J., & OLSON, R. K. (1992). The nonword reading deficit in developmental dyslexia: A review. *Reading Research Quarterly, 27,* 29–53.

SAWYER, D. (1992). Language abilities, reading acquisition, and developmental dyslexia: A discussion of hypothetical and observed relationships. *Journal of Learning Disabilities, 25,* 82–95.

SIMMONS, D. C, KAMEENUI, E. J. (in press). A focus on curriculum design: When children fail. In E. L. Meyer, G. A. Vergason, & R. J. Whelan (Eds.), *Strategies for teaching exceptional children in inclusive settings.* Denver, CO: Love Publishing Co.

SLAVIN, R. (1989). PET and the pendulum: Faddism in education and how to stop it. *Phi Delta Kappan, 90,* 750–758.

SMITH, S. B., SIMMONS, D. C., & KAMEENUI, E. J. (1995). *Synthesis of research on phonological awareness: Principles and implications for reading acquisition.* (Tech. Rep. No. 21). Eugene, OR: University of Oregon, National Center to Improve the Tools of Educators.

SNOWLING, M. J. (1991). Developmental reading disorders. *Journal of Child Psychology Psychiatry, 32,* 49–77.

SPEAR, L. D., & STERNBERG, R. J. (1986). An information processing framework for understanding reading disability. In S. Ceci (Ed.), *Handbook of cognitive, social, and neuropsychological aspects of learning disabilities* (Vol. 1, pp. 3–31). Hillsdale, NJ: Lawrence Erlbaum.

SPECTOR, J. E. (1992). Predicting progress in beginning reading: Dynamic assessment of phonemic awareness. *Journal of Educational Psychology, 84,* 353–363.

SPECTOR, J. E. (1995). Phonemic awareness training: Application of principles of direct instruction. *Reading and Writing Quarterly, 11,* 37–51.

STANOVICH, K. E. (1985). Explaining the variance in reading ability in terms of psychological processes: What have we learned? *Annals of Dyslexia, 35,* 67–96.

STANOVICH, K. E. (1986). Matthew effects in reading: Some consequences of individual differences in the acquisition of literacy. *Reading Research Quarterly, 21,* 360–407.

STANOVICH, K. E. (1991). Word recognition: Changing perspectives. In R. Barr, M. L. Kamil, P. B. Mosenthal, & P. D. Pearson (Eds.), *Handbook of reading research* (Vol. 2, pp. 418–452). New York: Longman.

STANOVICH, K. E. (1994). Romance and reality. *The Reading Teacher, 47,* 280–291.

STEIN, M. L. (1993). *The beginning reading instruction study.* Washington, DC: Office of Educational Research and Improvement, U. S. Department of Education.

TORGESEN, J. K. (1985). Memory processes in reading disabled children. *Journal of Learning Disabilities, 18,* 350–357.

TORGESEN, J., WAGNER, R., & RASHOTTE, C. (1994). Longitudinal studies of phonological processing and reading. *Journal of Learning Disabilities, 27,* 276–286.

U. S. DEPARTMENT OF EDUCATION. (1991). *America 2000: An education strategy.* Washington, DC: Author.

VELLUTINO, F. R. (1991). Introduction to three studies on reading acquisition: Convergent findings on theoretical foundations of code-oriented versus whole-language approaches to reading instruction. *Journal of Educational Psychology, 83,* 437–443.

VELLUTINO, F. R., & DENCKLA, M. B. (1991). Cognitive and neuropsychological foundations of word identification in poor and normally developing readers. In R. Barr, M. L. Kamil, P. B. Mosenthal, & P. D. Pearson (Eds.), *Handbook of reading research* (Vol. 2, pp. 571–608). New York: Longman.

VELLUTINO, F. R., & SCANLON, D. M. (1987a). Linguistic coding and reading ability. In S. Rosenberg (Eds.), *Advances in applied psycholinguistics* (pp. 1–69). New York: Cambridge University Press.

VELLUTINO, F. R., & SCANLON, D. M. (1987b). Phonological coding, phonological awareness, and reading ability: Evidence from a longitudinal and experimental study. *Merrill-Palmer Quarterly, 33,* 321–363.

WAGNER, R., & TORGESEN, J. (1987). The nature of phonological processing and its causal role in the acquisition of reading skills. *Psychological Bulletin, 101,* 192–212.

WOODWARD, J., & NOELL, J. (1992). Science instruction at the secondary level: Implications for students with learning disabilities. In Carnine, D., & Kameenui, E. J. (Eds.), *Higher order thinking: Designing curriculum for mainstreamed students* (pp. 39–58). Austin, TX: Pro-Ed.

AUTHOR NOTE

Preparation of this chapter manuscript was supported in part by The National Center to Improve the Tools of Educators (H180M10006), funded by the U. S. Department of Education, Office of Special Education Programs.

Correspondence concerning this chapter should be addressed to Edward J. Kameenui, Institute for the Development of Educational Achievement, College of Education, University of Oregon, Eugene, OR 97403-1211. Electronic mail may be sent via Internet to Edward_Kameenui@ccmail.uoregon.edu.

C H A P T E R

4

Effective Strategies for Teaching Writing

Robert C. Dixon
University of Oregon

Stephen Isaacson
Portland State University

Marcy Stein
University of Washington, Tacoma

WRITING IS A HIGHLY complex process that writers ultimately apply independently (Bereiter & Scardamalia, 1982). Conceivably, writing is one of the most complex human activities (Bereiter, 1980; Hillocks, 1987; Isaacson, 1989; Scardamalia, 1981.) The inherent complexity of writing suggests that acquiring writing proficiency might prove to be difficult for many students—a speculation borne out both by descriptive research and the experience of many teachers.

Applebee, Langer, & Mullis (1986) reported that students in fourth, eighth, and twelfth grades taking the National Assessment of Educational Progress (NAEP) performed poorly on measures of non-fiction writing: approximately half wrote adequate or better narrative and informative pieces, and only about a third wrote adequate or better persuasive pieces. Eleventh-grade students performed equally as poorly on the 1990 NAEP: they did not write much, and what they did write was of poor quality (National Assessment of Educational Progress, 1990). The NAEP data and other research (Applebee, Langer, Jenkins, Mullis, & Foertsch, 1990; Christenson, Thurlow, Ysseldyke, & McVicar, 1989; Flower & Hayes, 1981) suggest that students in general education experience many writing difficulties.

The students who experience the greatest difficulties with writing are those with learning disabilities and emotional and/or behavioral problems (Englert & Raphael, 1988; Graham, 1982; Graham, Harris, MacArthur & Graham, 1986; Morocco & Neuman, 1986; Montague, Maddux, & Dereshiwsky, 1990; Nodine, Barenbaum, & Newcomer, 1985; Thomas, Englert, & Gregg, 1987). Given the increasing diversity of children in classrooms (see section on learner characteristics in Chapter 2), there is a need to identify elements of writing instruction that are likely to be most effective at helping teachers improve the writing of the broadest possible range of students. That is, given the practical limitations of the classroom, which characteristics of a *single* writing curriculum are likely to contribute to improved performance for the majority of students?

In this chapter we describe a few fundamental characteristics of writing instruction that can contribute significantly to a single writing curriculum that is effective with a broad range of students at various performance levels. First, we briefly describe some current issues in writing instruction. Then we turn to the specifics of instructional design.

CURRENT ISSUES IN WRITING INSTRUCTION

Opportunity To Learn

We stress a *single* effective writing curriculum because frequently, little or no real writing instruction takes place in regular classrooms (Applebee et al., 1990; Bridge & Hiebert, 1985; Langer & Applebee, 1986). Therefore, it seems quite impractical to advocate the implementation of two or more writing curricula in diverse classrooms as a means of accommodating the needs of diverse learners.

It goes without saying that the minimal requirement for adequate writing achievement is that effective writing instruction be made available to students at all. In general, opportunity to learn has long been considered one of the major factors influencing achievement (in addition to pedagogical practice and aptitude; see Carroll, 1963). Students probably will not become better writers if they do not spend a relatively substantial part of most school days engaged in productive writing activities. Graves (1985) states, for example, that students should write for at least 30 minutes a day, at least four days a week, as opposed to a national average of writing one day in eight.

Author versus Secretary, or Author *and* Secretary

Not just any time allocated generally to "writing" is likely to result in notable writing improvement. For example, neither "free writing" nor instruction on grammar and writing mechanics have proven, by themselves, to be effective means for improving writing performance (Hillocks, 1984). The elements of meaningful allocated writing time are the principal subject of this chapter. (See Isaacson, in press, for a full discussion of academic learning time and writing instruction.)

Smith (1982, cited in Isaacson, 1991) characterizes writing as a complex undertaking in which the writer works both as author and secretary throughout the processes of writing. The writer-as-author is concerned primarily with matters of content, including the origination and organization of ideas, levels of diction, and so on. Simultaneously, the writer-as-secretary is concerned with the mechanics of writing. Sometimes the secretary role is characterized as a concern related almost solely to the revision phase of writing, but for students with learning difficulties, mechanical skills such as handwriting and spelling can present severe obstacles to participation in all authoring processes (Graham, 1990).

The author-as-secretary characterization provides a framework for identifying vastly different orientations toward writing instruction. The first is the skills-dominant approach, in which instruction focuses primarily on the mechanics of writing: secretarial concerns. Based on several descriptive studies, this approach has been the predominant one in American schools for many years (Applebee, 1981; Bridge & Hiebert, 1985; Langer & Applebee, 1986; Leinhardt, Zigmond, & Cooley, 1980). Within this approach, composition activities are minimal, often limited to writing short answers or transcribing.

Even less emphasis seems to placed on composition in skill-dominant approaches used with lower-performing students. Such students receive a great deal of skills instruction Englert et al., 1988, Graham et al., 1991; Isaacson, 1989; Roit & McKenzie, 1985), and even that instruction is poor, in that it occurs in isolation and is unconnected with its presumed eventual use (Graves, 1985).

Interestingly, skills-dominant approaches are polemical ghosts, in that they have little if anything to recommend them. To our knowledge, no one advocates skills-dominant approaches in the literature. If there is a rationale for such approaches at all, we can only speculate as to what it might be.

Perhaps someone believes that attention to mechanical skills will somehow result in improved composition. Perhaps someone believes that lower-performing youngsters are incapable of creating coherent text without first acquiring a full complement of mechanical skills. Or perhaps no rationale for skills-dominant approaches exists at all; for example, a teacher who is not comfortable with his or her own composition ability might inadvertently slight composition instruction in the classroom. We know for certain only that skills-dominated approaches are in widespread use, without the benefit of empirical or theoretical support.

A second, nearly opposite approach to writing may have evolved in reaction to skills-based approaches: the composition-dominant approach, concerned primarily with authoring aspects of writing. Advocates of this approach generally argue that instruction on mechanics should be restricted to those concerns students raise themselves in connection with the polishing stage of composition (DuCharme, Earl, & Poplin, 1989; Graves, 1983).

We have some general concerns with composition-dominant approaches. First, there is little research to support the hypothesis that the mechanics of writing will take care of themselves in the context of authentic writing experiences. Many of the gains reported anecdotally for students in composition-dominated programs could possibly be the result of maturation. In addition, some measures of collaborative efforts may mask individual achievement, or lack of it.

Second, there is strong evidence that mechanical difficulties can effectively preempt many students from meaningful participation in far more rewarding authoring roles (Graham, 1990; Morocco, Dalton, & Tivnan, 1990). The kinds of general difficulties experienced by many students with learning problems strongly suggest such students are not likely to acquire knowledge of any sort casually (Isaacson, 1991). In our well-justified haste to distance ourselves from skills-based approaches to writing, we should be cautious and thoughtful: mechanics are an integral part of writing.

If we envision writing as an interweaving of complexities involving both author and secretary roles, then perhaps parallel instruction is one means for resolving dominance conflicts. Within a parallel framework, instruction includes all aspects of writing from beginning to end—from conceptualization to "publication"—with a concerted focus on the integration of writing knowledge. (See Isaacson, 1989, for an in-depth discussion of this issue.)

PRINCIPLES FOR IMPROVING WRITING INSTRUCTION STRATEGIES

The implication of time allocated to writing instruction (or the lack of time allocated to writing instruction) is clear and, it seems, unanimously advocated: more time needs to be allocated. Any controversy that exists relates to different approaches to such allocation of time.

In this chapter we apply the six design principles highlighted in Chapter 1 to both the author role and the secretary role of writers. Although we separate the roles for the sake of illustration, we wish to re-emphasize that the roles co-exist and intertwine in authentic writing. Although the principles and applications we describe are research-based, we caution our readers that much of the substantial research conducted on writing in recent years is descriptive, anecdotal, quasi-experimental, or otherwise questionable as the basis for making broad generalizations about effective writing instruction (Graham et al., 1991). Still, data from a few very good studies, coupled with knowledge of diverse learners and instructional design research, provide the basis for cautiously identifying some important aspects of effective writing instruction for students at diverse levels of writing proficiency.

Designing Instruction Around Big Ideas

Big Ideas and the Author Role in Writing   In general, big ideas for writing instruction are those that seem to recur across successful writing programs. However, the notion of big ideas in general is not based as much on empirical evidence as on our intuitive analysis of the alternative: teaching small, inconsequential, or marginal aspects of writing.

Writing Process   One well-known big idea in writing is usually referred to as *the writing process*. The idea that writing instruction should center on the stages through which writers most frequently work goes back at least 25 years, when Herum and Cummings (1970) wrote on the writing process for college students. Those educators may have been ahead of their time, since the widespread acceptance of their approach in public schools is usually credited to Graves (1983).

Presumably, professional writers and those for whom writing is a major part of their profession have always reiteratively planned, drafted, and revised their work, dating back to the classical Greek rhetoricians. Surely it is past time for school children learning to write to be let in on this fairly public "secret" of good writers.

Text Structures   An awareness of the writing process by itself, however necessary to writing instruction, appears to be insufficient for consistent results, particularly for students with learning disabilities and with other learning difficulties (Englert et al., 1991). *Text structures* is another big authoring idea which has resulted in impressive achievement gains when combined with process writing. Each writing genre can be identified by its own set of structural characteristics. Stories, for example, always have a protagonist, a crisis, developing incidents, and a resolution. Students who are unaware of such common recurring elements might write "stories" that are more like rambling narratives than true stories.

Several studies have shown solid promise for teaching text structures and process writing in conjunction with one another (Graham & Harris, 1989; Hillocks, 1986; Meyer & Freedle, 1984). The work of Englert et al. (1991) is especially promising in terms of effective writing instruction for diverse learners in that it demonstrates how writing can be effectively taught simultaneously to mainstreamed learners with disabilities and their average-achieving peers.

Englert et al. (1991) also have shown a distinct advantage of focusing on big ideas: their instructional program taught *less*, but students learned *more*. That is, the program they developed taught only two text structures within a school year, but those structures (explanations and compare/contrast) were important to future schooling success, students learned them well, and the results on measures of transference were good. In contrast, our informal analysis of language arts texts reveals that between a dozen and two dozen text structures are typically "taught for exposure" within a single school year. When too much material is "taught for exposure" or merely "covered," many students appear to learn and retain little. The study by Englert et al. suggests that "less is more" when the content chosen is truly important.

Peer Interaction   Finally, peer interaction appears to be important for improved composition performance. Collaborative work has proven to be an effective instructional tool in many subject matter domains, but it has a partic-ular benefit to writing instruction: when working in cooperative groups, each student has the opportunity to participate in authoring, editing, and reading. Although the act of writing is often a covert and solitary endeavor for mature and able writers, those learning to write benefit from many opportunities to talk about writing with peers.

Big Ideas and the Secretary Role in Writing

We can conceive of several potential big ideas related to writing mechanics, ideas that promote understanding and reduce the learning burden for stu-dents. Morphology may be a big idea for spelling instruction (Dixon, 1991; Henry, 1988). The idea of combining manuscript and cursive writing into a sin-gle system, as in the D'Nealian writing program (Brown, 1984), promises sub-stantial efficiency for teaching handwriting. Effective keyboarding instruction also might help to reduce the burden of simply setting print to page (Brown, 1984) and promises substantial efficiency in teaching handwriting.

Hillocks' (1984) widely known research review of effective writing prac-tices suggested that although sentence combining alone is not the most effec-tive way to improve writing, it was more effective than other approaches exam-ined (teaching grammar, free writing, using good models of writing). Sentence combining and manipulation, then, might be considered a significant but non-dominant big idea for teaching writing mechanics. (We illustrate this possibil-ity more fully in later sections of this chapter.)

The notion of big ideas is less an "instructional design characteristic" than a foundation on which to build successful instruction. We do not *design* big ideas; we uncover them through a careful and complete analysis of content-area literature. Big ideas do not guide us on *how* to teach; they are a major fac-tor in determining *what* to focus on as we design instruction.

Designing Conspicuous Strategies

Conspicuous Strategies and the Author Role in Writing   Most students with learning difficulties, and many average-achieving students, do not automatically benefit from simply being exposed to big ideas, such as the steps in the writing process or text structures. A substantial body of research is accumulating that supports the teaching of conspicuous strategies for using those ideas (See Deshler & Schumaker, 1986; Pressley, Symons, Snyder, & Cariglia-Bull, 1989).

A teacher once described to the first author of this chapter the difference between the "old" and "new" ways of teaching writing for one of her students: "He used to sit, unable to get started, when trying to write about his summer vacation. Now, he sits, unable to get started, when trying to *plan* what he is going to write."

A conspicuous "planning strategy" could clarify for students some specific steps for starting and successfully completing their planning. The steps in such strategies derive from the best efforts of subject matter specialists to uncover or emulate cognitive processes that are normally employed covertly by experts. However, teaching just any set of steps to follow does not necessarily constitute a good strategy.

The best strategies appear to be those that are "intermediate in generality" (Prawat, 1989). If a strategy is too general, it is not likely to lead to reliable results. For example, "think before you write" is a general strategy and a good idea, but is too general to be of much practical value for many learners. On the other hand, a strategy that is too narrow is likely to result in the rote acquisition of some bit of knowledge with little potential for transference.

Conspicuous strategy instruction has been used with promising results to teach all phases of the writing process: planning (Harris & Graham, 1985), text structure (Englert et al., 1991; Graham & Harris, 1989), and revising (MacArthur, Graham, & Schwartz 1991). Such strategies have appeared to meet the "intermediate in generality" criteria.

For example, Graham and Harris (1989) taught students to generate and organize story ideas by asking themselves questions related to the parts of the story: "What does the main character want to do?" (p. 98). On the one hand, the strategy was not too broad. The questions taught in the study all involved parts of stories. On the other hand, the strategy was broad enough: it directed students' attention to the elements common to all stories.

Conspicuous Strategies and the Secretary Role in Writing   Assume that a student is puzzling over the following sentence while attempting to edit and revise a draft:

All of we young people seem to like ice cream.

Is it, the student wonders, *we* or *us* young people? In terms of grammar, the answer can involve a complex array of spiraling knowledge: nominative case, objective case, objects of verbs, objects of prepositions, predicate nominatives, appositives. It is little wonder that many teachers would choose to forgo a grammatical approach in favor of nearly almost any other option, such as telling the student the answer or suggesting that the student rewrite the sentence to make the problem disappear.

Yet the problem can be attacked via conspicuous strategy instruction, with relatively little effort and complexity, and with relatively high potential for transference. The strategy is to decompose or simplify the sentence in question, then examine the results:

#8

> *All young people seem to like ice cream.*
> *All of we/us seem to like ice cream.*

A native speaker of English who does not have a severe language disorder will instantly recognize *us* as the correct choice in the simpler sentence and realize that it is therefore the correct choice in the original sentence.

The same general strategy can be applied to far different instances of pronoun case, and to difficulties not involving pronoun case at all.

pronoun case: compounds

John gave Mary and I/me a new book.
John gave Mary a new book.
John gave me a new book.

subject/verb agreement

Original sentence: *None of the boys was/were on time.*
First simplification: *Not one of the boys was/were on time.*
Second simplification: *Not one was on time.*

Designing conspicuous strategies is challenging. We tend to readily recognize good strategies that others have designed, but most instructional designers agree that designing a good strategy from scratch is no simple matter. The best we can do is suggest that anyone attempting to design conspicuous strategies begin with *something*, then evaluate the early attempts critically, using "intermediate generality" as the principal criterion for analysis. Whenever possible, promising strategies should be field-tested with students.

Designing Mediated Scaffolding

Mediated Scaffolding and the Author Role in Writing   We are using the term "scaffolding" broadly to refer to many kinds of assistance that students may receive as they move toward deeper understanding of what is being taught. Scaffolding may be provided directly by teachers, through guidance and feedback; or it may be provided by peers, through collaboration, or built in to instructional materials, through devices that facilitate the successful completion of various tasks.

A primary characteristic of conspicuous strategy instruction, discussed above, is scaffolding and guided practice in various forms (Graham & Harris, 1991; Pressley, Harris, & Marks, 1992; Pressley et al., 1989).

Two aspects of such scaffolding seem worthy of special note. First, it is provided on an "as needed" basis and is gradually diminished over time. Second, it includes not only strategies for accomplishing writing goals but provides for self-regulation as well. That is, students are taught to regulate their own thinking about the use of composing strategies. Taken together, these features seem critical to the goal of independence for students with learning difficulties and their average-achieving peers alike.

In addition, collaborative work among students constitutes a form of scaffolding. When students work together on projects, they act as resources for one another for everything from planning a piece of writing to final revision and editing. We should caution, however, that practitioners might be careful to observe the same gradual reduction of scaffolding as advocated by Graham et al. (1991). Otherwise, there is the danger that some students will develop a dependency on collaboration.

The kinds of scaffolding that are built into tasks are sometimes referred to as *procedural facilitators*. The idea of using procedural facilitation for writing originated with Bereiter and Scardamalia (1982). It is a form of help that assumes students have underlying competencies, but that they are having difficulty implementing them due to the complexity of writing. For example, if a student really "knows" the structure of a given text type, such as a story, but can't effectively plan a draft around that structure because of the complexities involved, then a procedural facilitator could help lessen the cognitive burden of the task.

Graham et al. (1991) caution that the effective use of procedural facilitators is probably dependent on integration with other forms of help whenever the cause of student difficulties is something other than inability to execute complex cognitive demands. That is, if students know how to do something complex, but have trouble using that knowledge, then a procedural facilitator alone might be enough help. But if students have not learned the complex strategy to begin with, then other types of scaffolding are probably necessary. Englert et al. (1991) used procedural facilitation, in conjunction with big ideas, strategies, and other instructional characteristics, to teach writing simultaneously to mainstreamed students with learning disabilities and their nondisabled peers.

Figure 4–1 contains a series of think sheets that illustrate how procedural facilitators for the writing process can enhance the effectiveness of other instructional considerations. All five think sheets are designed to facilitate stages in the writing process: planning, drafting, revision, and editing.

Figure 4–1a gives students guidance in planning their writing. The potential in such a procedural facilitator is probably most likely to be realized when it is used in conjunction with scaffolded strategy instruction: teacher and student models of planning, frequent discussion with teachers and peers, and frequent monitoring of student work and feedback.

Figure 4–1b specifically facilitates the drafting of one particular text structure: explanations. A different genre, such as a story, requires a different think sheet. An example of a story organization think sheet is given in Figure 4–2.

Planning Think Sheet

Name of writer _____   Date _____

Topic _____

Who will the audience be?

What is my goal?

Everything I already know about this topic—anything I can think of:

_____   _____

_____   _____

_____   _____

_____   _____

Possible ways to group my ideas:

_____   _____   _____

_____   _____   _____

_____   _____   _____

_____   _____   _____

_____   _____   _____

_____   _____   _____

_____   _____   _____

_____   _____   _____

FIGURE 4–1A
Think Sheet for Helping Students Plan Their Writing

Figure 4–1c helps students understand the "inner dialogue" role of writers and helps encourage self-regulation. This self-editing think sheet gives students an opportunity to reflect on a draft and to possibly make changes before anyone else reads it.

The "Editor's Feedback Worksheet" illustrated in Figure 4–1d is based on the assumption that students might not only have difficulty with their own writing, but difficulty giving constructive feedback on the writing of others as well. We base that assumption less on descriptive research than on the observations of many teachers with whom we have worked.

Finally, Figure 4–1e illustrates a think sheet that could help facilitate revision. In addition to providing guided application of revision strategies, it helps put the role of editors in perspective: that of a valuable resource.

Not only can any given phase of instruction be scaffolded, but instruction on writing a given text structure from beginning to end can be scaffolded as well. Englert et al. (1991), for example, had students write their first explanation as a group project, with a great deal of interaction among students and between teachers and students. Next, students wrote individual papers, but also with substantial support from teachers and other students. Finally, students wrote a *third* explanation in which students were encouraged to write independently, but were given support as needs arose.

That sequence of events can be summarized as *four* extensive opportunities with a single text structure: a complete teacher model of all phases in the writing process as they apply to explanations; the complete development of a class explanation; and two individually written explanations. In the course of the study, students studied explanations extensively, and learned to write them well. This approach is in contrast to that of typical language arts texts, in which a single text structure is taught in a period of a week or less, with little evidence of effectiveness.

Mediated Scaffolding and the Secretary Role in Writing   Few students are likely to fully understand and apply sentence-manipulation strategies, such as

---

Organization Think Sheet
Explanation

What am I explaining? _____

What will the reader need (if anything)? Is there any special setting for this?

_____

What can I tell readers at the beginning to get them interested? _____

_____

List the steps:

1. _____

2. _____

3. _____

4. _____

5. _____

6. _____

First   Next   Then   After   Second   Third   Finally

FIGURE 4–1B
Think Sheet for Helping Students Organize an Explanation

Self-Editing Think Sheet
Explanation

My Impressions

The things I like best   The things I like least

_____   _____

_____   _____

A Good Explanation?

Everything is clear. ☐

There is a statement saying what is being explained. ☐

I've used good keywords. ☐   The steps are in order. ☐

I've added something of special interest to my readers. ☐

I've included what is needed, if anything. ☐

I've finished with a good summary statement. ☐

Questions I would like to ask my editor—friends, teachers, parents—before revising:

1. _____

2. _____

Ideas for Revision

_____   _____

_____   _____

_____   _____

_____   _____

FIGURE 4–1C
Think Sheet for Helping Students Edit Their Own Drafts

those outlined in the last section, without support. Such support can come in a variety of forms, including teacher guidance on the use of procedural facilitators such as those illustrated in Figure 4–3.

In Level 1 tasks, strategies are modeled and heavy scaffolding is provided to ensure that students' first attempts to apply the strategy are successful. At each successive level, a piece of scaffolding is taken away, leading to self-regulated, independent application—at Level 5 in this case. This is in sharp contrast to the approach taken in many textbooks, in which students are given a model, no explicit strategy based on big ideas, and then are expected to complete several application tasks independently.

A straightforward procedure for designing scaffolded tasks is that of beginning at the end. That is, the easiest tasks to design are generally those that represent the final, independent *outcome* that we would like to see students achieve. In the example given in Figure 4–3, the Level 5 task is the outcome task. From here, the designer can work backwards, modifying the outcome task slightly by making it slightly easier, then making that task slightly easier, until the designer reaches the beginning: a highly scaffolded task that ensures high success for all or nearly all students.

Designing Strategic Integration

Strategic Integration and the Author Role in Writing   The issue of knowledge integration is crucial at several levels in language arts instruction. At the

---

Editor's Feedback Worksheet

Title of paper I am editing: _____

Author _____

1. What I like most about this paper: _____

     _____

2. Parts I think are not clear: _____

     _____

     _____

3. Suggestions for improving:

   ☐ Better Introduction   ☐ Better Use of Keywords

   ☐ More Examples   ☐ Change Organization

   ☐ Other _____

     _____

     _____

     _____

FIGURE 4–1D
Think Sheet for Helping Students Give Feedback to Other Students

---

Revision Think Sheet

Suggestions from my Editor

1. Read editor's feedback worksheet carefully.

2. List the suggestions you are interested in using:

_____

_____

_____

Adding Polish

1. At this point, can you think of a good way to get your readers interested right at the beginning of the paper?

_____

2. Does each part of the paper make the reader want to read the next part? _____

3. How is your ending? Any additional ideas for summing everything up neatly?

_____

Revising

Use this page, your self-edit think sheet, and your editor's feedback worksheet as the basis for beginning to revise your draft.

Consider submitting your revision to an editor for further feedback.

FIGURE 4–1E
Think Sheet for Helping Students Revise Their Drafts

broadest level, reading and writing instruction can potentially be integrated based on the observation that writers are readers and readers, hopefully, are writers. This relationship between reading and writing has been illustrated by Raphael and Englert (1990).

Also of particular interest is the relationship between writing mechanics and composition. A genuinely holistic view of writing, we believe, must accommodate all those writing elements that in fact intertwine to produce "good writing."

Specific to composition, knowledge of basic text structure should be integrated as a means of efficiently teaching more advanced and complex structures—those used most frequently by "expert" writers. One major instructional contributor to such integration is cumulative review (discussed in a later section of this chapter).

The major ingredients of instruction aimed at achieving integration appear to be, first, that students acquire fluency with the knowledge to be integrated, and, second, that instruction deliberately focuses on the integration of such knowledge. All of the instructional characteristics discussed in this chapter potentially contribute to the former: a focus on big ideas, strategies, and so on. In fact, a focus on big ideas alone would tend to encourage knowledge integration because big ideas typically comprise other knowledge realms within a domain.

Strategic Integration and the Secretary Role in Writing In addition to integrating writing mechanics and composition, we believe that mechanics should be integrated among themselves. The Level 5 task illustrated in Figure 4–3 might be the end of isolated work on pronoun case, but it should be the beginning of integration. When students write, they must discriminately select from among their entire repertoire of writing knowledge. In authentic writing, they are not "prompted" to use the correct case for pronouns, for instance.

Organization Think Sheet
Story

Protagonist?_____

Antagonist? _____

What is the crisis or problem the protagonist must overcome?

_____

Developing Incidents

_____

_____

_____

_____

_____

Climax

_____

_____

Ending

_____

_____

FIGURE 4–2
Think Sheet for Helping Students Organize a Story

Level 1: Interactive Model/Heavy Scaffold

Sometimes it is difficult to know when to use words such as *I* and *me* or *she* and *her*. You can usually figure out the right word to use by breaking the sentence into two simpler sentences.

Circle the correct choice in the second simpler sentence. That is the correct choice in the longer sentence.

1. Longer sentence: The doctor gave Elicia and I / me a flu shot.
   Simpler sentences:
   The doctor gave Elicia a flu shot.
   The doctor gave I / me a flu shot.

Level 2: Relatively Heavy Scaffolding

You can usually figure out what word to use by breaking a sentence into two simpler sentences.

For each sentence, one simpler sentence is given for you. First, write the other simpler sentence. Then circle the right word in the longer sentence.

1. Longer sentence: She / Her and John lived next door to us for four years.
   John lived next door to us for four years.

   _____

Level 3: Minor Prompting for Scaffolding

For each sentence, write the two simpler sentences. Then circle the right word in the longer sentence.

1. Before going on our camping trip, Melinda and I / me prepared all our supplies.

   _____

   _____

Level 4: Only Reminder as Scaffold

Circle the correct word in each sentence. Remember, the word that's right in the simpler sentence is also right in the longer sentence.

1. After the team members left, they / them and some other friends went out for burgers.

Level 5: Independent—No Scaffolding

Circle the correct word in each sentence.

1. The movie started before Jaques and I / me arrived.

FIGURE 4–3
Levels of Scaffolding for a Sentence-Manipulation Strategy

Cumulative review serves as a means for making instructional tasks closely emulate the conditions of writing.

Integration is not difficult to design into instruction if the designer keeps one principle in mind: don't force it. It might be tempting to jump on a knowledge integration bandwagon, but an instructional designer should focus on those aspects of a content area that integrate naturally. For example, if morphology is a big idea in spelling instruction, then spelling, vocabulary, etymology, and even parts of speech interrelate with one another naturally. The morphological parts of the word *alchemist*, for instance, relate to spelling (*al* + *chem* + *ist*), vocabulary (*al-* means "the" and *chem* means "to pour"), word history (the part *al-* comes from the Arabic), and parts of speech (*-ist* means "one who" and forms nouns).

Designing Primed Background Knowledge

Primed Background Knowledge and the Author Role in Writing   With respect to composition, primed background knowledge is a less critical characteristic of effective instruction relative to other content areas. Learning a given text structure, for example, is not dependent upon a large base of other foundational knowledge. The knowledge that is required to learn text structures can be characterized as the kinds of basic "knowledge of the world" that most school children, other than those with the severest disabilities, are likely to possess.

Primed Background Knowledge and the Secretary Role in Writing Primed background knowledge is usually important with respect to the acquisition of writing mechanics skill and knowledge. Relative to grammar and usage, in particular, background knowledge can be of crucial importance, depending on the strategies employed to teach these areas. For example, the "traditional" approach to teaching pronoun case is through the use of grammatical rules. Those rules, in turn, depend heavily on a broad and deep range of background knowledge, including, possibly, the notion of case, objects of verbs and of prepositions, subjects, and pronouns.

An instructional designer can determine necessary background knowledge by examining strategies closely. Are there any concepts in the strategy that students might not know fluently? One option for accommodating background knowledge is to test for it. Students who already have prerequisite background knowledge are ready to learn the material. Other students either should not be placed in the instruction, or if they are placed, the instruction should include necessary background knowledge.

Designing Judicious Review

Judicious Review and the Author Role in Writing   Review in writing instruction has received little attention in the literature. However, the general benefits of review have been shown across content areas through relatively substantial research. Dempster (1991), for example, summarizes that effective review is adequate, distributed, cumulative, and varied. In addition, there is reason to believe that even excellent writing instruction might be further improved through use of effective review. Graham et al. (1991) point out that we need to "continue to investigate procedures for promoting strategy maintenance and generalization" (p. 103).

The study by Englert et al. (1991) illustrates the potential benefits of *adequate* review. With a complex cognitive process such as composing, it is not surprising to find that a large amount of application opportunity is necessary for mastery.

We are unaware of direct or indirect research on distributed review as it applies to composition. However, the procedures recommended by Englert and her associates (Englert et al., 1991; Raphael & Englert, 1990) tend to strongly support cumulative review, and to a lesser degree, distributed review.

Englert and her associates initially teach distinct text structures, such as explanation and compare and contrast. They teach those structures *thoroughly*: approximately half a school year each for explanations and compare and contrast. Compared with the typical basal "one-topic-per-week" organization, this approach might be thought of as *very* massed practice. However, because scaffolding is gradually reduced as students learn, this approach has some of the attributes of distributed practice as well.

Eventually, students combine basic text structures into more complex writing, scaffolded in part by "expert think sheets" which are more generic than those for specific text structures. Such practice, in effect, constitutes both a distribution and an accumulation of knowledge.

Finally, in order to promote transference and generalization, review should be varied. With respect to composition specifically, work on a particular text structure can be reasonably varied by simply allowing students to select different topics about which to write. There is evidence, too, of generalization from a set of basic text structures to more complex texts incorporating one or more of the basic structures. For example, in a persuasive essay it is common to find elements of non-fiction narrative, explanation, and comparison and contrast. The crucial prerequisite for such transference appears to be that the "transfer knowledge" (basic text structures) be taught thoroughly to begin with (Englert et al., 1991).

When review is not varied, the result is likely to be a rote-like acquisition of knowledge. The opposite extreme also is possible: review may be so varied that *something else* is actually being reviewed.

Judicious Review and the Secretary Role in Writing   How much review of sentence-manipulation strategies is adequate? The answer can be found only through field testing with students. However, that amount might be relatively small. First, the strategy is meaningful, which enhances memory (Torgeson, 1988). Second, if the review is well distributed, less total review should be required.

Reviewing cumulatively is critical to full understanding and to realistic integration with composition. In a sense, the Level 5 task shown in Figure 4–3 is still scaffolded to some extent, simply because it applies to only one of many possible applications of sentence-manipulation strategies: first-person plural pronouns in appositives. To learn just how sentence manipulation can be applied to solve a variety of writing mechanics problems, the strategy would need to be applied to those problems cumulatively, as each type is taught (pronouns in compounds, subject-verb agreement, several punctuation applications, etc.).

Finally, the review should include widely varying examples, in order to promote transference of the strategy, but the examples should not vary to the extent that something untaught is being "reviewed." We found a lesson in a language arts basal text, for example, that only addressed pronoun case in compounds, with no instruction on the appositives, but then almost immediately gave students practice on pronoun case in appositives.

SUMMARY

Our discussion of designing effective writing instruction is cast in the context that such instruction is *important* for so many students (Englert et al., 1988). Writing is not just an end in and of itself, but a means by which students demonstrate their knowledge within various content areas (Christenson et al., 1989; Graham, 1982; Harris & Graham, 1985).

We have looked at designing both composition instruction and instruction on writing mechanics. The research in recent years on teaching composition is heartening and promising for all students, but particularly for students with learning difficulties. Some well-designed studies have shown, for instance, that students with learning disabilities can achieve at a level equal to their average-achieving peers (Englert et al., 1991; Graham & Harris, 1989).

Big ideas in composition instruction appear to be supported strongly, if tacitly, in the work of researchers in the field. The biggest of the big ideas are process writing, text structures, and collaboration. The recommendation of making expert cognitive processes visible through explicit strategy instruction is quite directly supported by research on explicit strategy instruction, as is the scaffolding of instruction.

The effectiveness of teaching explicit strategies depends on the design of good strategies, but is likely, too, to be influenced by students' background knowledge. There is strong research to support the characteristics of effective review, and the need for maintenance and generalization in composition instruction is clear; however, more direct research is needed on the impact of review on composition. Finally, "complete understanding" in any sense implies the full integration of important knowledge—another area that might well benefit from more direct research.

When we turn our backs on instruction in writing mechanics, we are essentially turning our backs on many diverse learners. Without doubt, there exists an endless array of examples of poor—even terrible—writing skills sheets. That does not mean, however, that thoughtful educators, informed by research on composition, cannot find effective ways to teach mechanics and to integrate them smoothly into composition activities. The *principal* prerequisites for this, no doubt, are that effective composition instruction take place on a regular and sustained basis, and that instruction on writing mechanics be reasoned and systematically integrated with composition.

REFERENCES

APPLEBEE, A. (1981). *Writing in the secondary school: English and the content areas.* Urbana, IL: National Council of Teachers of English.

APPLEBEE, A., LANGER, J., JENKINS, L., MULLIS, I., & FOERTSCH, M. (1990). *Learning to write in our nation's schools.* Princeton, NJ: Educational Testing Service.

APPLEBEE, A., LANGER, J., & MULLIS, I. (1986). *The writing report card: Writing achievement in American schools.* Princeton, NJ: Educational Testing Service.

BEREITER, C. (1980). Development in writing. In L. Gregg, & E. R. Steinberg (Eds.), *Cognitive processes in writing* (pp. 73–93). Hillsdale, NJ: Lawrence Erlbaum.

BEREITER, C., & SCARDAMALIA, M. (1982) From conversation to composition: The role of instruction in a developmental process. In R. Glaser (Ed.), *Advances in instructional psychology* (Vol. 2, pp. 1–64). Hillsdale, NJ: Lawrence Erlbaum.

BRIDGE, C., & HIEBERT, E. (1985). A comparison of classroom writing practices, teachers' perceptions of their writing instruction, and textbook recommendations on writing practices. *Elementary School Journal, 86,* 155–172.

BROWN, V. L. (1984). D'Nealian handwriting: What is it and how to teach it. *Remedial and Special Education, 5*(5), 48–52.

CARROLL, J. (1963). A model for school learning. *Teacher's College Record, 64,* 723–733.

CHRISTENSON, S., THURLOW, M., YSSELDYKE, J., & McVICAR, R. (1989). Writing language instruction for students with mild handicaps: Is there enough quantity to ensure quality. *Learning Disabilities Quarterly, 12,* 219–229.

DEMPSTER, F. N. (1991). Synthesis of research on reviews and tests. *Educational Leadership, 4,* 71–76.

DESHLER, D. D., & SCHUMAKER, J. B. (1986). Learning strategies: An instructional alternative for low-achieving adolescents. *Exceptional Children, 52*(6), 583–590.

DIXON, R. C. (1991). The application of sameness analysis to spelling. *Journal of Learning Disabilities, 24*(5), 285–310.

DuCHARME, C., ERAL, J., & POPLIN, M. S. (1989). The author model: The constructivist view of the writing process. *Learning Disability Quarterly, 12,* 237–242.

ENGLERT, C. S., & RAPHAEL, T. (1988). Constructing well-formed prose: Process, structure, and metacognitive knowledge. *Exceptional Children, 54,* 513–520.

ENGLERT, C. S., RAPHAEL, T., ANDERSON, L., ANTHONY, H., FEAR, K., & GREGG, S. (1988). A case for writing intervention: Strategies for writing informational text. *Learning Disabilities Focus, 3,* 98–113.

ENGLERT, C. S., RAPHAEL, T., ANDERSON, L., ANTHONY, H., STEVENS, D., & FEAR, K. (1991). Making writing strategies and self-talk visible: Cognitive strategy instruction in writing in regular and special education classrooms. *American Educational Research Journal, 28,* 337–372.

FLOWER, L., & HAYES, J. (1981). A cognitive process theory of writing. *College Composition and Communication, 32,* 365–387.

GRAHAM, S. (1982). Composition research and practice: A unified approach. *Focus on Exceptional Children, 14*(8), 1–16.

GRAHAM, S. (1990). The role of production factors in learning disabled students' compositions. *Journal of Educational Psychology, 80,* 781–791.

GRAHAM, S., & HARRIS, K. R. (1989). A components analysis of cognitive strategy instruction: Effects on learning disabled students' compositions and self-efficacy. *Journal of Educational Psychology, 81,* 356–361.

GRAHAM, S., HARRIS, K. R., MACARTHUR, C. S., & SCHWARTZ, S. (1991). Writing and writing instruction for students with learning disabilities: Review of a research program. *Learning Disability Quarterly, 14,* 89–114.

GRAVES, D. (1983). *Writing: Teachers and children at work.* Exeter, NH: Heinemann.

GRAVES, D. (1985). All children can write. *Learning Disabilities Focus, 1*(1), 36–43.

HARRIS, K., & GRAHAM, S. (1985). Improving learning disabled students' composition skills: Self-control strategy training. *Learning Disabilities Quarterly, 8,* 27–36.

HENRY, M. K. (1988). Beyond phonics: Integrated decoding and spelling instruction based on word origin and structure. *Annals of Dyslexia, 38,* 258–272.

HERUM, J., & CUMMINGS, D. W. (1970). *Writing: plans, drafts and revisions.* New York: Random House.

HILLOCKS, G. (1984, November). What works in teaching composition: A meta-analysis of experimental treatment studies. *American Journal of Education, 93,* 133–170.

HILLOCKS, G. (1986). *Research on written composition.* Urbana, IL: National Conference on Research in English.

HILLOCKS, G. (1987). Synthesis of research on teaching writing. *Educational Leadership, 44,* 71–82.

ISAACSON, S. (1989). Role of secretary vs. author: Resolving the conflict in writing instruction. *Learning Disability Quarterly, 12,* 209–217.

ISAACSON, S. (1991). Written expression and the challenges for students with learning problems. *Exceptionality Education Canada, 1*(3), 45–57.

ISAACSON, S. (in press). Process, product, and purpose: Written expression and the role of instruction. *Reading Research Quarterly.*

LANGER, J., & APPLEBEE, A. (1986). Reading and writing instruction: Toward a theory of teaching and learning. In E. Rothkopf (Ed.), *Review of research in education* (Vol. 13, pp. 171–194). Washington, DC: American Educational Research Association.

LEINHARDT, G., ZIGMOND, N., & COOLEY, W. (1980). *Reading instruction and its effects.* Paper presented at the American Educational Research Association Annual Meeting, San Francisco, CA.

MACARTHUR, C. A., GRAHAM, S., & SCHWARTZ, S. (1991). Knowledge of revision and revising behavior among students with learning disabilities. *Learning Disability Quarterly, 14,* 61–73.

MEYER, B. J. F., & FREEDLE, R. O. (1984). Effects of discourse type on recall. *American Education Research Journal, 21,* 121–144.

MONTAGUE, M., MADDUX, C., & DERESHIWSKY, M. I. (1990). Story grammar and comprehension and production of narrative prose by students with learning disabilities. *Journal of Learning Disabilities, 23,* 190–197.

MOROCCO, C. C., DALTON, B. M., & TIVNAN, T. (1990, April). *The impact of computer-supported writing instruction on the writing quality of 4th grade students with and without learning disabilities*. Paper presented at the Annual Meeting of the American Educational Research Association, Boston.

MOROCCO, C., & NEUMAN, S. (1986). Word processors and the acquisition of writing strategies. *Journal of Learning Disabilities, 19,* 243–247.

NATIONAL ASSESSMENT OF EDUCATIONAL PROGRESS. (1993). *What's wrong with writing and what can we do right now?* (Research Report). Washington, DC: Office of Educational Research and Improvement. (ERIC Document Reproduction Service No. ED 356 477)

NODINE, B., BARENBAUM, E., & NEWCOMER, P. (1985). Story composition by learning disabled, reading disabled, and normal children. *Learning Disabilities Quarterly, 8,* 167–179.

PRAWAT, R. S. (1989). Promoting access to knowledge, strategy, and disposition in students: A research synthesis. *Review of Educational Research, 59*(1), 1–41.

PRESSLEY, M., HARRIS, K. R., & MARKS, M. B. (1992). But good strategy instructors are constructivists! *Educational Psychology Review, 4*(1), 3–31.

PRESSLEY, M., SYMONS, S., SNYDER, B. B., & CARIGLIA-BULL, T. (1989). Strategy instruction research comes of age. *Learning Disability Quarterly, 12,* 16–31.

RAPHAEL, T., & ENGLERT, C. S. (1990, February). Writing and reading: Partners in construction meaning. *The Reading Teacher, 43*(6), 388–400.

ROIT, M., & MCKENZIE, R. (1985). Disorders of written communication: An instructional priority for LD students. *Journal of Learning Disabilities, 18,* 258–260.

SCARDAMALIA, M. (1981). How children cope with the cognitive demands of writing. In C. H. Frederiksen (Ed.), *Writing: The nature, development, and teaching of written communication. Vol. 2, Writing: process, development, and communication* (pp. 81–103). Hillsdale, NJ: Lawrence Erlbaum.

SMITH, F. (1982). *Writing and the writer.* New York: Holt, Rinehart & Winston.

THOMAS, C., ENGLERT, C. C., & GREGG, S. (1987). An analysis of errors and strategies in the expository writing of learning disabled students. *Remedial and Special Education, 8,* 21–30.

TORGESON, J. K. (1988). Studies of children with learning disabilities who perform poorly on memory span tasks. *Journal of Learning Disabilities, 21,* 605–612.

AUTHOR NOTE

Preparation of this chapter manuscript was supported in part by The National Center to Improve the Tools of Educators (H180M10006), funded by the U. S. Department of Education, Office of Special Education Programs.

Correspondence concerning this chapter should be addressed to Robert C. Dixon, Institute for the Development of Educational Achievement, College of Education, University of Oregon, Eugene, OR 97403-1211. Electronic mail may be sent via Internet to rcdixon@ix.netcom.com.

CHAPTER

5

Effective Strategies for Teaching Mathematics

Douglas W. Carnine, Robert C. Dixon, Jerry Silbert
University of Oregon

THIS CHAPTER DESCRIBES considerations for improving instruction for learners at diverse performance levels. Improved instruction alone cannot meet all the challenges that the needs of such learners present. However, the contribution of improved instruction can be enormous and can play a central role in any serious school improvement effort. As noted in Chapter 1, a separate technical report summarizes the research basis for these considerations (Dixon, Carnine, & Kameenui, 1992). While these considerations also contribute to the learning of average and above-average students, the considerations are particularly important for diverse learners. Most of the examples in this chapter are taken from a mathematics program designed to accommodate diverse learners, *Connecting Math Concepts* (Engelmann, Carnine, Kelly, & Engelmann, 1994). The first consideration—organizing content around big ideas—is particularly beneficial for all students, including high-performing students.

The unique curricular needs of diverse learners in meeting high standards were acknowledged by the National Council of Teachers of Mathematics (NCTM) in their publication, *Curriculum and Evaluation Standards for School Mathematics* (1989):

> *Students with Different Needs and Interests.* The consequences of dealing with students with different talents, achievements, and interests have led to such practices as grouping and tracking and to special programs for gifted or handicapped students who need and deserve special attention. However, we believe that *all* students can benefit from an opportunity to study the core curriculum specified in the *Standards*. This can be accomplished by expanding and enriching the curriculum to meet the needs of each individual student, including the gifted and those of lesser capabilities and interests. We challenge teachers and other educators to develop and experiment with course outlines and grouping patterns to present the mathematics in the *Standards* in a meaningful, productive way (p. 253).

The focus of this chapter, then, can be thought of as specific recommendations for meeting the NCTM challenge.

CURRENT ISSUES IN MATHEMATICS INSTRUCTION

There is little, if any, real controversy over the goals of mathematics instruction, as exemplified within the NCTM *Standards* (1989): students should (a) learn to value mathematics, (b) become confident in their ability to do mathematics, (c) become mathematical problem-solvers, (d) learn to communicate mathematically, and (e) learn to reason mathematically. It is important to note that mathematics educators are not recommending watered-down or second-rate mathematics content for diverse learners. Rather, the goal is to devise curriculum and instruction techniques so that these students can think, solve problems, and reason.

Controversy arises when we look specifically at *how* learners in general, and students with learning difficulties in particular, can best achieve the goals of mathematics instruction. Even then, much of the controversy may be largely a result of relative emphasis.

For example, the NCTM *Standards* (1989) place a strong emphasis on the use of manipulatives in mathematics instruction, based on the assumption that students will subsequently discover an understanding of the algorithms associated with manipulatives activities. However, Evans (1990) found that students mastered concepts regardless of whether work with manipulatives preceded or followed work on algorithms, but that the students who started with algorithms mastered the concepts far more quickly. Given that students with learning difficulties need to "catch up" in some sense, such efficiency is notable. Throughout this chapter, therefore, our emphasis is on the efficiency, as well as the effectiveness, of mathematics instruction.

PRINCIPLES FOR IMPROVING MATH INSTRUCTION STRATEGIES

Designing Instruction Around Big Ideas

Educational tools that are going to facilitate students reaching world-class standard should be organized around big ideas (or fundamental knowledge or root meanings) because these represent major organizing principles, have rich explanatory and predictive power, help frame significant questions, and are applicable in many situations and contexts. For example, in *Factors and Multiples* from the Middle Grades Mathematics Project, the authors write that the program " . . . focuses on this fundamental theorem and related ideas, such as factor, divisor, multiple, common factor, common multiple, relative prime, and composite" (p. 2). The senior author of that book, Glenda Lappan, chaired the NCTM Commission on Teaching Standards for School Mathematics (1991).

Often, however, big ideas in mathematics are not at all clear to students, or even to the teacher. For example, in geometry, students are typically expected to learn seven formulas to calculate the volume of seven three-dimensional figures:

Rectangular prism: $l \cdot w \cdot h = v$
Wedge: $\frac{1}{2} \cdot l \cdot w \cdot h = v$
Triangular pyramid: $\frac{1}{6} \cdot l \cdot w \cdot h = v$
Cylinder: $\pi \cdot r^2 \cdot h = v$
Rectangular pyramid: $\frac{1}{3} \cdot l \cdot w \cdot h = v$
Cone: $\frac{1}{3} \cdot \pi \cdot r^2 \cdot h = v$
Sphere: $\frac{4}{3} \cdot \pi \cdot r^3 = v$

These equations emphasize rote formulas rather than big ideas. An analysis based on big ideas reduces the number of formulas students must learn from seven to slight variations of a single formula—area of the base times the height (B • h). This approach enhances understanding while simultaneously reducing the quantity of content to be learned, remembered, and applied. (See Figure 5–1.)

FIGURE 5–1
Volume as the "Big Idea" of Area of the Base Times a Multiple of the Height

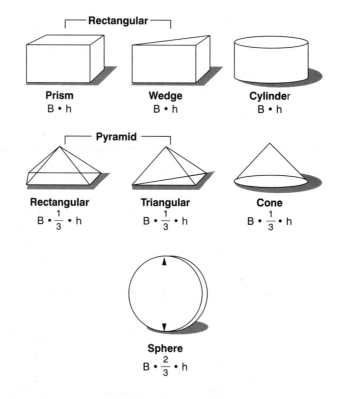

For the regular figures in Figure 5–1—the rectangular prism (box), the wedge, and the cylinder—the volume is the area of the base times the height (B • h). For figures that come to a point—the pyramid with a rectangular base, the pyramid with a triangular base, and the cone—the volume is not the area of the base times the height, but the area of the base times ⅓ of the height (B • ⅓ • h). The sphere is a special case: the area of the base times ⅔ of the height (B • ⅔ • h), where the base is the area of a circle that passes through the center of the sphere and the height is the diameter.

This analysis of root meaning fosters understanding of the big idea that volume is a function of the area of the base times some multiple of the height. As Gelman (1986) stated, "a focus on different algorithmic instantiations of a set of principles helps teach children that procedures that seem very different on the surface can share the same mathematical underpinning and, hence, root meanings" (p. 350).

Designing Conspicuous Strategies

When students orchestrate multiple concepts in some fashion, they are executing a strategy. Any routine that leads to both the acquisition and utilization of knowledge can be considered a strategy (Prawat, 1989). While the ultimate purpose of a strategy is meaningful application, acquisition is most reliable for diverse learners when initial instruction explicitly focuses on the strategy itself, rather than its meaningful application.

Consider, for example, the following problem, presented to each fifth-grade class in a school:

> At lunch, each student can choose a carton of white or chocolate milk. Estimate how many cartons of chocolate and white milk should be ordered for the entire school.

For students to work such problems successfully, they must have both computational ability and well developed strategies for data gathering, proportions, and probability which are relevant to a broad range of real mathematical problems.

In contrast to such well developed strategies, strategies may be so specific and narrow in application that they are little more than a rote sequence for solving a particular problem or a very small set of highly similar problems. For example, in a study by McDaniel and Schlager (1990) on water-jar problem solving, students in one of the teaching conditions learned a rote formula for adding and removing amounts of water with different-sized jars (+1 -2 +1), which, predictably, did not transfer well to solving other water-jar problems.

Too often, mathematics knowledge appears to be rote. Davis (1990) points out that "traditional school practice" tests mainly the ability to repeat back what has been told or demonstrated. There are really two significant problems with the "traditional school practice" described by Davis. First, such practice is often directed toward "small ideas"—for example, arbitrary procedures such as cross-multiplying to solve problems like $x/a = b/c$. Second, such procedures are frequently "repeated back" for rote recall, effectively preempting the possibility that students will even infer the important mathematical principles underlying them.

At the other extreme, a "strategy" may be so general that it is little more than a broad set of guidelines. Such strategies may be better than nothing, but they do not dependably lead most students to solutions for most problems. For instance, a broad strategy such as "draw a picture" or "read, analyze, plan, and solve" is probably far too general for reliably leading a majority of students to reasonable solutions for complex problems such as the milk-ordering problem above.

An important goal for strategy instruction is that the strategies taught are "good" in some sense. Some students develop strategies that are too narrow or too broad, while others develop strategies that are "just right." A major challenge of instruction—perhaps *the* major challenge—is to develop "just right" strategies for interventions with those students who do not develop strategies on their own, including, but not limited to, diverse learners.

Based on an exhaustive review of research, Prawat (1989) recommends that efficient strategy interventions should be "intermediate in generality." That is, efficient strategies fall somewhere between the extremes of being narrow in application but, presumably, relatively easy to teach successfully, and being broad but not necessarily reliable or easy to teach. This suggests that the principal feature of a "good strategy" is that it adheres to the Law of Parsimony as it applies to evaluating competing theories: "That theory is best that explains the most in the simplest way" (Mouly, 1978). As applied specifically to evaluating strategies, the Law of Parsimony might read: That strategy is best that results in the greatest number of students from a targeted student population (such as diverse learners) being able to successfully solve the greatest number of problems or complete the broadest range of tasks by applying the fewest possible strategic steps.

When experts implement strategies to acquire and utilize knowledge, only the result is overt; the steps in the strategy the experts follow are covert. The whole purpose of developing instructional strategies is to explicate expert cognitive processes so that they become visible to non-expert learners. The research support for explicitly teaching conspicuous strategies is quite strong (Carnine & Stein, 1981; Charles, 1980; Gleason, Carnine, & Boriero, 1990; Leinhardt, 1987; Resnick, Cauzinille-Marmeche, & Mathieu, 1987; Resnick & Omanson, 1987).

An example of a conspicuous strategy for the volume formula appears below. Note that the first step prompts the connection with a more concrete representation of volume in which students can count the cubes in a figure. Step 2 introduces the strategy. In step 3, the teacher does not assist the students because they have already been taught to compute the area of a rectangle. In contrast, step 4 calls for a new calculation, so the teacher is more directive.

1. *Linkage to prior knowledge:* "Touch box a. You know how to figure out its volume. Count the cubes and write the volume. What did you write? Yes, 50 cubic meters."
2. *Introduction of new strategy:* "Touch box b. You're going to learn how to calculate the volume by multiplying the area of the base times the height."
3. *Computing the area of the base:* "First calculate the area of the base for box b."
4. *Computing the volume:* "To figure out the volume of the box, you multiply the area of the base times the height. What are the two numbers you will multiply? Yes, 6×7."
5. *Writing the complete answer:* Write the answer with the appropriate unit. What did you write? Yes, 42 cubic inches.
   a. Count the cubes:
   b. Multiply the area of the base times the height:

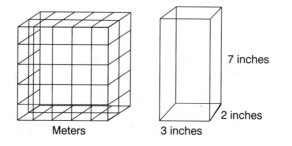

Meters   3 inches

The applicability of the big idea for volume with variations of a single strategy for three-dimensional figures is obvious. In contrast, it is not at all obvious how a single big idea with variations of a strategy could link these six problems:

1. Five packages of punch mix make 4 gallons. How many gallons of punch can Juan make for the party with 15 packages?
2. How long will it take a train to go 480 miles to Paris if it travels at 120 mph?
3. What is the average rate of a car that goes 450 miles in 9 hours?
4. How many pounds is 8 kilograms?
5. The oil transferred from the storage area has filled 44 tanks. There are 50 tanks. What percentage of the tanks are full?
6. There are 52 cards in a deck. Thirteen of them are hearts. The rest are not hearts. If you took trials (drew a card and then replaced it) until you drew 26 hearts, about how many trials would you expect to take?

However, it is with such seemingly unrelated problem types that a strategy based on a big idea is most valuable, particularly with learners for whom such connections usually remain elusive. The big idea that connects these different problems types is proportions. The strategy for proportions must be applied to each problem type in a systematic manner, to make clear that the same big idea underlies these very different problems. The application of proportions is most obvious in the first problem:

Five packages of punch mix make 4 gallons. How many gallons of punch can Juan make with fifteen packages?

A medium-level strategy for proportions might first have students map the units:

$$\frac{\text{packages}}{\text{gallons}}$$

Next, students insert the relevant information:

$$\frac{\text{packages}}{\text{gallons}} \quad \frac{5}{4} = \frac{15}{\square}$$

Finally, students solve for the missing quantity:

12 gallons

Rate problems, which are not typically viewed as proportion problems, also can be solved through a proportion strategy. Note that the key to setting up rate problems as proportions is realizing that the ratio in the proportion is a number of distance units over a single unit of time. This principle is applicable to solving the second problem:

How long will it take a train to go 480 miles to Paris if it travels at 120 mph?

First, map the units. The abbreviation mph can be represented as:

$$\frac{miles}{hour}$$

Next, insert the relevant information:

$$\frac{miles}{hour} \quad \frac{120}{1} = \frac{480}{\square}$$

Finally, solve for the answer:

4 hours

In the next rate problem, students solve for the average rate:

What is the average rate of a car that goes 450 miles in 9 hours?

Map the units:

$$\frac{miles}{hour}$$

Insert the relevant information:

$$\frac{miles}{hour} \quad \frac{\square}{1} = \frac{450}{9}$$

Solve for the answer:

50 miles per hour

Another application of proportions occurs with measurement equivalences. The key to this problem type is that students set up a ratio between the two units involved in the equivalence.

How many pounds is 8 kilograms?

Map the units:

$$\frac{pounds}{kilograms}$$

Insert the relevant information:

$$\frac{pounds}{kilograms} \quad \frac{2.2}{1} = \frac{\square}{8}$$

Solve for the answer:

17.6 pounds

Similarly, percent problems can be set up as proportions. For percents, the key to treating them as proportions is labeling the second ratio as telling about the percentage and pointing out that the denominator of the percentage ratio, which is almost always unstated, is 100.

The oil transferred from the storage area has filled 44 tanks. There are 50 tanks. What percentage of the tanks are full?

Map the units:

$$\frac{\text{filled tanks}}{\text{total tanks}}$$

Insert the relevant information:

$$\frac{\text{filled tanks}}{\text{total tanks}} \quad \frac{44}{55} = \frac{\overset{\text{percent}}{\square}}{100}$$

Solve for the answer:

88 percent

With the following, more difficult percentage problem, the proportion strategy makes the problem quite manageable, even for students with learning difficulties.

The oil transferred from the storage area filled 44 tanks. So far, 88% of the oil in the storage area has been transferred into tanks. How many tanks will be filled when all the oil is transferred from the storage area?

Map the units:

$$\frac{\text{filled tanks}}{\text{total tanks}}$$

Insert the relevant information:

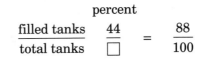

$$\frac{\text{filled tanks}}{\text{total tanks}} \quad \frac{44}{\square} = \frac{\overset{\text{percent}}{88}}{100}$$

Solve for the answer:

50 tanks

The next problem type, illustrating odds and probability, also has a key for tying it to proportions: Setting up a ratio of one type of member to another type or to the total number of members. In the example that follows, the one type of winning trials is related to the total trials.

> There are 52 cards in a deck. Thirteen of them are hearts. The rest are not hearts. If you took trials (drew a card and then replaced it) until you drew 26 hearts, about how many trials would you expect to take?

Map the units:

$$\frac{hearts}{trials}$$

Insert the relevant information:

$$\frac{hearts}{trials} \quad \frac{13}{52} \quad \frac{26}{\Box}$$

Solve for the answer:

104 trials

The next connection to be illustrated with proportions involves the coordinate system. Proportions can link simple proportion problems—rate, measurement equivalence, percentage, and probability—to the coordinate system. This linkage is illustrated in the graphs for each problem type in Figure 5–2.

The last connection—functions—is also apparent in Figure 5–2. A function table accompanies each graph in the figure.

The application of the proportion big idea with variations of a strategy for these problem contexts will deepen the student's understanding not only of proportions but also of rate, measurement equivalencies, percentage, probability, the coordinate system, and functions. One of the most important ways to develop this understanding is through learning how various concepts are linked by a single strategy. In other words, a deep understanding of proportions is constructed by applying the strategy across many contexts. For this reason, the application of a strategy can be thought of as more important in developing understanding and proficiency than how the meaning of a strategy is initially constructed. These applications do far more to develop deep understanding than allowing students to initially construct their own meaning for proportions in authentic activities. Becoming proficient at authentic activities is far more important than starting out with authentic activities.

Five packages of punch mix make 4 gallons. Fifteen packages would make how many gallons of punch?

$$\frac{\text{packages}}{\text{gallons}}\ \frac{5}{4}=\frac{15}{\square}$$

How long will it take a train to go 480 miles to Rome if it travels at 120 mph?

$$\frac{\text{miles}}{\text{hour}}\ \frac{120}{1}=\frac{480}{\square}$$

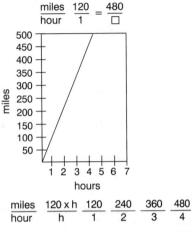

packages	p	1	2	3	4	5
gallons	.8 x p	.8	1.6	2.4	3.2	4.0

miles	120 x h	120	240	360	480
hour	h	1	2	3	4

How many pounds is 5 kilograms?

$$\frac{\text{pounds}}{\text{kilograms}}\ \frac{2.2}{1}=\frac{\square}{5}$$

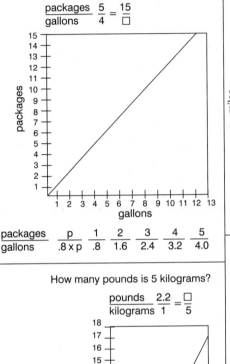

pounds	2.2 x k	2.2	4.4	6.6	8.8	11
kilograms	k	1	2	3	4	5

There are 52 cards in a deck. 13 of these are hearts. The rest are not hearts. If you took trials (drew a card and then replaced it) until you drew 26 hearts, about how many trials would you expect to takes?

$$\frac{\text{hearts}}{\text{trials}}\ \frac{13}{52}=\frac{26}{\square}$$

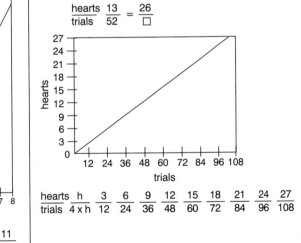

hearts	h	3	6	9	12	15	18	21	24	27
trials	4 x h	12	24	36	48	60	72	84	96	108

FIGURE 5–2
Using Proportions to Link Multiple Concepts to the Coordinate System

Designing Mediated Scaffolding

British educator A. J. Romiszowski has characterized traditional mathematics instruction as: "I'll work two on the board, then you do the rest." The "I'll work two" part of that approach can be thought of as a model, and the "you do the rest" is considered immediate testing. It has been said that the problem with learning from experience is that the lessons come too late. The same could be said of this traditional model of instruction. After "doing the rest," students might receive feedback, ranging from right/wrong, to an explanation of how to do missed problems, and possibly a grade. The feedback is too late and the grade too early.

Scaffolding is a means by which students receive support in various forms along the path to full understanding and "doing the rest" successfully. Along the way, teachers would remove more bits of scaffolding, but in no instance would they abruptly remove all the scaffolding and, in essence say, "You do the rest." For example, after modeling the formula the teacher would not have the students "do the rest." Instead, the teacher would scaffold the steps of the strategy, initially giving students feedback after every step. The steps for a scaffolded volume strategy involving a cone 5 inches tall with a radius of 1.6 inches might take this form:

1. "Write the formula for the volume of the figure."

Students write: B • ⅓ • h

2. "Calculate the area of the base for that figure."

Students write: $3.14(1.6)^2 = 8.04$

3. "Calculate the volume."

Students write: 8.04 • ⅓ • 5 = 13.4

4. "Write the complete answer with the appropriate unit."

Students write: 13.4 cubic inches.

This level of scaffolding is specific enough to be useful but general enough to be used flexibly with all three-dimensional figures. One test for flexibility is the degree to which the strategy can be applied to seemingly different problem types, as was illustrated earlier with proportions. This flexibility is also the means by which students come to understand how various big ideas can be linked, such as proportions, functions, and the coordinate system.

Designing Primed Background Knowledge

In all of the proportion examples, a strategy is applied to a variety of concepts. The concepts to which the proportions strategy is applied—rate, percentage, measurement, probability—are assumed to have been introduced previously. Similarly, when proportions are linked to other big ideas—coordinate system and functions—these big ideas would need to have been taught. Without such prior knowledge, the application of proportions could be a rote activity, extending students' understanding of neither the proportions strategy, nor the concepts to which the strategy is applied, nor the other big ideas to which the strategy is linked. Similarly, the strategy for volume assumes certain prior knowledge on the part of the students: an understanding of the concept of area as well as computational proficiency, e.g., squaring a number and then multiplying by π.

Providing students with both the necessary prior knowledge and flexible strategies based on big ideas that can link that knowledge is possibly the best way to prepare diverse learners for the challenges posed by the new NCTM *Standards*. Instruction should purposefully demonstrate a broad range of mathematics applications for students and enable them to successfully engage in such applications by providing the necessary prior knowledge.

Designing Strategic Integration

Students must not only understand important mathematics strategies as entities, but must also learn the relationships among strategies leading to an integrated, cohesive strategy (Nickerson, 1985; Prawat, 1989; Van Patten, Chao, & Reigeluth, 1986). It is conceivable that a student could learn several "good" strategies but not know when to apply them. However, instruction on individual strategies can be designed to anticipate situations in which several strategies are integrated, a practice also consistent with Piaget's (1973) model of assimilation of the new to the old and accommodation of the old to the new.

For example, if diverse learners are going to have opportunities to successfully engage in solving novel problems, they must not only be able to apply a strategy such as that for proportions but also be able to know when *not* to apply the particular strategy. Understanding involves knowing when a strategy applies and when it does not. Developing such understanding in diverse learners requires integrated teaching, not in the broad sense of interdisciplinary teaching, but within a discipline. Teaching for integration within mathematics can be illustrated with the proportion strategy. Problem A is a fairly straightforward proportion problem:

Problem A. A truck delivers cartons of juice to a store. 2/7 of the juice is grape. The truck has 8400 cartons of juice. How many are grape juice?

Map the units: $\dfrac{\text{Grape}}{\text{Total}}$

Insert the relevant information:

$$\underset{\text{Grape}}{\underset{\text{Total}}{}} \quad \frac{\text{Grape}}{\text{Total}} \quad \underset{7}{\overset{2}{}} = \frac{\boxed{}}{8400}$$

$$\text{Ratio} \qquad \text{Juice Cartons}$$

Solve for the answer: 2400 cartons

If students erroneously apply the same proportion strategy to the numbers in problem B, the answer will also be 2400.

Problem B: A truck delivers cartons of grape and apple juice to a store. 2/7 of the juice is grape. The truck will deliver 8400 cartons of apple juice. How many cartons of grape juice will the truck deliver?

Map the units: $\dfrac{\text{Grape}}{\text{Total}}$

Insert the relevant information:

	Ratio		Juice Cartons
$\dfrac{\text{Grape}}{\text{Total}}$	$\dfrac{2}{7}$	$=$	$\dfrac{\boxed{2400}}{8400}$

Solve for the answer: 2400 cartons

For Problem B, the answer 2400 is *incorrect*, of course, because the 8400 does not refer to the total number of cartons, but to apple juice cartons.

With integrated teaching, the students would be less likely to inappropriately apply the basic proportion strategy to problem B because an advanced proportion strategy would have been taught to "accommodate" these more complex problem types that deal with not just two elements (total juice and grape juice), but with three elements (total juice, grape juice, and apple juice). Conversely, the new strategy for three elements must be "assimilated" with the simpler strategy that handles only two elements.

This accommodation and assimilation is accomplished through an advanced proportion strategy for three elements. This strategy illustrated in Figure 5–3.

The advanced proportion strategy in Figure 5–3 is in itself a medium-level strategy that can be flexibly applied to more complex mathematics problems, such as those involving mixtures and discounts. Below is the map for the application of the advanced proportion strategy to a discount problem:

A shirt was on sale. The discount was $2. The sale price was $18. What percent was the discount?

	Dollars	Percent
Sale Price	18	☐
Discount	2	☐
Original Price	☐	100

The application of the complete strategy to a mixture problem is illustrated in Figure 5–4.

Designing Judicious Review

The term "review" can be an emotive one in education, conjuring up images of endless (and, perhaps, mindless) drill and practice. Yet research strongly sup-

FIGURE 5–3
Advanced Proportion Strategy

A truck delivers cartons of grape and apple juice to a store. 2/7 of the juice is grape. The truck will deliver 8400 cartons of apple juice. How many cartons of grape juice will the truck deliver?

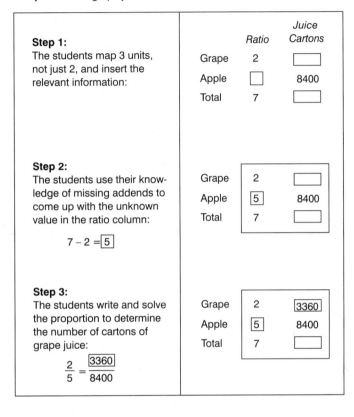

ports certain review practices as significantly effective. We include review as the last guideline because in many ways effective review depends on the extent to which other considerations are reflected in instructional tools.

It can be said that one gets out of review what one puts into it; that is, the quality of instruction—principally in terms of big ideas and strategies—influences the value of review. Regardless of how much review is devoted to "small ideas" or marginally significant material, the ideas remain small and the material marginally significant.

The following are considerations for effective review (Dempster, 1991):

1. *Review should be sufficient.* Is there enough review to achieve the goals of fluency and understanding? For example, solving a wide variety of proportion problems depends on fluency and understanding of computation with proportions, even if carried out with a calculator. If diverse learners, in particular, are to use proportions to solve problems, they will need to practice and review computation with many, many proportion problems.

FIGURE 5–4
Application of Advanced Pro-
portion Strategy Applied to a
Mixture Problem

Mixture Problem
A mix contains peanuts and almonds in a ratio of 4 to 3. If 35 pounds of mix are made, how many pounds of almonds will be used?

		Ratio	Pounds
Step 1: The students map the units and write the known values:	Peanuts	4	☐
	Almonds	3	☐
	Total	☐	35

Step 2: The students use their knowledge of missing addends to come up with the unknown value in the ratio column: $4 + 3 = \boxed{7}$	Peanuts	4	☐
	Almonds	3	☐
	Total	$\boxed{7}$	35

Step 3: The students write and solve the proportion to determine the number of pounds of almonds: $\dfrac{3}{7} = \dfrac{\boxed{15}}{35}$	Peanuts	4	$\boxed{20}$
	Almonds	$\boxed{3}$	$\boxed{15}$
	Total	7	35

2. *Review should be distributed.* Given a fixed number of review opportunities, that number will enhance learning better if it is distributed over time than if it is massed. Specifically, distributed review contributes to long-term retention and automaticity of knowledge. The distribution of review suggests that the many, many proportion problems that students might work should not all be crammed into a few days. Several problems should be reviewed over many days.

3. *Review should be cumulative.* This requirement is tied closely to the integration guideline. The notion of cumulative review means that material taught accumulates in review. For example, after learning to use a multiplication and division strategy to solve problems, and after learning a proportion strategy to solve problems, problem-solving exercises should consist of a mix, some calling for multiplication/division and some calling for proportions.

4. *Review should be varied.* With relatively few exceptions, the specific items that are reviewed should not be the same as the items used earlier in instruction. The reason for this is that varied items promote generalization

and transference. However, items should not be so varied that they actually represent new knowledge. For example, instruction on using proportions to calculate measurement equivalencies might focus on units of weight and length. Review exercises might include capacity, with standard units as well as metric units. However, review problems should not include conversions of Celsius to Fahrenheit because mapping that conversion goes beyond the use of the proportion strategy. New, difficult problem types such as this conversion merits instruction, rather than just inclusion in a review activity.

SUMMARY

The tool design considerations for mathematics presented in this chapter have significance for those working directly with students and for those developing and publishing mathematics instructional materials. Vygotsky (1978) uses the term *zone of proximal development* to describe situations in which students' cognitive ability matches the cognitive requirements demanded by an instructional activity. The importance of designing educational strategies to match students' zone of proximal development is critical to ensuring that students benefit from instruction and that the instructional experiences enhance the students' self-esteem.

In solving the milk-ordering problem described in the section on conspicuous strategies, students integrate the advanced proportion strategy with data gathering and probability-statistics strategies. (See Figure 5–5.) The students apply data gathering strategies—determining the ratio of chocolate milk to white milk for their class and finding out the total enrollment of the school. The students then evoke the advanced proportions strategy: mapping the relevant information. The fifth-graders would need to assume that the preference for types of milk in their class represents the whole school's preference, which entails applying the concept of sampling from statistics and probability. Finally, the concept of missing addends is evoked to solve for the number for white milk.

Many subtle variations are possible with a problem like this, but all are accommodated through the integrated strategies illustrated in Figure 5–5. One variation might be to use average attendance instead of total enrollment, which would cut down on milk ordered (and wasted). In another variation, students might have reason to believe that the preferences in their own class would not be representative of the entire school. The students could gather data from different classes, work the problem, compare the results, and discuss variations in solutions based on different samples. As a final variation, the students could compare results with actual figures on milk ordered to predict shortages or excesses of each type of milk.

The milk-ordering problem and its variations illustrate how goals of the NCTM—working together to enhance understanding, engage in conjecture and invention, and connect mathematical ideas—can be effectively met for diverse learners through judicious instruction in medium-level strategies based on big ideas. As students discuss their options for selecting a sample group, they are working together to enhance their understanding of mathematics. As they

FIGURE 5–5
Data Gathering, Advanced Proportions, and Probability-Statistics Strategies

Step 1: Data Gathering
The students conduct a survey in their class to determine the preferences for white and chocolate milk. The students also find out from the office the total enrollment for the school.

There are 32 students in the class; 22 prefer chocolate milk and the rest prefer white.

There are 479 students in the school.

Step 2: Advanced Proportions
The students map the units for the advanced proportions strategy and insert the relevant information.

	Fifth-grade Class	Entire school
Chocolate	22	
White	10	
Total	32	479

Step 3: Probability and Statistics
The students solve a proportion to estimate the number of chocolate milk cartons to purchase for the entire school:

$$\frac{22}{32} = \frac{329}{479}$$

Chocolate	22	329
White	10	
Total	32	479

Step 4: Missing Addends
The students determine the estimate for white milk using their knowledge of missing addends:

$$479 - 329 = 150$$

Chocolate	22	329
White	10	150
Total	32	479

weigh the relative merits of using total enrollment versus average attendance, they are engaging in conjecture and invention. As they link their understandings of various strategies, they are clearly learning to connect mathematical ideas, solve problems, and apply mathematics broadly.

REFERENCES

CARNINE, D. W., & STEIN, M. (1981). Organizational strategies and practice procedures for teaching basic facts. *Journal for Research in Mathematics Education, 12*(1), 65–69.

CHARLES, R. I. (1980). Exemplification and characterization moves in the classroom teaching of geometry concepts. *Journal for Research in Mathematics Education, 11*(1), 10–21.

DAVIS, R. B. (1990). Discovery learning and constructivism. In R. B. Davis, C. A. Maher, & N. Noddings (Eds.), *Constructivist views on the teaching and learning of mathematics*. Reston, VA: National Council of Teachers of Mathematics.

DEMPSTER, F. N. (1991). Synthesis of research on reviews and tests. *Educational Leadership, 4,* 71–76.

DIXON, R., CARNINE, D. W., & KAMEENUI, E. J. (1992). *Research synthesis in mathematics: Curriculum guidelines for diverse learners*. Monograph for National Center to Improve the Tools of Educators. Eugene, OR: University of Oregon.

ENGELMANN, S., CARNINE, D., KELLY, B., & ENGELMANN, O. (1994). *Connecting math concepts, A through F*. Columbus, OH: SRA.

EVANS, D. G. (1990). *Comparison of three instructional strategies for teaching borrowing in subtraction*. Unpublished doctoral dissertation, University of Oregon.

GELMAN, R. (1986). Toward an understanding-based theory of mathematics learning and instruction, or in praise of Lampert on teaching multiplication. *Cognition and Instruction, 3,* 349–355.

GLEASON, M., CARNINE, D., & BORIERO, D. (1990). Improving CAI effectiveness with attention to instructional design in teaching story problems to mildly handicapped students. *Journal of Special Education Technology, 10*(3), 129–136.

LEINHARDT, G. (1987). Development of an expert explanation: An analysis of a sequence of subtraction lessons. *Cognition and Instruction, 4*(4), 225–282.

McDANIEL, M. A., & SCHLAGER, M. S. (1990). Discovery learning and transfer of problem solving. *Cognition and Instruction, 7*(2), 129–159.

MOULY, G. J. (1978). *Educational research: The art and science of investigation*. Boston: Allyn and Bacon.

NATIONAL COUNCIL OF TEACHERS OF MATHEMATICS, Commission on Standards for School Mathematics (1989). *Curriculum and evaluation standards for school mathematics*. Reston, VA: Author.

NATIONAL COUNCIL OF TEACHERS OF MATHEMATICS (1991). *Professional standards for teaching mathematics*. Reston: Author.

NICKERSON, R. S. (1985). Understanding. *American Journal of Education, 93,* 201–239.

PIAGET, J. (1973). *The child and reality: Problems of genetic psychology*. New York: Viking Press.

PRAWAT, R. S. (1989). Promoting access to knowledge, strategy, and disposition in students: A research synthesis. *Review of Educational Research, 59*(1), 1–41.

RESNICK, L. B., CAUZINILLE-MARMECHE, E., & MATHIEU, J. (1987). Understanding algebra. In J. A. Sloboda & D. Rogers (Eds.), *Cognitive processes in mathematics* (pp. 169–203). Oxford: Clarendon Press.

RESNICK, L. B., & OMANSON, S. F. (1987). Learning to understand arithmetic. In R. Glaser (Ed.), *Advances in instructional psychology* (pp. 41–95). Hillsdale, NJ: Lawrence Erlbaum.

VAN PATTEN, J., CHAO, C., & REIGELUTH, C. M. (1986). A review of strategies for sequencing and synthesizing instruction. *Review of Educational Research, 56*(4), 437–471.

VYGOTSKY, L. S. (1978). *Mind in society: The development of higher psychological processes*. (M. Cole, V. John-Steiner, S. Scribner, & E. Souberman, Eds. & Trans.). Cambridge, MA: Harvard University Press.

AUTHOR NOTE

Preparation of this chapter manuscript was supported in part by The National Center to Improve the Tools of Educators (H180M10006), funded by the U. S. Department of Education, Office of Special Education Programs.

The authors would like to acknowledge Megan Nolan and Bernie Kelly for their contributions to this chapter.

Correspondence concerning this chapter should be addressed to Douglas W. Carnine, Institute for the Development of Educational Achievement, College of Education, University of Oregon, Eugene, OR 97403-1211. Electronic mail may be sent via Internet to DCarnine@oregon.uoregon.edu.

Effective Strategies for Teaching Science

Bonnie J. Grossen and Douglas W. Carnine
University of Oregon

Nancy R. Romance
Florida Atlantic University

Michael R. Vitale
East Carolina University

THIS CHAPTER PARALLELS the other chapters in this book by illustrating the same six key considerations in designing educational tools for enabling teachers to accommodate a wide range of students, including diverse learners (children of poverty, children with disabilities, linguistically different and minority children). The appendix contains a summary of each of the six considerations. For a more complete discussion of the implications of conceptualizing instructional textbooks, media, software, and teacher/student activities as teaching tools, see Chapter 1. For a discussion of the implications of the changing demographics of diversity among learners on the future of education, see Chapter 2.

The purpose of this chapter is to illustrate the six considerations in designing or selecting effective tools in the area of science education. These considerations derive from a thorough review of the educational research literature, described in Chapter 1. This chapter is not a research review; it is an illustration of the implications of that research review. The illustrations are directed toward the needs of both educational practitioners (e.g., teachers and supervisors) and designers of new instructional tools (e.g., publishers and developers).

Meeting the needs of all students, including diverse learners, is a purpose that is entirely consistent with recent efforts to reform science education. Two major national efforts to reform science curriculum have been initiated: Project 2061 of the American Association for the Advancement of Science (AAAS) (1993), and the National Committee on Science Education Standards and Assessment of the National Research Council (NRC) (1993). The emphasis of both groups is on a commitment to "science for all" that is highly significant for diverse learners. As an example, a National Science Education Standards Progress Report (National Research Council, 1993) asserts:

> In particular, the commitment to *science for all* implies inclusion not only of those who traditionally have received encouragement and opportunity to pursue science, but of women and girls, all racial and ethnic groups, students with disabilities, and those with limited proficiency in English. (p. 1)

The NRC standards also clearly state that high expectations should be held for diverse learners as well as for general population students:

> For those . . . concerned that high expectation standards will further widen the learning gap for disadvantaged students . . . we respond that there is considerable evidence that nearly all students can learn science at considerably higher levels than currently achieved. . . . Our focus group on science for students with disabilities tells us that the low expectations of teachers, parents, and students themselves are more limiting than their disabilities. (p. 2)

There are a number of common perspectives on problems in teaching science that have bearing on the present chapter. Among the most important are recently developed national science standards and benchmarks (e.g., NRC's Project 2061) intended to recommend guidelines for teaching the fundamental concepts, principles, facts, laws, and theories that exemplify scientific literacy by providing a foundation for understanding and applying science. Within this chapter, we refer to these fundamental understandings as the "big ideas" of science. In keeping with the NRC standards (1993, p. 4), a big idea is one that"

1. "represents central scientific ideas and organizing principles."
2. "has rich explanatory and predictive power."
3. "motivates the formulation of significant questions."
4. "is applicable to many situations and contexts common to every day experiences."

The present chapter adopts a curricular emphasis on "big ideas" as a fundamental characteristic for all effective science instructional tools.

Another important concern addressed in the research is the role of textbooks as the most commonly used tool for teaching science, and as the determiners of as much as 70 percent of the instructional activity in science (Raizen, 1988; see also Patton, Polloway, & Cronin, in press; Wood & Wood, 1988). Science texts have been the target of many criticisms, including that they contain too many concepts, present ideas in a list-like rather than an integrated fashion, have unclear prose and illustrations, and are generally ineffective in effecting conceptual change for meaningful learning (Lloyd, 1989; Newport, 1990; Osborne, Jones, & Stein, 1985; Smith, Blakeslee, & Anderson, 1993). Although the admittedly poor design of current science texts has caused many educators to totally reject their value, the view expressed in this chapter is that properly designed (or properly augmented) textbooks can be useful learning tools in science classrooms.

The poor design of science textbooks not only has caused many educators to reject textbooks, but also has lead some educators to reject instruction in science subject matter as a reasonable goal for pre-university science instruction (Shaw, 1983; Staver & Small, 1990; Yager & Penick, 1987; Yeany, Yap, & Padilla, 1986). They recommend instead that proficiency in science inquiry skills be the primary goal of science education, so that student-directed inquiry methods can be used exclusively, rather than the explicit, teacher-directed presentations that typify textbook-based instruction. Apparently, explicit instruction for content understanding has been denigrated because it is done so poorly in science texts.

However, in keeping with national science standards, stepping back from the challenge of effectively teaching science subject matter would be incompatible with the nation's emerging goals to achieve world-class standards in science by the year 2000. Toward that end, the new science content standards include, along with science inquiry, science subject matter (the concepts and principles of science) as a critical component in both the reform of science education and the achievement of scientific literacy for all students. Two additional goal areas addressed by the new national science education standards are scientific connections and science in human affairs.

The reader should view each of the following design considerations as the focus of efforts to develop, select, or enhance instruction so that it accommodates a broad range of students, including diverse learners:

1. Does the instruction focus on teaching the "big ideas" of science?
2. Does it make the strategies for using the big ideas conspicuous?
3. Are important component concepts of big ideas and component steps of strategies taught?
4. Does mediated scaffolding provide a smooth transition to independent success?
5. Is judicious review provided?
6. Is the content strategically integrated for greater efficiency in learning?

In the first part of this chapter, the first three highly interdependent design considerations—big ideas, strategies, component steps and concepts—are discussed, and examples from science inquiry and from subject matter knowledge are given. The sequence of illustrations models the order in which the analysis of instructional content occurs—starting with the desired student outcome and analyzing back to a reasonable starting point for instruction—rather than the reverse order, which would more closely correspond to the instructional sequence. In the second part of this chapter, the remaining three considerations—scaffolding, judicious review, and strategic integration—are discussed.

BIG IDEAS, STRATEGIES, AND THEIR COMPONENTS IN SCIENCE INQUIRY INSTRUCTION

Big Ideas in Science Inquiry

Science inquiry—the process of truth-seeking—is perhaps the "biggest" idea of science. The classic approach to science inquiry—the scientific method—consists of several well accepted steps: forming hypotheses to explain observed patterns or discrepancies, controlling and manipulating variables, planning investigations to test hypotheses, and interpreting the resulting data.

Science inquiry—the ability to test hypotheses—is a crucial truth-seeking skill in both formal scientific and informal contexts. Kuhn (1993) found that few adults have the minimal truth-seeking skills required to confront their informal beliefs in an honest manner. For example, only 40 percent of her subjects could describe the nature of the evidence that would cause them to falsify their theories for such questions as: What causes prisoners to return to a life of crime after they are released? What causes children to fail in school? What causes unemployment? Many adult subjects claimed that they did not have to consider any evidence because their opinion was their opinion and they were entitled to it.

The processes needed to establish and evaluate everyday beliefs and theories are essentially the same processes used in formal scientific hypothesis testing. For this reason, science inquiry (or the scientific method) is truly a big idea that is relevant to a much larger range of human affairs than simply the domain of science, one that connects across a wide range of disciplines.

Component Steps and Concepts in Science Inquiry

A key component of science inquiry is effectively controlling variables (Ross, 1988). As an inquiry skill, controlling variables means that in order to isolate the effect of a variable, students must be able to identify all other relevant variables and then design an experiment that keeps unchanged all but the variable being tested. An example of this critical strategy component—controlling variables—is included in the next section.

Conspicuous Strategies for Science Inquiry

A fairly common hypothesis in science education is that "inquiry" instructional methods (also sometimes called non-explicit, activity-based, student-centered, or discovery methods) are preferable to explicit instructional methods for teaching students how to *do* science inquiry. However, this hypothesis seems generally contradicted by experimental research. Research comparing "inquiry" (non-explicit) methods with instruction that makes the strategies for carrying out science inquiry explicit finds that the latter results in better learning (Ross, 1988; Rubin & Norman, 1992).

In spite of these findings, the hypothesis that persists is that inquiry instructional methods work better than explicit instruction for teaching science inquiry skills. A second group of studies are often cited to support this hypothesis (e.g., Shymansky, Kyle, & Alport, 1983; Staver & Small, 1990). However, the conclusions from this group of studies are misleading because the "explicit" treatments in these studies teach only scientific principles and do not explicitly teach the skills of science inquiry at all. For example, several studies compare an explicit treatment designed to teach the displacement principle (i.e., the amount of liquid displaced by an object is equal to the volume of the object) with inquiry instruction designed to teach students to derive the principle of displacement through their own inquiry (e.g., Bay, Staver, Bryan, & Hale, 1992). None of the explicit treatment conditions was designed to teach science inquiry skills.

It is not surprising that studies with this design generally find that inquiry teaching methods result in better science inquiry performance than "explicit" instruction (Bredderman, 1983; Shayer & Adey, 1993; Shymansky, Kyle, & Alport, 1983; Staver & Small, 1990). However, conclusions about explicit instruction for teaching science inquiry cannot be made on the basis of explicit treatments designed to teach only scientific principles. Studies that compare inquiry instruction with instruction designed to make the strategy for science inquiry explicit generally conclude that explicit instruction is more effective. Explicit methods that teach what students are expected to learn usually result in better learning than inquiry (non-explicit) teaching methods. The conclusions to be drawn from such research are: If students are to learn science inquiry, make the strategy for science inquiry explicit. Similarly, if students are to learn scientific principles, it is important to make the scientific principles explicit.

Our interpretation of this research is that effective instruction makes significant strategies "conspicuous" rather than simply "explicit." We make this distinction because educators often interpret "explicit instruction" to mean simply "verbalized instruction." However, the effective treatments in the first group of studies involved much more than simply teacher verbalization, and, in effect, they made the strategies for science inquiry very conspicuous.

To illustrate a conspicuous strategy that accommodates the needs of *all* learners, we present a modified activity from *Elementary Science Study* (1974), a popular inquiry-based curriculum of the 1970s. In the original inquiry activity, students viewed a row of figures called mellinarks and a second row of figures that were not mellinarks. The students then viewed a third row of mellinarks and non-mellinarks and identified which figures would be classified as mellinarks. The instruction did not model or describe any strategy for controlling variables that the students could use to think about the examples in order to figure out the concept of mellinark. Students continued the activity with similar concepts until they themselves discovered or "self-learned" the inquiry skill needed to derive a concept from examples and non-examples. Therefore, the instruction was described as an "inquiry" method.

Although this activity may seem quite simple, Lawson et al. (1991) found that only 22 percent of high school chemistry and biology students possess the science inquiry skills to successfully identify a mellinark and other such imaginary concepts. These findings indicate that nearly *all* students would benefit from a teacher-directed experiential activity designed to teach a conspicuous a strategy for controlling variables.

The instruction begins with the presentation of only one figure, Drawing A in Figure 6–1 (taken from the original activity). The students' goal is to determine with some certainty what it means to be a mellinark by designing additional examples, each of which the teacher identifies as mellinark or non-mellinark. For these examples to be most informative, students must control the possible variables; that is, they must design each example so that it is exactly the same as the original figure except for the one feature that students want to test. For example, Drawing B in Figure 6–1 is not very informative because it does not control many variables; that is, Drawing B differs from Drawing A in more than one way. On the other hand, Drawing C is quite informative because it controls for all variables except the spot, so the information that Drawing C is not a mellinark would allow students to conclude that a mellinark must have a spot. (A possible conspicuous strategy for initial teaching is presented later in the chapter.)

The activity continues with students designing more figures that change only one of the other variables listed on the board, or the drawings could test additional variables, such as the range of acceptable sizes for the spot, or even whether more than one spot is possible on a mellinark. The variable list is potentially endless.

FIGURE 6–1
*Controlling Variables to
Define a Concept*

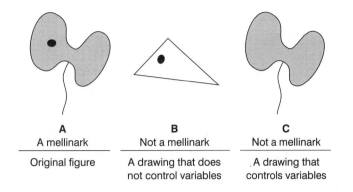

A	B	C
A mellinark	Not a mellinark	Not a mellinark
Original figure	A drawing that does not control variables	A drawing that controls variables

The steps made conspicuous in the strategy for identifying mellinarks form a generic strategy for controlling variables—a strategy that students can learn and apply not only to the mellinark problem, but to any problem requiring systematic scientific investigation. These elements are: Design the figure (the experiment) so that the new figure (the experimental treatment) differs from the original figure (the control treatment) in only one feature (the independent variable) and all the other features (variables) are kept the same (controlled). Gather information about whether each figure is a mellinark to identify whether the feature that was changed is critical to the figure's being a mellinark (interpret the results).

In the initial instruction, the teacher should not use the sophisticated vocabulary that is normally used to describe these steps (e.g., independent and dependent variable). The teacher's goal should be to make the actual *strategy* conspicuous, not necessarily the sophisticated *vocabulary* that normally is used to describe these procedures. Vocabulary words can be taught later, after students have acquired the meanings that go with them. The mellinark activity is easily managed and could readily teach most students, including diverse learners, science inquiry strategies by making them conspicuous to learners.

BIG IDEAS, STRATEGIES, AND COMPONENTS IN SCIENCE SUBJECT MATTER INSTRUCTION

Big Ideas in Science Subject Matter

As noted earlier, both the NRC and the AAAS science standards emphasize the importance of teaching the big ideas of science subject matter. For purposes of illustration, some significant big ideas in science subject matter include the nature of science, energy transformations, forces of nature, flow of matter and energy in ecosystems, and the interdependence of life. Such big ideas and their component concepts clearly cut across the science domains (e.g., physics, earth science, biology) and are essential in building a level of scientific literacy among all students that is necessary for understanding and problem-solving within the natural and created world.

Convection: An Example of a Big Idea   The principle of convection is a good example of a big idea that both explains and unifies many of the dynamic phenomena that occur within the earth (geology), oceans (oceanography) and atmosphere (meteorology)—three domains of science usually associated with earth science. For example, in the area of geology, plate tectonics, earthquakes, volcanoes, and the formation of mountains are all influenced by convection in the mantle. Global and local convection patterns influence the dynamics of the atmosphere. Similarly, the ocean currents, thermo-haline circulation, and coastal upwelling are influenced by global and local convection. In turn, the interaction of these phenomena in the earth and the atmosphere results in the rock cycle, weathering, and changes in landforms. The interaction of these phenomena in the ocean and in the atmosphere influence the water cycle, wind-driven ocean circulation, El Niño, and climate in general.

As is the case for many currently evolving big ideas, alternative and variant explanations for these phenomena have been offered, and the fact that competing theoretical explanations often exist is an aspect of science of which students should be made aware. However, not all the alternative and variant explanations need to be taught, particularly in initial instruction. Figure 6–2 illustrates the core principle of convection and the various phenomena it explains.

Benefits of an Analysis of Big Ideas   By design, big ideas have the potential to transfer or apply more widely to other areas (domains) of science and everyday phenomena than small (or less general) ideas. For example, as discussed above, the principle of convection can be used to explain dynamic natural phenomena in geology, meteorology, and oceanography. Also, well designed instruction in big ideas allows for more efficient use of time. Because of the foundational understanding and connections established with big ideas, the teacher can cover a greater amount of meaningful content while teaching fewer principles. And, as students apply big ideas across other domains of science, these big ideas function as prior knowledge within which students can easily assimilate new learning with appropriate elaboration rather than learning everything as if it were new. (While the use of big ideas is an effective and efficient strategy, other characteristics of instructional delivery, such as scaffolding and review, determine the extent to which students actually learn the big idea.)

In general, big ideas represent an adaptive curricular solution that amplifies meaningful understanding in a fashion that is of particular importance to diverse learners, rather than encouraging mere memorization of an array of disconnected facts, as too often occurs. This approach provides diverse learners with the opportunity to learn that scientific concepts and "real world" science phenomena are both understandable and logically related.

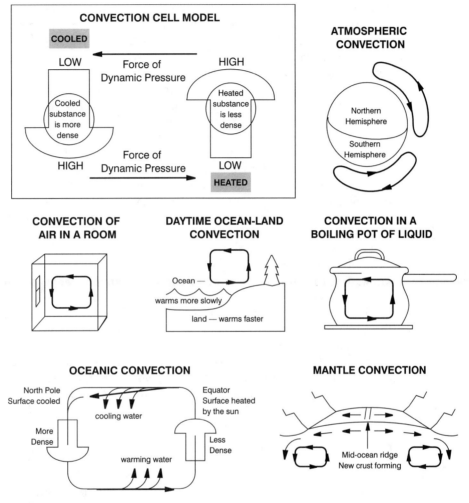

FIGURE 6–2
The Big Idea of Convection and Simple Visual Maps of Some of Its Applications

Components in Science Subject Matter

Component concepts are essential elements that must be identified when attempting to teach any big ideas, including those identified as benchmarks or standards within the national science reform initiatives of the NRC or AAAS. In order to explain and meaningfully apply a big idea such as convection, for example, students must understand and use its component or underlying concepts. In the case of convection, in-depth understanding depends on students' prior understanding of concepts such as cause-and-effect relationships between and among the phenomena of heating and cooling, density, force and pressure. By designing instruction to teach the component concepts conspicuously (in this example, a network of cause-and-effect relationships that underlie the larger causal principle of convection), a deeper understanding of the principle can be achieved by all students rather than a select few. In turn, the knowledge resulting from a deeper understanding of the underlying causes of convection (density, heat, the effect of heat on density and pressure, and so on) provides a meaningful foundation that can be used to explain everyday phenomena as well as more abstract phenomena, such as novas and black holes in the universe.

In fact, unless students have extensive specialized prior scientific knowledge, specific instruction in the component concepts is necessary in order to build understanding of convection. For example, students must understand that heat causes a substance to expand and become less dense, and that substances move from a place of high pressure to a place of low pressure. Simultaneously, in order to understand and apply the underlying component concepts and principle of convection, specific facts about the solar system, the ocean, the solid earth, and the atmosphere must be known. For example, students must know that the sun is the primary external source of heat, that the tilt of the earth as it orbits around the sun causes variations in the amount of heat received in different areas of the earth (i.e., changing seasons), that the core of the earth is hot, that the ocean is very, very deep, and so on.

As students learn to integrate the component concepts with other relevant knowledge, they gain an understanding analogous to a dynamic mental model of a generic convection cell (upper left box in Figure 6–2). By conspicuously teaching component concepts, understanding and application of the convection process becomes accessible to a wider range of diverse students.

Conspicuous Strategies in Science Subject Matter

Better problem solving in the form of applications of scientific knowledge is a major goal of science education reform. To solve problems, students need to learn strategies for using and applying the big ideas of science and their component concepts in a variety of contexts. The big ideas and component concepts represent scientific knowledge which, of necessity, must be brought to bear in the problem-solving process. Thus, the design of instructional tools and classroom instruction around big ideas is a critical dimension underlying the degree to which students can understand and apply the knowledge they have learned. Students should learn important big ideas in a form that optimizes their explanatory and predictive power, along with the kinds of questions to which the big ideas apply.

In fact, the strategies necessary for effective problem solving and learning in science are literally the applications of big ideas. For example, instructional strategies that connect component concepts to a big idea or scientific principle (such as convection) can be applied by students to predicting the location of and movement in a substance given the placement of the heat source. Such knowledge becomes dynamic whenever it helps students interpret events in the world or make more accurate predictions about what is likely or not likely to happen. Knowledge of big ideas and their component concepts forms the basis for meaningful conceptual learning and effective problem solving in science. Within this context, science learning for students is analogous to the current problem faced by scientists of predicting earthquakes and volcanoes given prior factual knowledge in conjunction with the conceptual understanding of the location of plates in the earth and their significance.

Building Understanding Through Wide Application of Big Ideas Once the big idea of convection and the component concepts underlying it are understood in simple forms and are used to explain and predict common experiences, they can then be broadened to explain more abstract phenomena, such as convection in the atmosphere and in the earth's mantle. Given these two applications, the big idea of convection is important to the meaningful understanding of each, for two reasons. First, the common convection models amplify their similarity: The source of heat is at the bottom of the convection cell in both cases because the sun heats the surface of the earth which causes convection in the atmosphere and the heated core of earth causes convection in the mantle. Second, aspects of the models amplify their differences: One convection model involves gases, the other involves solids. At a more abstract level, using the convection model to understand that movement in the mantle is similar to movement in the atmosphere and is similar to common experiences prevents a possible misconception that convection does not occur in solids.

Explaining the application of the big idea of convection to the ocean would ordinarily be taught after the mantle and atmosphere because it requires more complex understanding beyond convection. In oceans, the source of heat is at the top of the convection cell: The sun heats the surface of the ocean. This is only a minor elaboration of the convection model. However, convection in the ocean also interacts with convection in the atmosphere (i.e., winds), so that the surface currents of the ocean must be explained by both ocean and air convection patterns. Finally, an even more complex process is the interaction of local convection patterns in the atmosphere with global convection in the atmosphere. This interaction can be quite complex, which is why weather prediction is usually very difficult. However, an awareness of the problems involved in using an understanding of convection to make accurate predictions can add a final touch of realism to the instruction. While other factors are important in these applications (such as the rotation of the earth), the important point is not only that teacher-directed sequences involving the wide application of big ideas can enhance the understanding of big ideas for all students, but also that these forms of adaptation are of great importance in the success of diverse learners in science instruction.

Using Visual Maps to Model Strategies for Organizing Concepts and Big Ideas Science subject matter content, as represented by big ideas and component concepts, should be presented in such a way that the instruction facilitates the application of big ideas which often manifest themselves in problem solving. To accomplish this, instruction can use visual maps (i.e., concept maps, pictures, diagrammatic sketches) to emphasize the explanative nature of science and the organization of science's big ideas. This approach will further improve problem-solving performance (Mayer & Gallini, in press; Mayer, 1989; Woodward, in press). Ideally, such illustrations should correspond with how an expert organizes and uses the information in applying science concepts to solve problems. This requirement is important because in science, expert problem solvers differ from novice problem solvers in three important ways: Expert problem solvers have more knowledge; the knowledge is better organized in a hierarchical structure; and good problem solvers seem to organize this hierarchy around explanatory principles that function as big ideas.

As an illustration, Figure 6–2 shows a hierarchical organization around an explanative principle: convection. The central concept is a generic convection model (upper left box in Figure 6–2.) The other figures illustrate the various applications or effects of convection. The generic convection model—the big idea—can be used by students to explain everyday occurrences such as the movement of air currents in a room and the movement of water in a heated pan. Each application of the strategy is not unrelated but forms part of a unified, structured schema related to the principle of convection.

In general, visual maps of big ideas add to the overall "considerate" quality of an instruction tool. A considerate tool is one that eases comprehension in a supportive manner (Armbruster, 1984; Armbruster, Anderson, & Ostertag, 1989; Guzzetti, Snyder, Glass, & Gamas, 1993; Yates & Yates, 1990). In addition to visual maps, considerate communication uses cues in the text or textual elements such as headings and signal words to make the structure of the knowledge being communicated as clear and coherent as possible. Considerations of the structure, coherence, unity, and audience appropriateness (Kantor, Anderson, & Armbruster, 1983) and even accuracy (Champagne & Bunce, 1989) have been found to contribute to understanding. Clearly showing useful perspectives on how knowledge is best organized can provide important benefits to diverse learners.

Adding a "Refutational" Aspect to Communication of a Big Idea In addition to conspicuous strategies for visually representing concept relationships and applications, adding a "refutational" aspect to the communication can further facilitate understanding and conceptual change for students (Guzzetti et al., 1993; Muthukrishna, Carnine, Grossen, & Miller, 1993; Niedelman, 1992; Smith, Blakeslee, & Anderson, 1993). Along with conspicuously presenting a coherent new strategy, a refutational text anticipates common misconceptions and builds into instruction examples that directly confront such misconceptions. Because students have many preconceived notions or misconceptions about science (e.g., "big objects float and small objects sink"), it is important that instruction clearly confront common misconceptions in an conspicuous manner. Many studies have found that a refutational, considerate, explicit text is very successful in achieving conceptual change; some studies have shown that student performance reaches a ceiling of conceptual change (e.g. Guzzetti, 1990). The following example illustrates how conceptually based strategy instruction can be designed to refute misconceptions.

The first step in teaching students to understand density is to have them compare the masses of substances of equal volume and predict which substances will sink when mixed. Two same-sized cubes with differing numbers of dots can be used to teach this step, as in Task 1 in Figure 6–3. In the figure, each dot represents 1 gram of mass. In this case, the more dots there are inside a cube (the greater the mass), the greater the density of the cube.

Next, students can learn to identify equivalent volumes of substances of unequal sizes and predict which will sink when the substances are mixed. In Task 2 of Figure 6–3, figures of different sizes are shown, with empty cubes placed over segments of equal size to confront the misconception that more mass means greater density. By looking at the number of dots in the equal-sized cubes, students can tell that substance B is more dense than substance A, although substance B is smaller in volume. Students are able to compare the density of a series of substances like those in Task 2 where the size and number of dots varies.

Next, as students form a conceptual understanding of mass and volume, such understanding can provide a foundation for subsequent activities using actual substances in a naturalistic environment in which (in conjunction with appropriate measurement skills) students predict which substance will sink when the substances come together (Task 3 in Figure 6–3).

Recent research has shown that planned refutations (built-in teaching examples that counter commonly observed misconceptions) were more effective in changing students' naive conceptions to scientific understandings than instruction that left the teacher to provide refutational material spontaneously during instruction. The teachers using the curricular material with planned refutations achieved better learning outcomes than the teachers who introduced refutations spontaneously (Smith, Blakeslee, & Anderson, 1993).

FIGURE 6–3
Strategy Example with Density

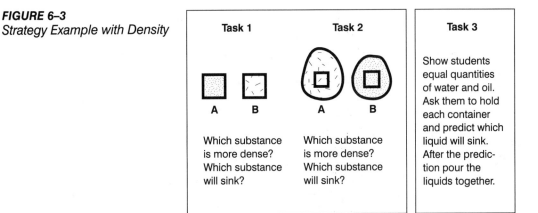

Task 1

A   B

Which substance is more dense? Which substance will sink?

Task 2

A   B

Which substance is more dense? Which substance will sink?

Task 3

Show students equal quantities of water and oil. Ask them to hold each container and predict which liquid will sink. After the prediction pour the liquids together.

Because curricular materials are designed before they reach the classroom, they must necessarily incorporate planned refutation if they are to include any refutation at all. As an illustration, Task 2 in Figure 6–3 is a planned example that refutes the common misconception that density is the same as weight. Having all students respond to this example reduces the likelihood that this misconception will occur. By anticipating predictable misconceptions such as this, instruction can be more effective for all students, particularly diverse learners, than instruction that relies on the teacher to respond spontaneously to presumably unpredictable misconceptions that might differ from individual to individual, and then design the teaching examples on the spot.

Providing Relevant Experiential Learning   It is often falsely assumed that if knowledge is conspicuously introduced, it must be in a lecture setting in which the teacher is active (i.e., telling) and the students are passive. Similarly, it is falsely assumed that in order to involve students actively in learning, science instruction must utilize hands-on experiences and the teacher should not communicate information conspicuously. Neither of the preceding assumptions is valid because the initial communication of scientific concepts to naive learners can be very interactive and conspicuous. With this in mind, Table 6–1 contrasts traditional telling methods, inquiry methods, and conspicuous communication methods.

Conspicuous communication methods are interactive and experiential, just as inquiry methods are. However, conspicuous communication methods include only learning experiences that are relevant to understanding big ideas. In this regard, "hands-on" learning experiences may or may not be relevant. Certainly, simple mechanical participation in a hands-on activity without conceptual understanding is analogous to the meaningless memorization of facts. In many cases, it is often impossible to design relevant hands-on activities that effectively communicate underlying causal big ideas. For example, students would have difficulty discovering an acceptable theory of electricity from a pile of wires, batteries, and switches, or from operating the lights and electrical appliances in their homes. Students may believe that a wire that is cut through cannot carry electric current and therefore is safe to touch, when in fact it can still deliver quite a shock if it is still connected to the power source. While this is not to say that hands-on activities for applying electricity concepts are inappropriate; they would, for example, be very appropriate for applying strategies

TABLE 6–1
Features of Traditional Telling Methods and Inquiry Methods Contrasted with Conspicuous Communication Methods for Initially Teaching Naive Learners

Traditional Telling Methods	Inquiry Methods	Conspicuous Communication Methods
Traditional	Innovative	Innovative
Teacher-directed	Student-directed	Teacher-directed
Non-experiential	Experiential	Experiential
Non-interactive	Interactive	Interactive

about electrical circuits. The important distinction is that students could not be expected necessarily to derive or construct a reliable understanding and explanation of electricity solely from hands-on experiences.

To avoid misconceptions, hands-on activities should be used in initial instruction only when they are concretely relevant to the concept being taught. Hands-on experience would certainly be relevant where physical texture is an important feature of understanding, as it is in most identification and categorization activities, such as the identification of rocks, leaves, or flowers. In most cases, hands-on experience seems to detract from initial learning when texture is not a key feature of meaningful learning, as in learning about electricity, for example (Hider & Rice, 1986).

MEDIATED SCAFFOLDING IN SCIENCE INQUIRY AND SUBJECT MATTER INSTRUCTION

The Concept of Scaffolding in Instruction

The emphasis of scaffolding is that, to be effective, instruction must always be adapted to the initial level of student proficiency. It is important to stress that scaffolding addresses and operates on the processes (or means) through which desired instructional goals are accomplished, not on changing (and in particular not simplifying or not limiting) achievement goals. Scaffolding, then, emphasizes dynamic efforts that provide initial learners with substantial support early in learning, support that is then purposively reduced as they gain additional proficiency. Because of its importance in supporting initial learning, scaffolding is also of great importance to ensuring the success of instruction with many diverse learners. The implication of scaffolding is that educators must strive to design, select, or adapt instruction in order to make the goals of science literacy available to all students.

Illustrations in the preceding section characterized ideal initial instruction as being interactive, conspicuous, and teacher-directed. In this context, the notion of scaffolding applied to initial instruction assumes that students are faced with learning instructional content that is new to them. Whenever students experience the key features of a new science concept or inquiry strategy, scaffolding stresses that the initial presentations should strive to make all key features conspicuous through a variety of techniques that include explicit verbal prompts or very clear representational models and examples that provide guidance and support.

When the idea of scaffolding (e.g., through prompts) is combined with other instructional design characteristics, such as a focus on big ideas and conspicuous strategies, the result is effective initial learning in which students are actively and meaningfully involved in experiential learning. In this sense, teacher-directed (or teacher-supported) initial instruction is far more powerful for initial learning than independent, student-directed activities. However, as initial learning activities evolve and students become more proficient, the reduction of support purposefully eliminates teacher direction until learning is, in fact, independent and student-directed. The purpose of scaffolding, thus, is to allow *all* students to become successful in independent activities, not just the select few who do not require initial learning support.

Figure 6–4 shows additional aspects of initial instruction that work to create a supportive learning environment that can enable naive students to enter into new learning successfully. In this sense, the term "scaffolding" is an apt metaphor for describing this dynamically supportive environment. As students, with the support of a scaffold, progress toward proficiency in a learning objective, the scaffolding is removed and the instructional activities become less teacher-directed and more student-driven.

Understanding the Two Categories of Scaffolding Techniques

There are at least two distinct ways to scaffold instruction. The first is through teacher assistance and the second is through the design of the examples used in teaching. Both assume that the student is actively involved in learning tasks rather than being a passive learner.

Scaffolding Teacher Talk   As illustrated in Figure 6–5, the initial presentation of the conspicuous strategy for controlling variables (at the top of the figure) involves more telling, while the later scaffolding (at the bottom of the figure) involves more questioning or scaffolding. In the example, the conspicuous steps of the initial strategy and of the scaffolded strategy are: (1) select one variable (hypothesis) to test; (2) vary the tested variable only and keep the other variables the same; (3) interpret the results. Only the degree of teacher guidance varies. As noted earlier, students will eventually be expected to control variables as they direct their own projects.

Scaffolding Examples   The example presented previously in Figure 6–3 illustrates a way to scaffold instruction through the design of sequences of teaching examples. In the example, each task corresponds to a step in a strategy for applying the concept of density. Task 1 requires students to compare the masses in an equivalent volume and predict which substance will sink. Task 2 requires students to identify equivalent volumes in two unequal-sized sub-

FIGURE 6–4
Continuum of Effective Instructional Practices as They Relate to the Learner's Level of Performance in the Specific Type of Learning Activity

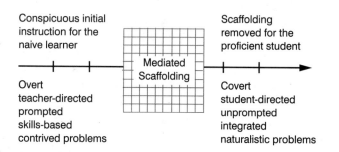

Conspicuous initial instruction for the naive learner

Scaffolding removed for the proficient student

Mediated Scaffolding

Overt
teacher-directed
prompted
skills-based
contrived problems

Covert
student-directed
unprompted
integrated
naturalistic problems

Initial Conspicuous Strategy Presentation

Step 1: (*Introduction*) You're going to figure out what a mellinark is by drawing pictures that might be mellinarks.

Step 2: (*Generating hypotheses*) This is a mellinark. (Teacher makes Drawing A in Figure 1.) What variables might be important in determining whether something is a mellinark or not? (As students name possibilities, the teacher lists them on the board: the barbell shape of the body, the curved shape of the body, the presence of a dark spot, the position of the spot, the presence of a tail, the size, the color, and so on, with the list of features [variables] representing a list of hypotheses.)

Step 3: (*Controlling variables*) The best way to figure out what a mellinark is, is to draw a new figure that changes only one variable. The first variable I want to test is whether a mellinark needs a spot. Watch. (Teacher draws Drawing C in Figure 1.)

Step 4: (*Interpreting data*) This figure is not a mellinark. From that information you can figure out one variable that defines a mellinark. What variable is that? (A spot.) After you draw a figure, I will tell you if it is a mellinark or not. From what I tell you, you should be able to figure out more about the variables that tell about a mellinark.

Later Scaffolded Instruction

Step 1: (*Hypothesis*) (Point to this figure.) This is a glerb. ⟶
Pick a feature to test to see if it defines a glerb. What feature did you select?

Step 2: (*Controlling variables*) Draw a figure that allows you to test for that feature.

Step 3: (*Interpret data*) (For example, if the student ⟶ drew this figure.)

This is not a glerb. Now, what do you know about glerbs? . . .Yes, they need an opening. (Corrective feedback for drawings that do not control variables, such as this one, for example.) ⟶

You did not draw a glerb. But there are a lot of reasons why this is not a glerb. It could be too big; it could be the wrong shape; it could have the wrong number of sides; it could be the wrong color. You can't tell why because you changed too many things from the original figure. When you test a variable, you must keep all the other variables the same.

What variable were you trying to test?
Whether it needs straight sides.

What about the other variables?
Keep them the same.

So what variable would you change?
The straight sides.

FIGURE 6–5
Using Teacher Assistance to Scaffold Instruction

stances and predict which substance will sink. Task 3 (with some additional assumptions) requires application of the strategy to real examples.

Because scaffolding is a dynamic process, as learners become more competent, the scaffolding is removed by purposively moving slightly ahead of the learner on the continuum of instructional practice shown in Figure 6–4. As learners grow in competence and independence, effective instruction moves forward on the continuum. This process is illustrated below, using activities presented earlier in the chapter.

1. Progress from overt descriptions of the thinking strategies to covert practice of those strategies.

Example: In initial instruction, the teacher states and/or models overtly the thought process involved in drawing a mellinark to test whether it needs a spot. With covert practice, the teacher says nothing. Students carry out a single step by drawing a figure that changes only one variable.

2. Progress from teacher-directed to student-directed activity.

Example: When students first begin testing variables, the teacher directs students by telling them which variable to control for (e.g., the spot), how to control for that variable, and so on. When students are proficient, the directions for the activity become more general and students select their own variables (hypotheses) and control for them without assistance.

3. Progress from prompted to unprompted assistance.

Example: The teacher initially prompts students as they work by giving specific feedback on their mellinark drawings or specific instructions that prompt better control of the next variable. As students become more proficient at controlling variables, the prompts are no longer needed, and students successfully control the variables without teacher prompts.

4. Progress from instruction in component concepts to instruction that integrates the concepts into a whole.

Example: The instruction in the convection cell begins with instruction in the components of the convection cell, including concepts of density and pressure; understanding of the source of heat; the cause-and-effect relations of heat, density, and pressure; and the effects of these on the movement of cells. Later instruction in the convection cell presumes knowledge of these components and provides an integrated model explaining their interactions.

5. Progress from more contrived problems to naturalistic ones using real objects.

Example: The density drawing in Tasks 1 and 2 of Figure 6–3 are contrived in order to scaffold the strategy for using density. When students are proficient in the strategy, they can then use it in Task 3 to predict which of two real substances will sink or float.

An example of an activity that incorporates all of these unscaffolded features for students who are more proficient at science inquiry would be a lab activity in which students identify rules that will predict which of various tubes—some made of iron, others aluminum; some hollow, others solid; some short, others long—will roll faster down a ramp (as described in Main & Rowe, 1993). Students will need to apply their knowledge about controlling variables to determine which variables increase the speed of the tubes. The students would need to select appropriate pairs of tubes to roll down the ramp to test possible variables. The variables might include hollow versus solid, large versus small, heavy versus light, short versus long, and so on. Similar experiences with varied unscaffolded applications such as this provide opportunities for details in understanding to be further clarified.

It seems generally that the more the teacher interacts with the students by scaffolding important content, the more effective the instruction. Teacher-directed instruction that is characterized by frequent interactions (i.e., checks for understanding and applications) can scaffold content-specific instruction so that students with learning disabilities acquire an understanding of scientific concepts that Harvard graduates frequently do not have (Muthukrishna et al., 1993).

JUDICIOUS REVIEW

Science is a difficult subject for most students. Therefore, the following requirements of effective review are particularly important in science instruction:

1. *Review should be sufficient.* Problem-solving ability is diminished by insufficient review. Students must recall relevant knowledge in order to be able to use it to understand and solve problems. The mere presentation of a definition or formula for density (i.e., density is the amount of mass in a volume) or a description of convection are insufficient. Ample opportunities to apply the concept are necessary if students are to fully understand the relevance and utility of a concept or big idea.

2. *Review should be distributed.* Review that is distributed over time, as opposed to massed in one learning unit, contributes to long-term retention and problem solving. For example, after intensive study of density in a series of introductory lessons, density can be reviewed sporadically as it is applied in the context of learning about pressure, the effects of heat on density and pressure, the effects of changes in density on movement and pressure, and so on.

3. *Review should be varied.* Besides gradually removing scaffolding, later instruction should provide application practice that provides widely varied examples. Varied practice allows students to further deepen understanding. From the initial presentation, students can acquire only a basic understanding

of concepts. For example, after learning about density, students may not realize that relative density holds for fragments from a piece of substance. Students might predict that a large glob of mercury would sink, but when asked about a tiny ball from that glob, they might predict that it would float. Similarly, after the initial presentation in controlling variables, students will need much more practice in a wide variety of contexts.

Varied practice contributes to students' generating more ideas for solving problems, having higher quality ideas, asking better questions, and more successfully solving problems (Covington & Crutchfield, 1965; Schmidt & Bjork, 1992; Wardrop et al., 1969). When real-world application practice follows instruction using contrived examples, students are able to apply the strategies to different types of problems and retention improves (Olton & Crutchfield, 1969). When students fail to use knowledge, it is usually associated with very few practice examples (Gick & Holyoak, 1980; Lesgold & Perfetti, 1978) or examples from an overly limited context (Bransford, Vye, Adams, & Perfetti, 1989; Levin, 1979; Nitsch, 1977; Schmidt & Bjork, 1992).

4. *Review should be cumulative.* Review is cumulative when new concepts are integrated into big ideas. Cumulative review is important for developing an integrated understanding of the big ideas of science. For example, the initial instruction in the generic convection cell represents a cumulative review of the component concepts of density, pressure, and so on.

STRATEGIC INTEGRATION

In a domain that is hierarchically organized, such as science, review can be designed in such a way that all four of the above dimensions are incorporated almost automatically in the design of the curriculum. Instruction can be organized so that new learnings provide a new context for old learnings. In addition, review naturally occurs as subordinate concepts and strategies are incorporated in more complex, integrated concepts and strategies. Figure 6–6

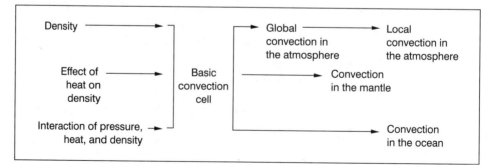

FIGURE 6–6
A Strand Design

illustrates a strand design that can provide this built-in practice and review. Designing instruction in overlapping strands (topics) facilitates the naturalness of integrated review. The strands that teach the concepts of density, heat, and pressure overlap until they are integrated in the model of the basic convection cell. The concept of density is taught first, then the scaffolding is removed and unscaffolded practice using the concept of density is provided in the context of teaching about the effects of heat on density. Similarly, in initial instruction about pressure, unscaffolded practice with density and heat are provided in the context of learning the interaction of heat, density, and static and dynamic pressure. All of these concepts are further reviewed when they are integrated in the basic convection strategy.

This basic strategy is then applied to explain global convection in the atmosphere, the earth's mantle, and the ocean. Each of the applications provide review of the convection cell and its related concepts. In this way, one of the central goals of the new science standards—connectedness—can be achieved.

SUMMARY

This chapter illustrates six instructional design considerations that can improve science instruction and result in higher achievement, particularly for diverse learners. Higher achievement for *all* learners is a national goal in four areas of science: science as inquiry, science subject matter, scientific connections, and science and human affairs.

The big ideas of science inquiry can be applied to any domain of study. The big ideas of science subject matter can be linked with the measurement skills of mathematics to add precision to the predictions of science. Furthermore, the relevance of science to human affairs is a fairly natural consequence of selecting big ideas based on their explanative quality which in part depends on their utility in human affairs. To enable better problem solving, the structure of science knowledge should be clearly communicated using considerate, user-friendly tools, including visual maps, to illustrate the connections of science. Instruction should teach carefully the component concepts that underlie big ideas, build understanding by showing the utility of strategies in problem solving, include examples that confront common misconceptions, and provide relevant experiences.

For initial learning, teacher-directed experiential methods that scaffold the acquisition of meaningful learning are superior to teacher-directed, passive learning methods and also seem superior to student-centered, experiential methods, particularly for diverse learners. As learners become more proficient, scaffolding should be removed. Whether students should work under close teacher direction or independently depends on careful consideration of the learner's proficiency level in the desired learning objective. Review that is sufficient, distributed over time, varied across contexts, and cumulative can serve to prevent the fragmentation of knowledge. Review can be organized into overlapping strands so that all the component concepts are consistently reviewed and then integrated into the larger models.

These six considerations can be evaluated in the context of student performance using guidelines developed by Romance, Vitale, and Widergren (in press). If the principles illustrated in this chapter are applied to the design of science instruction, better problem solving and higher level thinking for all learners will result. In addition, the instruction can provide the opportunity for diverse learners, not just university-bound students, to acquire a usable knowledge base in the content and reasoning of science. Providing educational opportunities for diverse learners requires more than simply placing these students in a science class typically earmarked for university-bound students and adding a few teaching tips for making the content accessible to diverse learners (Parmar & Cawley, 1993).

If the only instructional methods used are those that seldom work for diverse learners, the opportunity to learn science remains denied. Considerate, user-friendly instruction in the big ideas of science is most likely to open the doors to understanding science. Diverse learners who receive the above-described instruction in convection may not become expert meteorologists, but they will be able to explain scientific principles such as why mountains form or why seasons change (Muthukrishna et al., 1993). Certain aspects of user-friendly tools and approaches that make science accessible to less able students can also make science accessible to more able students. In contrast, an approach that is designed only for more able students is difficult to modify so that less able students can also learn, because the teacher must design and create the needed missing components.

REFERENCES

AMERICAN ASSOCIATION FOR THE ADVANCEMENT OF SCIENCE. (1993). *Benchmarks for science literacy: Project 2061.* Washington, DC: Author.

ARMBRUSTER, B. (1984). The problem of "inconsiderate text." In G.G. Duffy, L.R. Roehler, & J. Mason (Eds.), *Comprehension instruction* (pp. 202–217). New York: Longman.

ARMBRUSTER, B., ANDERSON, T. H., & OSTERTAG, J. (1987). Does text structure / summarization instruction facilitate learning from expository text? *Reading Research Quarterly, 22,* 331–346.

BAY, M., STAVER, J., BRYAN, T., & HALE, J. (1992). Science instruction for mildly handicapped: Direct instruction versus discovery teaching. *Journal of Research in Science Teaching, 29*(6), 555–570.

BRANSFORD, J. D., VYE, N. J., ADAMS, L. T., & PERFETTI, C. A. (1989). Learning skills and the acquisition of knowledge. In A. Lesgold & R. Glaser (Eds.), *Foundations for a psychology of education* (pp. 199–249). Hillsdale, NJ: Lawrence Erlbaum.

BREDDERMAN, T. (1983). Effects of activity-based elementary science on student outcomes: A quantitative synthesis. *Review of Educational Research, 53*(4), 499–518.

CHAMPAGNE, A., & BUNCE, D. (1989, April). *Electricity in 6th grade tests: Too much, too fast.* Paper presented at the American Educational Research Association Conference, San Francisco.

COVINGTON, M. V., & CRUTCHFIELD, R. S. (1965). Facilitation of creative problem solving. *Programmed Instruction, 4,* 3–5, 10.

ELEMENTARY SCIENCE STUDY. (1974). *Attribute games and problems: Teacher's Guide.* New York: McGraw-Hill.

GICK, M. L., & HOLYOAK, K. (1980). Analogical problem solving. *Cognitive Psychology, 12,* 306–355.

GUZZETTI, B. J. (1990). Effects of textual and instructional manipulations on concept acquisition. *Reading Psychology, 11,* 49–62.

GUZZETTI, B., SNYDER, T. E., GLASS, G. V., & GAMAS, W. S. (1993). Promoting conceptual change in science: A comparative meta-analysis of instructional interventions from reading education and science education. *Reading Research Quarterly, 28*(2), 116–159.

HIDER, R. A., & RICE, D. R. (1986). *A comparison of instructional mode on the attitude and achievement of fifth and sixth grade students in science*. Technical research report. Mobile, AL: University of South Alabama.

KANTOR, R. N., ANDERSON, T. H., & ARMBRUSTER, B. B. (1983). How inconsiderate are children's textbooks? *Journal of Curriculum Studies, 15,* 6–72.

KUHN, D. (1993). Science as argument: Implications for teaching and learning scientific thinking. *Science Education, 77*(3), 319–337.

LAWSON, A., MCELRTH, C., BURTON, M., JAMES, B., DOYLE, R., WOODWARD, S., KELLERMAN, L., & SNYDER, J. (1991). Hypothetico-deductive reasoning skill and concept acquisition: Testing a constructivist hypothesis. *Journal of Research in Science Teaching, 28*(10), 953–970.

LESGOLD, A. M., & PERFETTI, C. A. (1978). Interactive processes in reading comprehension. *Discourse Processes, 1,* 323–236.

LEVIN, T. (1979). Instruction which enables students to develop higher mental processes. *Evaluation in education: An international review series, 3*(3), 174–220.

LLOYD, C. V. (1989, December). *The relationship between scientific literacy and high school biology textbooks*. Paper presented at the annual meeting of the National Reading Conference, Austin, TX.

MAIN, J., & ROWE, M. (1993). The relation of locus-of-control orientation and task structure to problem-solving performance of sixth-grade student pairs. *Journal of Research in Science Teaching, 30*(4), 401–426.

MAYER, R. E. (1989). Models for understanding. *Review of Educational Research, 59*(1), 43–64.

MAYER, R. E., & GALLINI, J. (in press). When is a picture worth a thousand words? *Journal of Educational Psychology*.

MUTHUKRISHNA, A., CARNINE, D., GROSSEN, B., & MILLER, S. (1993). Children's alternate frameworks: Should they be directly addressed in science instruction? *Journal of Research in Science Teaching, 30*(3), 233–248.

NATIONAL RESEARCH COUNCIL, National Committee on Science Education Standards and Assessment. (1993). *National science education standards: A sampler*. Washington, DC: Author.

NEWPORT, J. F. (1990). Elementary science texts: What's wrong with them? *Educational Digest, 59,* 68–69.

NIEDELMAN, M. (1992). Problem solving and transfer. In D. Carnine & E. Kameenui (Eds.), *Higher order thinking: Designing curriculum for mainstreamed students* (pp. 137–156). Austin, TX: Pro-Ed.

NITSCH, K. E. (1977). *Structuring decontextualized forms of knowledge*. Unpublished doctoral dissertation, Vanderbilt University.

OLTON, R. M., & CRUTCHFIELD, R. S. (1969). Developing the skills of productive thinking. In P. Mussen, J. Langer, & M. Covington (Eds.), *Trends and issues in developmental psychology* (pp. 68–91). New York: Holt, Rinehart and Winston.

OSBORNE, J. H., JONES, B. F., & STEIN, M. (1985). The case for improving textbooks. *Educational Leadership, 42*, 9–16.

PARMAR, R. S., & CAWLEY, J. F. (1993). Analysis of science textbook recommendations provided for students with disabilities. *Exceptional Children, 59*(6), 518–531.

PATTON, J., POLLOWAY, E., & CRONIN, M. (in press). A survey of special education teachers relative to science for the handicapped. *Science Education.*

RAIZEN, S. (1988). *Increasing educational productivity through improving the science curriculum.* Washington, DC: The National Center for Improving Science Education.

ROMANCE, N. R., VITALE, M. R., & WIDERGREN, P. (in press). *Student conceptual understanding in science: Knowledge-based perspectives for enhancing teaching practices.* Monograph series. Washington, DC: National Science Teachers Association.

ROSS, J. A. (1988). Controlling variables: A meta-analysis of training studies. *Review of Educational Research, 58*(4), 405–437.

RUBIN, R., & NORMAN, J. (1992). Systematic modeling versus the learning cycle: Comparative effects on integrated science process skill achievement. *Journal of Research in Science Teaching, 29*(7), 715–727.

SCHMIDT, R., & BJORK, R. (1992). New conceptualizations of practice: Common principles in three paradigms suggest new concepts for training. *Psychological Science, 3*(4), 207–217.

SHAW, T. (1983). The effect of a process-oriented science curriculum upon problem-solving ability. *Science Education, 67*(5), 615–623.

SHAYER, M., & ADEY, P. (1993). Accelerating the development of formal thinking in middle and high school students IV: Three years after a two-year intervention. *Journal of Research in Science Teaching, 3*(4), 351–366.

SHYMANSKY, J., KYLE, W., & ALPORT, J. (1983). The effects of new science curricula on student performance. *Journal of Research in Science Teaching, 20*(5), 387–404.

SMITH, E., BLAKESLEE, T., & ANDERSON, C. (1993). Teaching strategies associated with conceptual change learning in science. *Journal of Research in Science Teaching, 30*(2), 111–126.

STAVER, J. R., & SMALL, L. (1990). Toward a clearer representation of the crisis in science education. *Journal of Research in Science Teaching, 27*(1), 79–89.

SYSTEMS IMPACT, INC. (1987). *Earth science* [videodisc program]. Washington, DC: Author.

WARDROP, J. L., GOODWIN, W. L., KLAUSMEIER, R. M., OLTON, R. M., COVINGTON, R. S., CRUTCHFIELD, R. S., & RONDAY, T. (1969). The development of productive thinking skills in 5th grade children. *Journal of Experimental Education, 37*, 67–77.

WOOD, T. L., & WOOD, W. L. (1988). Assessing potential difficulties in comprehending fourth grade science textbooks. *Science Education, 72*(5), 561–574.

WOODWARD, J. (in press). Effects of curriculum discourse style on eighth graders' recall and problem solving in earth science. *Elementary School Journal.*

YAGER, R. E., & PENICK, J. E. (1987). Resolving the crisis in science education: Understanding before resolution. *Science Education, 71*(1), 49–55.

YATES, G. C. R., & YATES, S. (1990). Teacher effectiveness research: Towards describing user-friendly classroom instruction. *Educational Psychology, 10*(3), 225–238.

YEANY, R. H., YAP, K. C., & PADILLA, M. J. (1986). Analyzing hierarchical relationships among modes of cognitive reasoning and integrated science process skills. *Journal of Research in Science Teaching, 23*(4), 277–291.

AUTHOR NOTE

Preparation of this chapter manuscript was supported in part by The National Center to Improve the Tools of Educators (H180M10006), funded by the U. S. Department of Education, Office of Special Education Programs.

Correspondence concerning this chapter should be addressed to Bonnie J. Grossen, Institute for the Development of Educational Achievement, College of Education, University of Oregon, Eugene, OR 97403-1211. Electronic mail may be sent via Internet to Bgrossen@oregon.uoregon.edu.

CHAPTER

7

Effective Strategies for Teaching Social Studies

Douglas W. Carnine
University of Oregon

Donald B. Crawford
Western Washington University

Mark K. Harniss
Northern Illinois University

Keith L. Hollenbeck and Samuel K. Miller
University of Oregon

EQUAL ACCESS TO an education does not mean using the same instructional strategies with all children, but using strategies that are effective for every child. This chapter discusses how the six considerations for improving instructional strategies presented in Chapter 1 can be applied to social studies education. The application of these six considerations are derived from a comprehensive review of the educational research literature on social studies curriculum and instruction. The purpose of this chapter is to illustrate how the six considerations can be used to modify or develop educational strategies to be effective for teaching social studies to students with diverse learning needs. (Refer to Chapter 2 for a discussion of the characteristics of students with diverse learning needs.)

CURRENT ISSUES IN SOCIAL STUDIES

Current reforms within social studies education warrant a discussion of its fundamental issues. Social studies are among the most complex and fractious of all academic fields and classroom subjects. The field of social studies is based on a loose confederation of disciplines which includes anthropology, archaeology, economics, geography, history, law-related education, philosophy, political science, psychology, religion, and sociology. Educators and curriculum designers have struggled for years over which of the various disciplines to include under the social studies umbrella and the relative weight that should be given to each.

A second struggle over expectations seemingly has been resolved: There is now widespread agreement that competency in social studies is essential for everyone. This goal is exemplified by the recommendation of The National Center for History in the Schools (1992) that "a reformed social studies curriculum should be required of all students in common, regardless of their 'track' or further vocational and educational plans" (p. 9).

This new emphasis means that social studies teachers face increased expectations for teaching a diverse student population with a wide range of cognitive abilities. The challenge for students is that many of the changes associated with the "new social studies" of the 1960s—inductive teaching, discovery learning, and content drawn from the newer social sciences—continue to influence social studies reform today. These programs were of great interest to scholars and university professors but were not a great success in the classroom and "emphasized the brightest students without much consideration of other students" (Hertzberg, 1981, p. 359, cited in Brophy, 1990). Clearly, yesterday's instructional strategies will not be adequate for teaching today's diverse learners.

In recent years the debate about which topics social studies education should stress has prompted a series of recommendations from national commissions, task forces, and professional organizations, including the National Council for the Social Studies, the Bradley Commission, the National Commission on Social Studies in the Schools, and the National Center for History in the Schools. The recommendations generally advocate that the purpose of social studies education is to develop well educated citizens who share a common body of knowledge drawn in a coordinated and systematic way from a range of disciplines, and that content knowledge from the social studies should not be treated as knowledge to memorize, but as knowledge through which important questions can be explored.

As an example of these recommendations, the National Council for the Social Studies (NCSS) articulated a set of ten thematic strands that form the basis of the social studies standards (National Council for the Social Studies, 1994). The scope of the social studies curriculum remains disconcertingly broad, as one can see from the ten NCSS strands:

Social studies programs should include experiences that provide for the study of . . .

1. culture and cultural diversity.
2. the ways human beings view themselves in and over time.
3. people, places, and environments.
4. individual development and identity.
5. interactions among individuals, groups, and institutions.
6. how people create and change structures of power, authority, and governance.
7. how people organize for the production, distribution, and consumption of goods and services.
8. relationships among science, technology, and society.
9. global connections and interdependence.
10. the ideals, principles, and practices of citizenship in a democratic republic. (pp. 365–368)

Developers of national standards for social studies have the difficult task of translating these recommendations into meaningful benchmarks for learning, while struggling to reconcile problems associated with content selection and an overloaded curriculum. In general, elementary-grade social studies instructional materials are criticized for teaching too little content, and secondary-level materials are viewed as two-minute reviews of the earth's history which emphasize coverage rather than depth. United States history curricula exemplify these problems:

The typical American history survey course . . . comprises everything from Mayans to moon landings. We are, as far as I know, the only country in the Western world that tries to teach the whole of our history to students in a single year. It's just insane. (Gagnon, cited in O'Neil, 1989, p. 5)

From this discussion it is clear that the current concern about social studies centers on what content is worthwhile to teach and how to teach it effectively. The challenge of teaching social studies is to provide students with both breadth and depth. In response to this problem, many social studies educators advocate developing curricula and instruction around selected concepts, rather than perpetuating the superficial parade-of-facts approach. Emerging national standards and recommendations for teaching social studies reflect a sentiment that can be characterized as "pausing for depth":

There is the ever-present problem of time. Social history, no less than political history, requires careful selection from among the numberless topics available. The sheer scope of the historical record requires the imaginative synthesis of political and social, cultural, economic, and religious history around central, significant themes and questions (National Center for History in the Schools, 1992, p. 17).

Taking the time to teach depth of knowledge has its cost, and as yet consensus has not been reached on what content to leave out to give time for more depth of study. Students who learned about one particular theme, culture, region, or historical era in depth would likely do poorly on a national exam that samples broadly from the domain of social studies knowledge, and even worse on a statewide performance assessment that tests in-depth understanding of a different theme, culture, region, or historical era. The struggle to develop a consensus about what content to teach in our nation's social studies classrooms continues to divide the field (Brophy, 1990).

PRINCIPLES FOR IMPROVING INSTRUCTIONAL STRATEGIES

One challenge specific to improving the instructional strategies for teaching social studies has to do with how to assist diverse learners in identifying and remembering what is truly important to learn. Social studies teachers widely recognize the difficulties that diverse learners experience when attempting to garner the critical information from textbooks. Considerable research has shown that employing a variety of mediators of content—advance organizers, study guides, interspersed questions, concept maps, and other graphic organizers—can greatly improve the ability of diverse learners to successfully acquire the essential content. These various forms of content mediation have three basic functions: They direct students' attention to the most important ideas in the textbook, they focus attention on the organizational structures of the texts, and they require rehearsal by asking students to recite or write down critical information.

Rich, authentic learning experiences are not sufficient for eliminating the difficulties that diverse learners experience in acquiring knowledge by reading textbooks. The same mediators of content needed by diverse learners when they read textbooks are required when they engage in other learning activities: watching videos, interviewing adult informants, listening to plays, going on field trips, having discussions, or participating in simulations. Even when the source of information is more user-friendly than the typical textbook, teachers must still create mediational materials that insure that diverse learners attend to the most important concepts, understand the organization of the information, and have an opportunity to recite or write down the key ideas. Teacher creation of mediational materials that assist diverse learners in acquiring, comprehending, and remembering social studies content demands a critical analysis of the curriculum and admittedly can be very time consuming. Ellis and Sabornie (1990) reported that teachers being trained to create these kinds of mediational materials expressed concern about the extra time required. These teachers were also particularly critical of textbook publishers for failing to include effective advance organizers, study guides, interspersed questions, and concept maps.

As the teachers in Ellis and Sabornie's study noted, it is unreasonable to expect teachers to assume sole responsibility for supplementing all the deficiencies of social studies textbooks. However, teachers who are knowledgeable about what is needed for instructional materials to be effective for diverse learners will be better prepared to select appropriate, and modify inappropriate, instructional materials.

A second challenge complicating efforts to improve instructional strategies for teaching social studies has to do with how to assess student outcomes. The multiple-choice tests traditionally associated with social studies texts are increasingly coming under attack, as are the somewhat similar multiple-choice national norm-referenced tests in social studies. Recommendations for replacing such tests with performance assessments of projects, essays, oral reports, simulation activities, and the like have yet to be accompanied by stringent assessment criteria that would help identify students who have not learned what was expected. In addition to lack of stringent assessment criteria, performance assessments have been very difficult to score reliably. Further, when diverse learners lack skills in writing or public speaking, it is often impossible to discern from their low scores on performance assessments what they have learned. Without assessment criteria that can discriminate between successful and unsuccessful student results, teachers receive minimal useful feedback on the effectiveness of their social studies teaching. Without useful feedback on the effectiveness of their teaching efforts, teachers find it very difficult to improve their instructional strategies.

Designing Instruction Around Big Ideas

Rather than teaching for coverage, one approach for bringing order to social studies content is to organize it around "big ideas." Big ideas are important concepts or principles that are more specific than the thematic strands recommended by NCSS and fundamentally different from traditional social studies concepts such as "democracy" and "community." Not all big ideas in social studies are equally useful. Big ideas must be chosen that facilitate efficient and broad acquisition of knowledge. To be instructionally effective, big ideas in social studies must be chosen which enable learners to organize, interrelate, and apply information so that meaningful connections can be made within social studies and between social studies content and their own lives. The following sections describe several examples of big ideas and discuss their value for preparing meaningful social studies curriculum and instruction.

Problem-Solution-Effect The problem-solution-effect structure is one example of a big idea. When applied to the study of social studies, it has the potential to help students understand that individuals, groups, and governments tend to react to common problems with identifiable causes and solutions. At the same time, the elements of the problem-solution-effect analysis can have great relevance to the daily lives of students. The structure and examples described below are based upon a United States history text (Carnine, Crawford, Harniss, & Hollenbeck, 1994).

Problems   Common problems in social studies can be attributed to the economic or human rights issues described below.

1. Economic problems generally can be linked to conditions that create difficulty for people trying to acquire or keep things they need or want. At a basic level, people need and want to maintain the availability of food, clothing, and shelter. In their personal lives, students can identify the struggle with economic problems—trying to acquire or keep things they need or want—and have an intuitive understanding of the motivational power of economic issues.

2. Human-rights problems in social studies are usually linked to groups of people trying to achieve rights associated with religious freedom, freedom of speech, equal protection under the law, equal rights for women, minorities, different social classes, and so forth. Adolescents are especially concerned about issues related to equal rights and freedom of expression in their own lives.

Solutions   When students can classify common historical problems, they can relate this knowledge to recurring actions people use to solve problems. Recurring solutions to historical problems can be categorized as attempts by individuals or groups to either move, invent, dominate, tolerate, or accommodate. These five solutions are described below.

1. *Move.* When people move to solve a problem, they hope to find a new place where the problem does not exist. United States history is filled with examples of immigrants who moved here in response to problems somewhere else. While students seldom have the option of moving themselves to solve problems, they all are acquainted with family members or friends who have moved to solve problems, and with the limitations of this type of solution to problems.

2. *Invent.* Throughout history people have tried to solve problems by inventing new ways or abilities to do things they could not do before. For example, people could not farm on the Great Plains because the soil was too heavy to plow. The invention of the steel plow solved this economic problem. Students' experience with inventions rarely extends to seeing them as solutions to problems, but through an examination of historical examples they can develop this understanding.

3. *Dominate.* Another way people historically have solved problems involves controlling or dominating other people. For example, the United States and its allies fought against Germany, Japan, and Italy in World War II. The opposing sides tried to dominate each other in response to economic problems such as inflation, unemployment, and limited natural resources. From personal experience, students know that attempting to dominate others can

result in a fight in which both sides lose. Students can apply this knowledge to understand historical events involving domination.

4. *Accommodate.* When people accommodate each other, they adjust or adapt to solve a problem. Historically, people have accommodated each other by negotiating or compromising. For example, delegates from the Northern and Southern states, despite their serious differences, effected a series of compromises that enabled passage of the Constitution. Young people are aware of the power of negotiations in their dealings with adults, and that understanding can be applied to historical situations as well.

5. *Tolerate.* When a group of people decides not to move, invent, dominate, or accommodate, they tolerate a problem. Sometimes this solution is applied because there is no other choice. Before 1863, many African Americans had to tolerate the problems of being slaves and of not having equal rights. Again, students can use their own lives to appreciate the connection between power and one's choice of solution. Adolescents know they only tolerate a situation when they do not have the power to change it.

Understanding the relationship between common problems and solutions can help students view social studies as a dynamic subject. Common solutions to problems in one era often become less viable as times change. Today, moving to solve the problem of acquiring land to grow food is less practical than it was 150 years ago, when territory could still be taken from the Native Americans. Moving to acquire land to grow food has been replaced by the invention of new ways to grow more food on land that has already been settled.

Effects   Solutions to problems produce consequences or effects. One effect is that a problem may cease to exist, but an examination of social studies shows that solutions to problems often create new problems. For example, tribes of the Pueblo culture in the Southwest desert solved the problem of building shelters in an environment where wood was hard to find. Their solution was to build the walls of their homes with stones and use logs only to support the roof.

Building the walls with stone had the effect of creating a new problem: the extremely hard work required to carry heavy stones for constructing shelters. The Pueblo tribes solved this problem by eliminating the space between homes so they shared a common wall.

The problem-solution-effect structure described can be useful to teachers as a framework for helping students organize their thinking during oral reading, classroom discussions, and written essays. This framework can be especially useful to students in reading both textbooks and primary source documents.

Figure 7–1 is an excerpt from a social studies textbook (Carnine et al., 1994) which incorporates a problem-solution-effect structure to describe how the Chinook tribe solved problems related to food, clothing, and shelter and the effects of those solutions.

This narrative is also an example of clearly written text students can easily comprehend. It is important for teachers and authors of instructional materi-

The Chinook Culture's Solutions to Basic Problems

The Chinook and the Problem of Food. The Chinook found plenty to eat. The rivers of the Pacific Northwest Coast were a great place to catch fish. The Chinook knew that the best time to catch fish was during the runs when the salmon left the ocean to go up the rivers to spawn. The Chinook would work so hard during the salmon runs that the tribe would catch enough salmon to last all year. They took so many salmon at one time that it was more like harvesting a crop than it was like fishing. The salmon were cleaned and then smoked or dried to preserve them as food for the rest of the year.

In general, Native American tribes had to meet their basic needs by adjusting and adapting to use the natural resources and their environment. The Chinook also had to use the solution of accommodating to their environment in order to survive. The Chinook accommodated to the generous supply of salmon in their environment by making salmon a main staple of their diet.

However, the Chinook wanted to have something to eat besides fish all the time. Another way the Chinook got food was by gathering food from edible plants in the forests, especially blackberries which grow wild in the region.

There was a third way of getting food, besides fishing and gathering, on the Northwest Coast. The men also hunted game, but that was a much less important source of food than fishing.

The Chinook would also go out to sea and bring back other kinds of fish and even whales to eat. The Chinook were the same as the Inuit because they both needed boats of some kind to use to go out to fish in the sea and also travel from village to village. The Chinook were different from the Inuit because they had plenty of trees in their environment. Because they had trees the Chinook did not need to make boats and canoes out of animal skins. The Chinook used the plentiful forests along the Northwest Coast to make their canoes and boats out of wood. The largest boats were 60 to 70 feet long. These huge boats were hollowed out of a single trunk of one of the huge cedar trees in their forests.

The Chinook and the Problem of Clothing. The northernmost tribe in the Northwest Coast, the Tlingit (tling-git, rhymes with fling kit), made use of tailored garments of deerskin, with leggings (pants) and moccasins, a style of clothing that was common throughout North America.

The milder temperature of the rest of the Northwest Coast region meant that the Chinook did not need as much clothing as the Tlingit. South of the Tlingit, the Chinook wore minimal clothing, usually a deerskin leather shirt and breechcloth, which is like the bottom part of a bikini. However, in rainy weather, the deerskin leather clothing became wet and uncomfortable. The Chinook found a way to make use of their plentiful forests to provide clothing that was cooler and more comfortable to wear than deerskin leather. The soft, stringy inner bark of cedar trees was softened and then woven into cloth to make cooler clothes. The tribes south of the Tlingit, where the climate was more rainy and warmer, preferred clothing made of shredded and woven bark. This softened cedar bark was also used to make blankets.

The Chinook and the Problem of Shelter. Because of the plentiful forests in the Northwest Coast region, the Chinook made many things from the trees in the forest. They used wood to construct buildings that were large enough for several families to live in at the same time. The wooden buildings were organized into villages of as many as 1,000 people.

The Effect of the Chinook Solutions. The Chinook accommodated to the plentiful supply of salmon by making salmon their main food. As a result of adapting to their environment the needs of the Chinook were well met. The effect was that the Chinook had more free time for celebrations and for artistic works. The art of the Chinook is still prized today. These are the effects of making good use of the abundant natural resources of the Northwest Coast.

FIGURE 7–1
Example of Problem-Solution-Effect Passage from Textbook
From: Carnine D., Crawford, D., Harniss, M., & Hollenbeck, K. (1994). *Understanding U.S. History. Volume 1: Through the Civil War.* Eugene, OR: Considerate Publishing. Reprinted by permission.

als to understand that improving social studies curricula requires more than simply changing the length of words and sentences. For an instructional tool to do more than provide information, every aspect of its design must be carefully engineered to bring about understanding.

Stages of Group Cooperation   A second strategy for relating historical conditions to group behavior could be taught to students who understand that group cooperation evolves in identifiable developmental stages. Students at a young age can be taught the specific features of this big idea as a strategy for examining cooperative group activities. Figure 7–2 summarizes four common conditions and their relationship to the development of group cooperation.

Multiple Perspectives   Another big idea in social studies is the notion that events can be viewed from more than one perspective and that these different perspectives are important to fully understanding social events. The following discussion of multiple perspectives is placed within the context of the problem-solution-effect big idea.

Something that will be a problem from one perspective may not be a problem from another perspective. In fact, what is a solution from the perspective of one person or group may actually create problems for another person or group. Understanding this relationship can help students recognize that groups of people often have different perspectives about the same event. Figure 7–3 illustrates the big idea of multiple perspectives at an elementary level.

Factors of Group Success   Another big idea is that the success of group efforts, such as wars or the establishment of colonies, are frequently associated with the four factors described below.

FIGURE 7–2
Stages of Group Cooperation

Stages of Group Cooperation

1. **Gather together and discuss common problems.**
   IF some members agree on a solution to a common problem, THEN people will begin occasional voluntary cooperation.

2. **Occasional voluntary cooperation**
   IF cooperative solutions are effective and the problems recur, THEN people will begin to cooperate regularly.

3. **Regular voluntary cooperation**
   IF the need for cooperation continues but voluntary cooperation fails, THEN people may agree to legally binding cooperation.

4. **Legally binding cooperation**
   The group is forced by rules to cooperate.

Perspective of Local Community	Perspective of People Who Live Near the Airport

Problem: Not enough jobs.

Solution: Build an airport.

Effect: People get jobs at the airport.

Problem: Airplanes cause a lot of noise.

Solution: People try to sell their houses.

Effect: The noise of the airplanes makes it difficult for people to sell their houses and they lose money.

FIGURE 7–3
Graphic Representation of Example of Multiple Perspectives

1. *Motivation*. Successful groups have group members or supporters who are committed to a common goal.
2. *Leadership*. Successful groups have highly qualified, knowledgeable, and effective leaders.
3. *Resources*. Successful groups have sufficient resources (usually money) to accomplish their goals.
4. *Capability*. In addition to resources and leadership, successful groups have personnel and material of sufficient quality to accomplish their goals.

These factors can help explain why different groups throughout history either succeeded or failed in reaching their goals. For example, when the Constitution was first proposed, many Americans were reluctant to support its passage. They saw no need to change from the voluntary form of cooperation that had worked for the colonies up to that time. Initially, only wealthy, established leaders known as the Federalists supported the Constitution. The four factors associated with group success can help students understand why the Federalists were able to get the Constitution ratified despite widespread opposition.

1. *Motivation*. The Federalists were motivated to secure passage of the Constitution because they strongly believed it would help protect their consid-

erable business interests. Their desire for success was much greater than that of their opposition, who simply did not like the idea of a federal government.

2. *Leadership.* Both the Federalists and their opponents had capable leaders who were able to persuade followers to support their position.

3. *Resources.* The Federalists had superior monetary resources compared to their opponents. This gave the Federalists an advantage in organizing and mobilizing their followers.

4. *Capability.* The Federalists carefully planned and organized how to achieve their goal during, and possibly even prior to, the Constitutional Convention. This provided the Federalists with a head start over their opponents and ultimately led to passage of the Constitution.

The Contribution of Big Ideas to Meaningful Social Studies Instruction

The problem-solution-effect structure, multiple perspectives, and the four factors of group success are three examples of big ideas in social studies instruction. When social studies is taught in this way, it becomes possible for students to comprehend historical events as an interrelated network.

At one level, big ideas are useful because their explanatory power can help students more easily understand content material. Equally important is that big ideas can help students recognize connections between the content of social studies and their personal lives.

Students can learn how to use the four factors of group success to analyze the strengths and weaknesses of group efforts in almost any realm. An elementary teacher might use this framework to discuss plans for a fund drive for playground equipment. A high school teacher might use this structure to lead students to discuss their high school football team in terms of the motivation, leadership, resources and capability of the team. A political science instructor might use the four-factors structure to analyze and predict the outcome of an upcoming general election.

Problem-solution-effect analysis is another big idea students can apply to their own lives, as shown in this real-life example: Two eighth-grade boys who had learned this big idea in social studies class got into a fight and were sent to the office. While the boys were awaiting their fate outside the principal's office, one of authors of this chapter stopped to ask what happened. When the boys explained that they had got into a fight, the author remarked, "I guess someone was trying to dominate, eh?" One of the boys replied, "Yeah, next time we ought to try accommodating."

Designing Conspicuous Strategies

Teaching higher-order thinking is another highly valued goal of social studies education reform. Although social studies educators tend to distinguish among *problem-solving, decision-making, analysis,* and *critical thinking,* all of these terms represent higher-order thinking in that students must apply an organizational strategy to understand and apply content knowledge. Extensive empirical evidence suggests that all students benefit from having such organizational strategies made conspicuous for them, and that diverse learners are especially in need of conspicuous presentation of the organization of knowledge. In practice, however, social studies curricula and materials rarely include explicit organizational strategies designed to help students understand and apply content knowledge.

A strategy is a general set of steps used to solve a problem or analyze content. Very often in the social studies, effective strategies are literally the application of a big idea. Higher-performing students are more likely to invent their own useful organizational strategies, given adequate time. The purpose of explicit strategy instruction is to ensure that all learners have equal and timely access to the details which lead to success in solving a problem. The emphasis in social studies on critical thinking provides a natural context for including strategies in instruction on social studies content.

Teaching students to apply the big idea of problem-solution-effect when examining the behavior of groups would be an example of a conspicuous strategy that could be profitably taught initially in the early grades. Problem-solution-effect develops naturally out of the narrative text structure with which students are familiar. Given social studies passages that used problem-solution-effect as an expository text structure, students could learn to anticipate and predict the elements of social studies material as well as they do with stories. Looking for the motivating problems, attempts at solutions, and the effects of those attempts could serve as a heuristic strategy for initial efforts at research.

In a multi-year social studies curriculum designed around big ideas and conspicuous strategies, young learners could begin by learning a basic strategy in social studies: looking for identifiable patterns in human behavior. Then, students could be taught the developmental stages of cooperation in the context of a problem they are likely to encounter in their own lives, such as what to do after school. Students could learn the stages of cooperation in the context of a story about how the occasional after-school baseball games of a group of children became more regular and finally became organized into a league with rules. Later, the curriculum could use the stages of group cooperation as a strategy for organizing the study of the how the local city government became organized. In another year the strategy could be applied to the development of the state. Students would learn that the strategy of looking for identifiable patterns of human behavior pays off. The power of a conspicuous strategy in social studies is heuristic; it helps students anticipate what questions to ask and what information is important.

For example, the application of the strategy of looking for the stages of cooperation can be even more powerful in deriving political science principles from history. The stages of cooperation can help explain why the Second Continental Congress gave almost no power to the central government in the Articles of Confederation. Students often regard the Articles of Confederation as somehow being imperfect because they failed to give the government essential powers needed to run the government. Instructional materials often do not explain that, when the Articles of Confederation were conceived, voluntary cooperation between the states had successfully resulted in the elimination of

British taxes and a Revolutionary War victory. Without a strategy for under-standing the development of group cooperation, even capable students have difficulty understanding that the weak nature of the Articles and the govern-ment were due to the level of cooperation between the states at that time.

However, if students acquire the big idea that groups who regularly cooper-ate with success are not compelled to adopt legally binding agreements until it is necessary, this knowledge becomes a sophisticated strategy for understand-ing history and its application to other social sciences at a deeper level. Using the stages of cooperation, students can relate their understanding of the Arti-cles and the weak role of a central government to political science questions, such as the current struggle for cooperation among the republics of the former Soviet Union, rather than being dependent on the teacher for that insight.

Designing Mediated Scaffolding

Temporary assistance along the path to self-regulated learning can help students become independent learners. In social studies, this support or "scaffolding" is often necessary for diverse learners to comprehend what they read, whether a textbook or primary source document. Ideally, instructional materials should provide carefully designed sequences of tasks that involve concept organizers such as maps, timelines, and study guides. However, if materials do not present such techniques, then the teacher must provide supplemental instruction. Simi-larly, scaffolding is also needed for diverse learners to comprehend the critical concepts and ideas of non-textbook sources of social studies information, such as discussions, videos, interviewed informants, and simulation activities.

Supplementing instruction requires a careful analysis of the content aimed at identifying which concepts and ideas are critical for all learners to acquire. Since preparation time for teachers is a scarce commodity, this content analy-sis should focus on methods for scaffolding instruction that are achievable. One reasonable approach to scaffolding is for a teacher to prepare questions prior to a lesson, and then to intersperse the questions while students read, view, or discuss the topic at hand.

Questions prepared in advance and interspersed during instruction can help reduce the number of irrelevant or obscure questions posed by a textbook or teacher. Questions should be designed to help students identify critical information and relationships that lead to conceptual understanding.

Interspersed questions are more helpful if they are posed in close proximity to the material that answers them. A question that is widely separated from its answer changes from a facilitator of understanding to a test of memory. It is crit-ical to interrupt reading, lectures, videos, and discussions to intersperse carefully prepared questions that help insure that students capture, express, and summa-rize the ideas and concepts that they are expected to glean from the activity.

Another useful and common technique for scaffolding students' compre-hension of social studies texts is oral reading. When students read a text aloud, it provides an opportunity for teachers to correct decoding and comprehension errors, prevents students from skipping material, and provides sufficient time for all students to process information.

An example of scaffolding associated with reading aloud involves the teacher's identifying in advance essential prerequisite information to present to students prior to reading a social studies selection. Oral reading prefaced in this manner is especially helpful for diverse learners, who often have limited background knowledge of common social studies content.

While it is possible for teachers to apply these scaffolding techniques to primary source documents and their existing social studies textbooks, the effort to do so is considerable. Figure 7–4 presents an example which carefully presents the big idea of economic problems as a component of the problem-solution-effect big idea. The example supports elementary-level students' understanding of economic problems through a clearly written narrative and interspersed questions in close proximity to new concepts.

Figure 7–5 demonstrates how a middle-school-level textbook on U. S. history (Carnine et al., 1994) applies the big idea of economic problems to different groups—families, businesses, governments, and other organizations–and scaffolds the concept by relating it to a graphic model which uses a balance scale.

Introduction to Problem–Solution–Effect

Studying history is like looking back in time through a window. When we look through this window, we can relive important problems and the solutions people used to solve them.

Sometimes these solutions cause positive effects. Often, however, solutions have unintended effects that create new problems.

Problems faced by large numbers of people together are usually *economic problems* or *people's rights* problems. People have problems when they are unable to get things they want or need.

ECONOMIC PROBLEMS
An economic problem involves difficulty in getting and keeping items that people need or want.

• *What is an economic problem?*

   At a basic level, people need three things: (a) food to eat, (b) shelter to keep them dry and out of the weather, and (c) clothing to keep them warm. People require these three basic items to live. For centuries, people have found ways to meet these basic needs.

• *What three basic things must people have to live?*

FIGURE 7–4
Example of Textbook Introduction to Problem-Solution-Effect

Over the past 400 years, the way people have met their basic needs has changed dramatically. Four hundred years ago, Native American families grew crops and hunted and killed their own food, helped build their own shelters, and made their own clothes. Now not many people grow their own food, build their own shelters, or make their own clothes. Today, families earn money by working. When members of a family work, they exchange their time and skills for money. The money they earn is spent on food, shelter, clothing, and things such as entertainment. If a family earns more money than it spends, the family will have extra money. When a family saves money, they are accumulating wealth. If a family spends more money than they earn, they would end up in debt. A family that gets too much into debt has an economic problem. They cannot afford the things they want and need.

Larger groups also can have economic problems. Factory owners, for example, earn money by selling their products. Some factories make and sell clothes, while others make and sell computers. A factory spends money for many things, such as paying for materials, machines, buildings, and workers' salaries. Factory owners have economic problems if they spend more money making things than they receive by selling those things.

Governments can have economic problems, too. Governments receive money by collecting taxes from their citizens. Governments spend money to pay for protection by the military, education, social services, and many other services. They have problems if they spend more money than they receive from taxes.

Businesses and governments are like families. When businesses and governments save money, they are accumulating wealth. When they spend more money than they earn, they have economic problems and cannot get all the things they want and need.

The figure below shows three different economic situations that families, businesses, governments, and other organizations may experience.

1. If families, businesses, governments and other organizations earn as much as they spend, they will be **economically balanced**. This situation is shown in box A. For example, if a family earns $4000 a month and spends $4000 a month, then it is economically balanced.

2. If a group earns more than it spends, the group will **accumulate wealth**. This situation is shown in box B. For example, if a business earns $50,000 a month and only spends $30,000 a month, then it is accumulating wealth.

3. If a group spends more than it earns, it will have an **economic problem**. This situation is shown in box C. For example, if a government takes in one billion dollars in taxes a month but spends two billion dollars a month, then it has an economic problem.

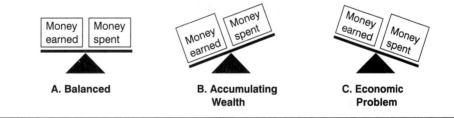

A. Balanced   **B. Accumulating Wealth**   **C. Economic Problem**

FIGURE 7–5
Graphic Representation of Economic Problems Analysis
From: Carnine D., Crawford, D., Harniss, M., & Hollenbeck, K. (1994). *Understanding U.S. History. Volume 1: Through the Civil War.* Eugene, OR: Considerate Publishing. Reprinted by permission.

Figure 7–6 shows how an example of how an elementary-level textbook could conclude its initial presentation of economic problems with scaffolded application questions. Note that the problem is already set up so that the focus is on the implications of the answer rather than setting up the problem.

The amount of scaffolding a teacher or instructional material provides will vary depending upon the difficulty level of a concept and the needs of the students. Diverse learners typically require more scaffolding, while more able students are able to develop effective comprehension strategies independently. Regardless of a student's instructional level, scaffolding must be gradually withdrawn over time. It makes little sense to develop learners who can only understand social studies with textbook or teacher-mediated support.

Designing Strategic Integration

Big ideas and strategies related to problem-solution-effect, factors of group success, and the stages of group cooperation should initially be presented as

---

Economic Problems Activity

1. Darleen's parents give her $5.00 a week as her allowance. She spends $2.50 a week to buy candy.

    5.00
    − 2.50

    Will Darleen have a balance of money earned and spent, be accumulating wealth, or have an economic problem?

2. Roy earns $2,500.00 a month as a bank teller. He borrows from his parents and spends $2,700.00 a month on car and house payments.

    2,500.00
    − 2,700.00

    Will Roy have a balance of money earned and spent, be accumulating wealth, or have an economic problem?

3. Larry earns $1,300.00 a month as a radio announcer. He spends $1,300.00 a month on rent and groceries.

    1,300.00
    − 1,300.00

    Will Larry have a balance of money earned and spent, be accumulating wealth, or have an economic problem?

FIGURE 7–6
Examples of Math Practice for Learning Economic Problems Analysis

discrete concepts. However, instructional materials should go on to help students integrate this knowledge. The goal of integration is to help students achieve a deeper understanding of social studies by providing them with opportunities to apply several big ideas and strategies to previously introduced topics. Practice in the application of big ideas and strategies can best be achieved through careful selection and sequencing of material. Following are principles for integrating big ideas and strategies in social studies instruction:

1. *Integrate several big ideas and strategies*. Students can integrate their knowledge of problem-solution-effect and the stages of group cooperation to analyze historical events such as the Federalists' effort to get the Constitution ratified and the resistance to the new Constitution.

Voluntary cooperation between the states after the Revolutionary War could not prevent interstate taxation, which was limiting trade between the states, nor raise a peacetime navy to protect shipping activities, nor raise enough money to pay off debts incurred by the war. These problems led to economic chaos and a general insurrection in Massachusetts (Shay's Rebellion), which in turn convinced the wealthy colonial establishment that voluntary cooperation defined by the Articles of Confederation needed to be replaced by a stronger central government, via a constitution. Understanding these relationships requires students to apply and integrate their knowledge of problem-solution-effect and the stages of group cooperation.

2. *Integrate potentially confusing concepts*. Lower-performing students often become confused when exposed to similar ideas. McKeown and Beck (1990), in a study of elementary students' knowledge of United States history after a year of instruction, found that students could no longer discriminate between the Declaration of Independence and the Constitution. Because the textbook did not anticipate that students would need help remembering important facts about each document, the students were left with a "document stew" level of understanding.

Thus, well designed knowledge integration in instructional materials and teacher presentations involves the initial separation of similar ideas to reduce confusion. Later, however, the potentially confusing concepts must be carefully integrated and explicitly contrasted.

3. *Integrate a big idea across multiple contexts*. A third aspect of integration involves providing students with opportunities to establish connections between current topics and those which were previously introduced. An example of this type of integration involves having students throughout all levels of social studies use the four factors of group success to analyze and understand why some group efforts fail. Elementary studies of Roanoke, Jamestown, the Pilgrims, and the Puritans could use the four factors to see why some colonies failed and others succeeded. These factors also can be used to analyze middle-school studies of the changes the British made during the French and Indian War, which resulted in victory after an initial series of defeats. And, as previ-

ously noted, at the high-school level the factors can help students analyze the efforts of the Federalists to ratify the Constitution. The application of a big idea across multiple contexts can help students understand their usefulness for comprehending social studies. It also models for students the process of making connections between seemingly diverse content.

Designing Primed Background Knowledge

Research has shown that students with diverse learning needs have less background knowledge of social studies content than their normally-achieving peers (Lenz & Alley, 1983). This lack of knowledge impedes such students' comprehension of social studies instructional materials, which in turn reduces the quality of understanding that a student can construct (McKeown, Beck, Sinatra, & Loxterman, 1992).

The components of big ideas and the steps that constitute strategies often require explicit instruction. For example, to understand the following primary source material from the writings of Geronimo, students must have prerequisite knowledge about the world views of the Apache and of Native Americans in general.

> For each tribe of men Usen [the Apache word for God] created, He also made a home. In the land created for any particular tribe He placed whatever would be best for the welfare of that tribe.
>   When Usen created the Apaches He also created their home in the West. He gave them such grain, fruits, and game as they needed to eat. To restore their health when disease attacked them He taught them where to find these herbs, and how to prepare them for medicine. He gave them a pleasant climate and all they needed for clothing and shelter was at hand. (McLuhan, 1971, p. 154)

In preparation for reading this passage, students need to know that Native American tribes had over thousands of years evolved very intimate and unique relationships between themselves and their local environments. Far from being one Indian culture, the tribes living in different ecological environments solved their basic needs in very different ways.

This background knowledge would enable students to apply one component of the problem-solution-effect big idea—accommodation—and conclude that Native Americans accommodated their environment. This understanding would enable them to comprehend the deeper meaning of the primary source material. Additionally, having learned the big idea of accommodating versus dominating, students are prepared to understand fundamental differences between how Native Americans and Western cultures relate to the environment. This knowledge can also be used to examine the impact of humans upon ecological systems and events associated with the environmentalists' desire that citizens accommodate the environment.

Without prerequisite knowledge, full application of a big idea or strategy is not possible and students are not prepared to make sophisticated connections between seemingly diverse content.

Designing Judicious Review

A major goal of instruction is that all students remember what they have learned. Retention of social studies content can be especially difficult for diverse learners, especially if the instruction they receive covers too many topics superficially. Retention is dependent on the use of effective review practices that are widely supported by research. Reviewing material that is the same or nearly the same *ad nauseam* promotes rote learning; however, effective review can lead to long-term retention and generalization.

Effective review is achievable when the guidelines pertaining to big ideas, strategies, and scaffolding are inherent in the design of instruction for social studies. In other words, if the presentation—from either a textbook or non-textbook source—lacks clarity and coherence, it will also lack a foundation for providing effective review. However, if instructional presentations are designed using big ideas, then the following principles of effective review can be applied:

1. *Review should be sufficient.* Adequate practice should be provided to enable students to reach a point of performance without hesitation. New knowledge is generally "massed" during initial and scaffolded instruction so students have adequate opportunities to apply new knowledge. For example, the application items shown earlier on economic problems were massed.

2. *Review should be distributed.* As students approach self-regulation of knowledge, review should be distributed across time and in increasing increments. The purpose of incrementally increasing review is to help students establish long-term retention and automatic retrieval of meaningful information. If students are given several opportunities during the year to apply their knowledge of factors that determine group success to analyzing different historical events, they will develop a more conceptual rather than rote understanding of the value of those factors. Such conceptual understanding is essential to develop a meaningful curriculum that students can relate to other aspects of their lives.

3. *Review should be cumulative.* Reviewing knowledge cumulatively means simply that the knowledge reviewed accumulates as knowledge accumulates. For example, after the big ideas of problem-solution-effect and four factors of group success are taught separately, both big ideas are reviewed together. To be effective, review must be meaningful and associated with big ideas.

4. *Review should be varied.* Introducing novel situations which require the use of previously learned knowledge can promote generalization and transference of knowledge. Varied review also preempts the possibility of students' resorting to shallow, rote recall. For example, once students learn the four factors that determine group success, the factors can be reviewed through an analysis of various group efforts such as the settlement of Jamestown, the Federalist drive for ratification of the Constitution, and the Civil War. Varied review is also linked to big ideas that can be related to current events. In the absence of an understanding of the stages of cooperation, for example, it is difficult for stu-

dents to recognize connections between the events leading up to the adoption of the United States Constitution and recent events in the former Soviet Union.

It is easy to confuse the "delivery vehicles" of review—concept maps, mnemonic graphics, study guides, and tests—with the attributes of effective review. Social studies programs sometimes include these instructional aids, but rarely do they incorporate effective review principles.

SUMMARY

Many of the guidelines for improving instructional strategies for teaching social studies to diverse learners apply to other learners as well. Understanding the guidelines can help teachers determine how best to attempt program modifications and what principles characterize an effective social studies program for diverse learners. In summary, those principles are:

1. *Design instruction around big ideas.* Important concepts or principles which enable learners to organize and interrelate information are "big ideas." Organizing social studies curriculum around big ideas such as problem-solution-effect, the developmental stages of group cooperation, multiple perspectives, and the four factors of group success is essential to help learners to make connections among the facts and concepts they learn in social studies. The principle of big ideas applies to learners at all levels: What is essential for high-performing students to know is essential for all other students. Big ideas facilitate the process of making what students learn from content-area instruction meaningful and appropriate to their own lives.

2. *Design conspicuous strategies.* A strategy is a general framework used to solve problems and analyze content. In social studies the strategy is often simply the application of the big ideas to the content. Able learners may not require explicit strategy instruction; however, the purpose of explicit strategy instruction is to ensure that all students learn strategies which lead to success in solving problems and understanding content.

3. *Design mediated scaffolding.* Social studies instruction should provide students with temporary support until their learning becomes self-regulated. Mediated scaffolding in social studies includes oral reading, interspersed questions, concept organizers of various sorts, and application questions. While the need for assistance varies according to the needs of the students, with lower-performing students requiring more scaffolding, effective instruction must include enough assistance to insure success for all.

4. *Design strategic integration.* For diverse students to integrate social studies content meaningfully with the rest of their lives, the curriculum must begin that process of integration for them. First, the curriculum must offer students an opportunity to successfully integrate several big ideas. Second, content learned in one context must be applicable to multiple contexts. Third,

potentially confusing concepts and facts should be integrated. The strategic integration of content within the curriculum can help students learn when to use specific knowledge. Furthermore, it "primes the pump" for further integration with the world beyond the social studies classroom.

5. *Design primed background knowledge.* In social studies as much as any discipline, the concepts unified by a big idea or strategy must be explicitly introduced in advance. Failing to make certain that all students possess the requisite background knowledge for deep understanding of the content is one the most pernicious oversights in social studies instruction today.

6. *Design judicious review.* In general, lower-performing students require more review than higher-performing students. Effective review of social studies content must be designed to be an integral and meaningful part of later lessons and must be sufficient, distributed, cumulative, and varied. All students require cumulative review to achieve transfer and generalize information.

Although the challenges of a new direction in social studies and the needs of diverse learners cannot be entirely resolved through the use of effective educational strategies, the prospects for advancing the quality of social studies education for all students, especially those with diverse learning needs, will be greatly improved if the principles presented in this chapter are applied.

REFERENCES

BROPHY, J. (1990). Teaching social studies for understanding and higher-order applications. In M. Wittrock (Ed.), *The Elementary School Journal, 90*(4), 353–417.

CARNINE D., CRAWFORD, D., HARNISS, M., & HOLLENBECK, K. (1994). *Understanding U. S. History. Volume 1: Through the Civil War.* Eugene, OR: Considerate Publishing.

ELLIS, E. S., & SABORNIE, E. J. (1990). Strategy-based adaptive instruction in content-area classes: Social validity of six options. *Teacher Education and Special Education, 13*(2) 133–144.

LENZ, B. K., & ALLEY, G. R. (1983). *The effects of advance organizers on the learning and retention of learning disabled adolescents within the context of a cooperative planning model.* Final research report. Washington, DC: U.S. Department of Education, Office of Special Education.

McKEOWN, M. G., & BECK, I. L. (1990). The assessment and characterization of young learners' knowledge of a topic in history. *American Educational Research Journal, 27*(4), 688–726.

McKEOWN, M. G., BECK, I. L., SINATRA, G. M., & LOXTERMAN, A. (1992). The contribution of prior knowledge and coherent text to comprehension. *Reading Research Quarterly, 27*(4), 78–93.

McLUHAN, T. C. (1971). *Touch the earth: A self-portrait of Indian existence.* New York: Promontory Press.

NATIONAL CENTER FOR HISTORY IN THE SCHOOLS (1992). *Lessons from history.* Los Angeles: Author.

NATIONAL COUNCIL FOR THE SOCIAL STUDIES (1994). Ten thematic strands in social studies. *Social Education, 58*(6) 365–368.

O'Neil, J. (1989). Social studies: Charting a course for a field adrift. *ASCD Curriculum Update,* pp. 1–8.

AUTHOR NOTE

Preparation of this chapter manuscript was supported in part by The National Center to Improve the Tools of Educators (H180M10006), funded by the U.S. Department of Education, Office of Special Education Programs.

Correspondence concerning this chapter should be addressed to Douglas W. Carnine, Institute for the Development of Educational Achievement, College of Education, University of Oregon, Eugene, OR 97403-1211. Electronic mail may be sent via Internet to Douglas_Carnine@ccmail.uoregon.edu.

C H A P T E R

8

Modulating Instruction for Language Minority Students

Russell Gersten
University of Oregon/Eugene Research Institute

Robert Jiménez
University of Illinois

THE CURRENT WAVE of immigration has drastically reshaped the nature of education in the United States. The 1990 census revealed that one out of every seven individuals over the age of five grows up speaking a language other than English. In California, one out of every four students comes from a home where English is not the primary language (Barrington, 1993).

Providing quality instruction for students for whom English is a second language has become one of the major educational issues of the decade, one which we are only beginning to address (Cziko, 1992; de la Rosa & Maw, 1990; Moll, 1992; Pallas, Natriello, & McDill, 1989; Waggoner, 1991). The large number of students involved and the enormity of the problem go beyond training a relatively small cadre of English-as-a-second-language (ESL) and bilingual specialists. Knowledge of instructional strategies for language minority students is critical to being a successful educator in this country at the present time.

Academic achievement levels for many groups of low-income language minority students continue to decline and show few signs of improvement (Pallas, Natriello, & McDill, 1989). For example, approximately 35 percent of all Latino students discontinue their education before completing high school, a figure that has remained stubbornly consistent for over 15 years (Waggoner, 1991). As a result of the surge in immigration, many teachers have become, often by default, teachers of second-language students. Teaching this group of students is a complex endeavor. A serious issue is the "double demands" required of language minority students: they need to acquire a second language and at the same time master traditional subject matter. Many teachers who are confronted with a struggling language minority student are baffled by the student's seemingly unpredictable rate of academic progress (Gersten & Woodward, in press). Inappropriate referrals into special education are common in some parts of the country (Mercer & Rueda, 1991).

The goal of this chapter is to present promising practices for teaching language minority students and to present a framework that can be used to better understand and analyze the quality of instruction provided. In particular, present specific procedures are provided for adapting or adjusting teaching practices so that they are successful with students for whom English is a second language. As Gersten and Woodward (1985) noted, "bilingual education . . . (is) relatively easy to write about, yet difficult to implement sensitively on a day to day basis" (p. 78). This chapter highlights key findings from instructional research on language minority students that have relevance for teachers and curriculum developers. Unlike the preceding chapters, this chapter deals less with curriculum design and more with how to adapt existing curricula in order to sensitively and effectively teach this group of students. Our goal is to begin to delineate instructional strategies that will help teachers perform the complex task of teaching academic content while developing students' English language abilities. The framework and strategies are based on contemporary research as well as our own ongoing research on the topic.

Throughout this chapter, we intentionally try to merge the findings from second-language acquisition research and bilingual education research with those on effective teaching, literacy instruction, and cognitive strategy instruction. These traditions have rarely been integrated in the past, with a few notable exceptions (Carter & Chatfield, 1986; Tikunoff, 1985).

We begin by sensitizing the reader to some common recurrent problems that have been documented by prior research (e.g., Moll, Estrada, Diaz, & Lopes, 1980; Yates & Ortiz, 1991). We then proceed to provide a framework for delineating productive instructional practice.

Because of the complexity of the issues and the extreme diversity of the population, we often point in directions that are likely to be productive, rather than toward a single methodology. All the examples in this chapter are taken from our observational field notes of actual classroom instruction.

PROBLEMS IN CURRENT INSTRUCTION OF LANGUAGE MINORITY STUDENTS

Until recently, much research has documented problems in the instruction of language minority students. There was a clear need for research documenting the need for improvement. When students are presented with conventional curriculum with no modifications, they tend to flounder, become overwhelmed, and mentally tune out or withdraw from active classroom participation (Saville-Troike, 1984).

Over a decade ago, the research of Moll et al. (1980) poignantly delineated the pain and frustration that language minority students struggling to learn English sometimes feel when taught in all-English settings. Students may fail to understand what the teacher is talking about, and may become frustrated when they have an idea but cannot adequately express their thoughts in English. Moll et al. found that teachers tended to correct pronunciation errors (e.g., *seyd* for "said") or interrupt passage reading with attempts to define simple English words (e.g., "surprise," "guess"), thereby breaking the flow of the story. Moll et al. decried "the deliberate, slow pace of lessons with students in the low reading groups" (p. 305), and the lack of intellectual challenge and conceptual development provided to them.

This focus on the details of accurate English language production makes the students appear less competent than they really are. When Moll et al. followed the same students into a Spanish reading lesson, they observed that the students, although considered "low ability" by their teacher, were able to answer comprehension questions correctly on grade-level material, to develop and expand on ideas in the stories, and to process more complex text. Further, the students could read texts usually reserved for "high-ability" students.

Yates and Ortiz (1991) found that many teachers view language minority children as simply low-performing native English-speaking children. This tendency has led many to merely adopt a watered-down curriculum, including reading material well below the students' ability to comprehend. This recurrent problem denies language minority children access to the type of instructional material they need in order to make adequate academic progress. This curriculum mismatch, in all likelihood, is one reason for the extremely low academic performance levels of many language minority students.

According to Fradd (1987), teachers who work with language minority students often tend to use "brief utterances such as 'What is this?' or 'What color is that?'" (p. 146). Students learn to reply in like form, in one- or two-word utterances. Not surprisingly, little curriculum content or social expectation is communicated in this type of verbal exchange. In classroom observations of language minority students, Ramírez (1992) noted the same phenomenon *regardless of teachers' or district's philosophy of bilingual education.*

For years, program evaluation research attempted to determine which model of bilingual education produced the highest levels of student academic achievement (Baker & de Kanter, 1983; Danoff, Coles, McLaughlin, & Reynolds, 1977–1978; Ramírez, 1992; Willig, 1985). In a recent synthesis of almost 20 years of program evaluation research, Cziko (1992) concluded, "it may well be unlikely that this question [of which is the best approach for teaching language minority students in the United States] will ever be satisfactorily answered regardless of the quantity and quality of additional evaluative research" (p.15).

In addition to the program model comparisons, much of the early educational research on language minority students focused on determining the rate at which English language instruction should be introduced. Many of the recommmendations made have emanated from program evaluation efforts, often quite massive in scope (Danoff et al., 1977–1978; Ramírez, 1992). These evaluation efforts were guided at times by theoretical issues, at other times by political issues involving bilingual education (Crawford, 1989; Hakuta, 1986). The heavy emphasis on learning English, to the virtual exclusion of concern for subject matter learning, reflected the mainstream conviction that language minority communities must be compelled to learn the new language (Cummins, 1986; Willig, 1985).

The type of bilingual program model employed and the language of instruction, while important, have received far more attention in research and in public debate than the equally critical issue of how ideas and concepts are taught. Recently, however, the research focus has shifted shift away from searching for the "best" program model and toward identifying useful and feasible instructional practices (Berman et al., 1992; Hakuta, 1986; Reyes, 1992; Tikunoff, 1985).

Differing Theories About and Approaches to Second Language Instruction

The goal of building competence in English without unduly frustrating students requires a complex balance between the utilization of the native language and the language to be acquired. In reality, many models of bilingual education exist (Ramírez, 1992). For the purposes of this discussion, however, we will briefly describe two of the major approaches advocated for educating language minority students, and the underlying rationales of each.

Native Language Emphasis For Latino students, the most commonly utilized model of bilingual education has a strong native-language component (Cummins, 1989; Hakuta & Snow, 1986; Troike, 1981; Wong-Fillmore & Valadez, 1986). We use the term "native language emphasis" to describe this approach.

The conceptual framework for native language emphasis was cogently presented by Troike (1981):

1. People are more likely to learn anything, including English, if they understand what they are being taught.
2. Students with limited English ability will not fall behind their English-speaking peers if they can keep up with subject matter content through their native language while they are mastering English. (p. 498)

Hakuta and Snow (1986) have argued that information and abilities learned via students' native language can be transferred to learning in English:

> The child who knows how to write a topic sentence or look up a word in the dictionary in Portuguese or Chinese will have these skills available for use in the English classroom. (p. 18)

Wong-Fillmore and Valadez (1986) applied Troike's rationale for a native-language emphasis to reading:

> It is not possible to read in a language one does not know. . . . (pp. 660–661)

In other words, until students obtain a reasonably good knowledge of English, particularly in such conceptually complex areas such as reading/language arts and social studies, instruction should be in the native language. This approach ensures that students are not deprived of the experience of learning core concepts in the school curriculum during the years when their English language vocabulary is limited.

Second-language acquisition theorists such as Krashen (1982) and Cummins (1989) assert that once students succeed at comprehending complex academic material in their native language, they will transfer this knowledge to the same subjects taught in English. Therefore, it would seem more sensible to teach complex academic content to students in their native language first so that they can understand and discuss challenging material without the added demand of constantly translating or expressing ideas in a second language. As Troike (1981) stated, "folk wisdom . . . teaches us that the longest way around is sometimes the quickest way home" (p. 498).

There remains great diversity in opinion and practice as to how rapidly students should be introduced to English language instruction and how long native language instruction should be maintained (Chamot & O'Malley, 1989; Crawford, 1989; Ramírez, 1992). One thing seems certain: Abrupt transitions from virtually all-Spanish to virtually all-English instruction is often detrimental for students (Berman et al., 1992; Ramírez, 1992).

Another problem is that during the transition years teachers often are unable to help students use their cognitive abilities and knowledge developed during the years of native-language instruction. It is almost as if students are asked to begin schooling anew in the fifth or sixth grade.

Sheltered English/Structured Immersion: Merging English Language Instruction with Content Learning   Contemporary conceptualizations of education for language minority students acknowledge the participation of many monolingual teachers. Newer approaches, often called sheltered English (Northcutt & Watson, 1986), structured immersion (Baker & de Kanter, 1983; Gersten & Woodward, 1985; Lambert & Tucker, 1972), or cognitive-academic language learning (Chamot & O'Malley, 1989; Saville-Troike, 1982), emphasize the merger of English language instruction with content-area instruction. Such an approach does not preclude native language instruction. The approach is currently used most frequently with Southeast Asian students in the elementary grades, and it is being used increasingly with all types of language minority students, including Latino students, at all grade levels (Chamot & O'Malley, 1989; Ramírez, 1992). This approach is steadily replacing the rather sterile "conversational" ESL instruction that predominated a decade ago.

According to contemporary theorists, understanding of English can be obtained through well designed content area instruction where English is used, *but at a level that is constantly modulated—* that is, adjusted and adapted so that it is comprehensible (Chamot & O'Malley, 1989; Long, 1983). Teachers attempt to control their classroom vocabulary, avoid use of synonyms and idioms, and use concrete objects, gestures, and visuals such as story maps to enhance student understanding of the essential concepts in academic material.

Teachers using the sheltered English approach do not shy away from teaching age-appropriate concepts such as "migration" to third-graders or "peninsula" or "compromise" to sixth- or seventh-graders. Consciously making instruction highly interactive affords students many experiences to verbalize their thoughts (even if the grammar or syntax is imperfect), so that they are able to grasp age-appropriate material.

In an articulate plea for the integration of reading with English language development, Anderson and Roit (1993) note: "Spoken language is fleeting and inconsistent over time. Text is stable and does not pass the learner by. It allows one to reread and reconsider that which is to be learned in its original form" (p. 2). Anderson and Roit demonstrate how the "potential reciprocity between learning to read and reading to learn has strong implications for developing oral language in language minority students, even as early as first grade" (p. 1).

Less than a decade ago, there were fierce controversies between proponents of structured immersion/sheltered English (Baker & de Kanter, 1983) and proponents of native language-emphasis bilingual approaches (Wong-Fillmore & Valadez, 1986). In recent years, however, research and thinking has moved away from this dichotomy towards a search for coherent programs that employ an optimal mix of instructional methods. Researchers such as Barrera

(1984) and Saville-Troike (1982) have stressed consistently that the key problem and issue is not the determination of the exact age or grade level at which to introduce English language instruction, but rather how to merge English language acquisition with academic learning in a fashion that is stimulating and not overly frustrating to students. In the remainder of this chapter we present examples of how teachers have succeeded in meeting this challenge. Before presenting the examples, we provide a framework for understanding aspects of effective instruction for students making the transition into English.

CONSTRUCTS FOR CONCEPTUALIZING EFFECTIVE INSTRUCTIONAL PRACTICE

In recent years, a growing consensus has begun to recognize that effective instruction for language minority students encompasses far more than knowledge of second-language acquisition (Chamot, Dale, O'Malley, & Spanos, 1993; Ramírez, 1992). Relevant research on literacy instruction for diverse learners, including research on cognitive strategy instruction, must be incorporated.

In this section we describe constructs for promoting learning and language acquisition that can serve as a basis for assessing the extent to which instruction is appropriately modified or adapted for language minority students. These constructs, listed in Table 8–1, were developed from extensive research syntheses (Garcia, Pearson, & Jiménez, 1990; Gersten & Woodward, 1992). They embody underlying principles of effective instruction that cross a wide range of theoretical orientations.

In a sense, all of these constructs for promoting learning and language acquisition are meant to delineate actions teachers can take to scaffold students' learning experiences. The term *scaffold* embodies notions of ongoing teacher support and active teacher involvement in helping students express ideas in a new language.

Most of these practices and instructional strategies can be utilized by monolingual teachers for working successfully with language minority students (Chamot & O'Malley, 1989; Gersten, 1993). These include:

▼ Selection of key vocabulary that will enhance understanding.
▼ Provision of a range of activities involving these key vocabulary concepts.
▼ Provision of meaningful English language input to students by responding to the intent of their utterances rather than pedantically correcting their speech.
▼ Active encouragement of students to practice expressing ideas and concepts in English.

Increasingly, the need for the systematic approach implied by the constructs for promoting learning and language acquisition in language minority

TABLE 8–1
Constructs for Promoting Learning and Language Acquisition

---

1. Structures, Frameworks, Scaffolds and Strategies

    a. Provide support to students by "thinking aloud." Build on and clarify input of students.
    b. Use visual organizers/story maps or other aids to help students organize and relate information.

2. Relevant Background Knowledge and Key Vocabulary Concepts

    a. Provide adequate background knowledge to students and/or informally assess whether students have background knowledge.
    b. Focus on key vocabulary words.
    c. Use consistent language.
    d. Incorporate students' primary language meaningfully into instruction.

3. Mediation and Feedback

    a. Provide feedback that focuses on meaning, not grammar, syntax, or pronunciation.
    b. Provide mediation and feedback frequently.
    c. Provide mediation and feedback that is comprehensible.
    d. Provide prompts or strategies.
    e. Pose questions that encourage students to clarify or expand on their initial statements.
    f. Provide activities and tasks that students can complete.
    g. Indicate to students when they are successful.
    h. Assign activities that are reasonable to avoid undue frustration.
    i. Allow use of native language responses (when context is appropriate).
    j. Exhibit sensitivity to common problems in second-language acquisition.

4. Involvement

    a. Encourage active involvement.
    b. Encourage involvement of *all* students, including low-performing students.
    c. Foster extended discourse.

5. Challenge

    a. Ensure that instruction poses challenges that are implicit (cognitive challenge, use of higher order questions).
    b. Ensure that instruction poses challenges that are explicit (high but with reasonable expectations).

6. Respect for and Responsiveness to Cultural and Personal Diversity

    a. Show respect for students as individuals and for students' cultures and families. Respond to things students say. Possess knowledge of cultural diversity.
    b. Incorporate students' experiences into writing and language arts activities.
    c. Attempt to link content to students' lives. Provide experiences that enhance understanding.
    d. View diversity as an asset. Reject notions of cultural deficit.

---

students is recognized by researchers (Cazden, 1992; Goldenberg, 1992–1993; Reyes, 1992).

In the remainder of this section, a range of examples of effective instructional practices taken from naturalistic research are presented (Allen, 1989; Au, 1992; Gersten, 1993; Gersten & Jiménez, in press; Goldenberg, 1992-1993; Jiménez & Gersten, 1993; Reyes & Molner, 1991). They focus on language arts/reading because of its centrality in the curriculum of most American schools, and because of its potential to serve as a vehicle for learning English (Anderson & Roit, 1993; Williams & Snipper, 1990).

Another reason for stressing language arts/reading instruction is that this is the area in which language minority students tend to experience the most difficulty. This was revealed both in student interviews (Gersten & Woodward, in press) and in patterns of achievement (de la Rosa & Maw, 1990; Ramírez, 1992) These techniques can be—and have been—used in other content areas, such as science and social studies (Chamot & O'Malley, 1989).

Merging Language Learning with Reading Instruction

The following example demonstrates how literature and language development can be merged for a group of third-graders with very little English proficiency. Constructs 1, 2, and 3 described in Table 8–1 are in evidence. These students also received native language instruction during a portion of their school day. The example comes from our observational research (Gersten & Jiménez, in press).

The teacher began by reading a story to the class in the form of a big book, *Bringing the Rain to Kapiti Plain*, by Verna Aardema (1981). She spoke to the students in a clearer, less hurried pace than she used in normal conversation. She also intentionally avoided synonyms. Both of these strategies seemed to increase students' levels of involvement in the lesson (as judged by eye contact), and most importantly, their comprehension.

After reading two or three pages of the story, she paused to check the students' understanding:

TEACHER:	What does the bow do?
SIPYANA:	Shoots arrow.

Note that the question is intentionally literal, so that the teacher could assess whether students understood a crucial vocabulary word, *bow*. Because the protagonist of the story is portrayed as a hero who causes rain to fall by shooting a feather from his bow into a cloud, it made sense that some children might benefit from hearing an explanation of this key word (Construct 2: Relevant Background Knowledge and Key Vocabulary Concepts).

A second question called for a moderate inference. It elicited a correct but truncated answer from a student:

TEACHER:	What does he hope will happen when he shoots the arrow?
TRAN:	The rain (He motions rain falling).
TEACHER:	Right, the rain will fall down.

This student understood both the intent of the story and the question posed by his teacher, but was unable (or was afraid to) fully express his thoughts in English. The teacher extended and elaborated on the child's utterance. Her action had the dual effect of affirming the student's response and modeling a more complete English sentence structure for the others, *but without shaming the student* (Construct 1a: Provide support to students, and Construct 3: Mediation and Feedback). Note that this teacher speaks none of the five languages represented in her class (Lao, Cambodian, Thai, Spanish, and Vietnamese), yet her approach enables her to support students' understanding of the reading material.

Building Intellectual Accountability During Literacy Instruction

In this example, when a teacher found that her third-grade class could not come up with a complete description or analysis of a character in the story they were reading, she provided one. For example, none of the students could explain precisely why a character was disobedient. Partial responses, such as "She was dying for gum," were provided. Finally, the teacher integrated comments by several students into a full response: "She is disobedient because she eats gum despite what her mother tells her" (Construct 1a: Build on and clarify input of students).

However, providing students with a complete response was used only as a last resort. Typically the teacher elicited more elaborate and sophisticated responses from the students. She stressed words, such as *disobedient, generous, anxious,* that not only helped them understand the story, but also would be key words in an ESL curriculum (Construct 2b: Focus on key vocabulary words).

The teacher used a bit of Spanish now and then to clarify complex concepts. For example, when she realized that students were not sure what the word *generous* meant, she used the Spanish word *generoso.* Most importantly, she spent a good deal of time framing a discussion of the generosity of a character by asking students to provide evidence located in the text. Because of the meaningful incorporation of students' primary language and the comprehensible support structures provided for locating needed information, this instructional activity exemplified Construct 3j: Exhibit sensitivity to common problems in second-language learning.

Before reading, the teacher always asked students to generate predictions, which she placed on an overhead transparency. After reading the text, each prediction was evaluated by the class. The teacher explicitly pointed out that the main character was "nice and sweet" rather than the "troublemaker" that one student had predicted based on the title of the story. No negative value was placed on making predictions that were not validated, but the teacher made it clear that all predictions would always be taken seriously, reviewed, and evaluated. This sense of intellectual accountability not only facilitated students' ability to perform these same functions later, but also served as motivational devices: Students looked forward to seeing how closely their predictions actually matched the information they encountered in text (Construct 4: Involvement, and Construct 5: Challenge).

Accessing First-Language Knowledge During Literacy Instruction

A recent trend has been to develop strategies that teachers can use to activate the skills and strategies that students possess in Spanish and to encourage them to use this knowledge in their English language classrooms (Chamot, 1992). This section contains examples that illustrate the powerful role the use of children's native language can play in teaching and learning. The two examples are from classrooms in which students were beginning to make the transition from Spanish academic instruction to English language content instruction. Note that, in both cases, students who appeared incompetent in an all-English context actually could produce credible responses to teacher requests when given the chance to respond in their native language.

In the first example, a teacher asked her third-grade students to orally report a brief summary of books previously read. She wanted students to provide a one- or two-sentence general description of the text. The teacher is a fluent speaker of both English and Spanish. One 8-year-old child, Ana, stood in front of the class, as did many of her classmates, but was silent. The teacher's prompts and knowledge of what this child knew and could report appeared to guide her scaffolding (support) during this short exchange. In the bilingual excerpt below, the student's Spanish responses to the teacher's English questions are followed by the English translation in parentheses.

TEACHER: What is it you don't know how to say? Say it in Spanish first.

ANA: *Los niños están asustados porque su abuelito les contó un cuento.* (The children are frightened because their grandfather told them a story.)

TEACHER: Okay, because grandfather told them a story about a dragon. Was there a real dragon? What happened?

ANA: *Ellos estaban corriendo y se encontraron con sus abuelitos.* (They were running and they met their grandparents.)

TEACHER: Okay, they were running and they met their grandparents. Do you have anything else to say, Ana? Okay, your next book report is going to be in English because I've heard you talk English outside and you do a good job.

A few interesting features of the teacher-student exchange above are that the teacher used only English in her interactions with Ana, even though the exchange could not have occurred without her knowledge of Spanish. Also, the teacher paraphrased Ana's responses in English, and asked questions that attempted to focus Ana's somewhat incomplete statement (Construct 3: Mediation and Feedback).

In other words, the teacher provided *bilingual scaffolding* to this student (Construct 1: Structures, Frameworks, Scaffolds, and Strategies). Although Ana spoke in Spanish, she expressed ideas about an English language book she read. The teacher was building Ana's (receptive) English-language abilities in the context of reading instruction. Ana was thus able to draw on her knowledge and express information gained from reading an English language book. This exchange was successful for Ana because of what her teacher knew about her and her language (Construct 3: Mediation and Feedback, and Construct 6: Respect for and Responsiveness to Cultural and Personal Diversity).

In the next example, a teacher conducted a conversation with his fifth-grade students in preparation for a story they were about to read in English about cowboys and cowgirls. The teacher and his students collaboratively created a list of English vocabulary words related to this topic. This technique, checking for understanding, is simple but effective as the comment by one student, José, attests:

TEACHER:	If you don't understand all those words, raise your hand.
CRISTINA:	Holster
CHELI:	Chaps

Teacher draws a picture of chaps and a holster.

JOSÉ:	*O, sí, sí, sí. Ya sé que son.* (Oh, yes, yes, yes. Now I know what they are!)

Like the teacher in the preceding example, this teacher shows a sensitivity to problems in second-language learning. Note that he intentionally used visual representations to assist children to think in English (Construct 1b: Use visual organizers to help students organize and relate information). José's comments indicate that he possessed the necessary information for comprehending the vocabulary presented, but without the proper mediation by the teacher (in this case, use of visuals), he might have been incapable of convincing either himself or his teacher that he did.

In both examples, the strategies used by the teachers to involve students actively in the reading lesson demonstrate Construct 3: Mediation and Feedback. In particular, these teachers allow use of native-language responses (Construct 3j) and provide relevant prompts (Construct 3d) that show sensitivity to common problems in second-language acquisition (Construct 3i). In addition, the mediation and feedback provided by these teachers encourage students to expand on their earliest responses (Construct 3e). Clearly, these teachers focus on meaning (Construct 3a) rather than form. The first example may be best conducted by teachers or others who know their students' native language, while the second example appears to be the kind of instruction within the grasp of monolingual English-speaking teachers with sensitivity to the difficulties involved in language learning.

Both these teachers are bilingual. There is no question that in the area of responsiveness to native-language utterances, bilingual teachers have a distinct advantage over those who speak only English. However, we wish to clarify that even teachers who speak only one language can accept responses in the child's home language, gently urge children to express the same idea in English, and use peers to collaboratively develop a response that both the teachers and students can understand.

Finding ways to adequately assess students' knowledge and abilities in complex cognitive domains is a difficult task for any teacher. This task is compounded when students are learning English as a second language. These students often experience problems when attempting to respond in English to teacher questions and requests, even though they may know the necessary information.

Integrating Responsiveness to Cultural and Personal Diversity into Literacy Instruction

Listening to students is a distinguishing feature of this next example. The classroom observed was a fourth-grade "transition room"—that is, a class of students in their first year of virtually all-English language instruction. The teacher is monolingual and has no formal background in second language acquisition, but does have a real commitment to teaching minority students. This teacher utilizes a relatively pure process approach involving a writers' workshop, students' selections of books that they will read (in English), and a heavy emphasis on projects and journal writing.

The teacher had just finished a conference with a student named Ruben. Ruben was a quiet, bookworm type of student. Ruben wanted to next read a book about Michael Jordan. A boy in the room said, "Ruben has no business doing that. He doesn't know anything about sports." The teacher overheard this remark and intervened. He said, "That's not true. Ruben and his brother watch soccer and basketball games all the time. He knows a lot about basketball." This is an illustration of Construct 6, Respect for and Responsiveness to Cultural and Personal Diversity.

A minute later, another student, Cynthia, asked if it was all right to read a book about the Monitor and Merrimack again. She had read it in the fall, but felt her English was much better at the time of our observation and she knew a lot more about history. The teacher said "Sure" and then described to the class what Cynthia was doing and told them that it was okay to do this and it may make sense for a lot of the rest of them. Because they've become much better readers, the may want to go back and reread something they have previously read.

These types of authentic interactions (Goodman, 1988) are interesting in that the students are treated like real people, with likes, dislikes, and idiosyncrasies. The teacher actually remembered what they said, and usually he found it interesting. Note how the teacher in the above example used this strategy to directly draw students' attention to the benefits associated with rereading.

These techniques allow teachers to encourage and assist in oral English language development because:

▼ Remarks and comments of students were taken seriously.
▼ Students were provided with opportunities to engage in extended discourse in English, using complex concepts and attempting to explain concepts in their own words (Construct 4: Involvement).

As evidenced by the above example, mere knowledge of Spanish is clearly not sufficient and not always necessary. Although teachers observed in this study who tended to really treat their students as individuals also tended to do more "thinking aloud" and modeling of cognitive processes, the correlation was far from perfect. The interplay of this human aspect of instruction and the more cognitively or behaviorally oriented aspects of effective teaching requires further investigation.

CONCLUSIONS

The teachers discussed in the preceding section achieved a delicate balance of high structure, clear focus, and rich objectives that was rare. In order to accomplish these goals with students with limited English-speaking ability, the teachers needed to utilize many of the effective teaching techniques: use of clear and consistent language to describe difficult concepts (Gersten, Woodward, & Darch, 1986), clear statement of objectives, a range of activities to review and clarify applications of new concepts and material, and clear rules not only for social behavior in class, but for instructional conversations (Leinhardt, 1988). Most importantly, high levels of teacher-student interaction were virtually always prevalent.

The most impressive strategy we observed—and it was rare—was for teachers to actually focus on a single aspect of written language for a short period of time, such as verbs, adjectives, or questions and question marks, and to essentially ignore other aspects of language during that time frame. This approach is akin to the focus on "big ideas" recommended throughout this book. Note, however, that the big ideas stressed for second-language learners are geared toward helping students focus on critical aspects of English language production, both oral and written.

When teachers focus on only one critical aspect of language at a time, students know what is expected of them and can direct their energy and attention to that one aspect of the new language. For example, one teacher asked students to rewrite their story using several "words that describe" (adjectives). The teacher wrote a list of possible words that describe on the board, but students could not succeed by merely copying them; they had to know which words fit the context of their story (Construct 1b: Use aids to help students organize and relate information).

The teacher's feedback for that day focused solely on words that describe; no comments were made on spelling or punctuation (Construct 3a: Provide feedback that focuses on meaning). "Correcting" students' grammatical errors has a potentially negative effect on students' self-esteem. Instead, teachers should provide feedback that is based more on the content than on the form of the student's response.

Teachers with expertise in more structured approaches such as direct instruction, active teaching, or any of the other approaches that have become so popular in the last decade have a battery of techniques and strategies and ways of conceptualizing instruction that have the potential to be successful with language minority students. When students falter or flounder in their attempts to work out a solution, are unable collectively to articulate how they figured out a character's motive, or cannot draw an appropriate inference, our observations (Gersten & Woodward, 1993; Jiménez & Gersten, 1993) consistently suggest that it is essential for the teacher to step in and provide a model.

We believe that the guidelines presented in this chapter for modulating instruction will allow for more sensitive, cognitively challenging, and ultimately, more effective teaching of language minority students.

REFERENCES

AARDEMA, V. (1981). *Bringing the rain to Kapiti Plain.* New York: Dial Press.

ALLEN, V. G. (1989). Literature as a support to language acquisition. In P. Rigg & V. G. Allen (Eds.), *When they don't all speak English* (pp. 55–64). Urbana, IL: National Council of Teachers of English.

ANDERSON, V., & ROIT, M. (1993). *Reading as a gateway to language for primary students of limited English proficiency.* Manuscript submitted for publication.

AU, K. (1992, April). *Student purposes in peer-and teacher-guided literature discussions.* Paper presented at the annual meeting of the American Educational Research Association, San Francisco.

BAKER, K. A., & DE KANTER, A. A. (1983). *Bilingual education: A reappraisal of federal policy.* Lexington, Massachusetts: Lexington Books.

BARRERA, R. (1984). Bilingual reading in the primary grades: Some questions about questionable views and practices. In T. H. Escobar (Ed.), *Early childhood bilingual education* (pp. 164–183). New York: Teachers College Press.

BARRINGER, F. (1993, April 28). When English is foreign tongue: Census finds a sharp rise in 80's. *New York Times,* pp. 1, 10.

BERMAN, P., CHAMBERS, J., GANDARA, P., McLAUGHLIN, B., MINICUCCI, C., NELSON, B., OLSON, L., & PARRISH, T. (1992). *Meeting the challenge of language diversity. Volume I: Executive summary.* Berkeley, CA: BW Associates.

CARTER, T. P., & CHATFIELD, M. L. (1986). Effective bilingual schools: Implications for policy and practice. *American Journal of Education, 95*(1), 200–232.

CAZDEN, C. B. (1992). *Whole language plus: Essays on literacy in the United States & New Zealand.* New York: Teachers College Press.

CHAMOT, A. U. (1992, August). *Changing instruction for language minority students to achieve national goals.* Paper presented at Third National Research Symposium on Limited English Proficient Students, Office of Bilingual Education and Minority Languages Affairs, Arlington, VA.

CHAMOT, A. U., DALE, M., O'MALLEY, J. M., & SPANOS, G. A. (1993). Learning and problem solving strategies of ESL students. *Bilingual Research Journal, 16*(3 & 4), 1–34.

CHAMOT, A. U., & O'MALLEY, J. M. (1989). The cognitive academic language learning approach. In P. Rigg & V. Allen (Eds.), *When they don't all speak English* (pp. 108–125). Urbana, IL: National Council of Teachers of English.

CRAWFORD, J. (1989). *Bilingual education: History, politics, theory and practice.* Trenton, NJ: Crane.

CUMMINS, J. (1986). Empowering minority students: A framework for intervention. *Harvard Educational Review, 56*(1), 18–36.

CUMMINS, J. (1989). A theoretical framework for bilingual special education. *Exceptional Children, 56*(2), 111–119.

CZIKO, G. A. (1992). The evaluation of bilingual education. *Educational Researcher, 21*(2), 10–15.

DANOFF, M. N., COLES, G. J., MCLAUGHLIN, D. H., & REYNOLDS, D. J. (1977–1978). *Evaluation of the impact of ESEA Title VII Spanish/English Bilingual Education Program.* Palo Alto, CA: American Institutes for Research.

DE LA ROSA, D., & MAW, C. (1990). *Hispanic education: A statistical portrait.* Washington, DC: National Council of La Raza.

FRADD, S. H. (1987). Accommodating the needs of limited English proficient students in regular classrooms. In S. Fradd & W. Tikunoff, (Eds.) *Bilingual education and special education: A guide for administrators* (pp. 133–182). Boston: Little, Brown & Co.

GARCIA, G., PEARSON, P., & JIMÉNEZ, R. (1990). *The at risk dilemma: A synthesis of reading research.* Champaign, IL: University of Illinois at Urbana-Champaign, Reading Research and Education Center.

GERSTEN, R. (1993). *The parameters of literacy instruction for language minority students: Findings from three years of observational research.* Paper presented at annual conference of the American Educational Research Association, Atlanta, GA.

GERSTEN, R., & JIMÉNEZ, R. (in press). A delicate balance: Enhancing literacy instruction for language minority students. *The Reading Teacher.*

GERSTEN, R., & WOODWARD, J. (1985). A case for structured immersion. *Educational Leadership, 43*(1), 75–78.

GERSTEN, R., & WOODWARD, J. (1992). The quest to translate research into classroom practice: Strategies for assisting classroom teachers' work with "at risk" students and students with disabilities. In D. Carnine & E. Kameenui (Eds.), *Higher cognitive functioning for all students* (pp. 201–218). Austin, TX: Pro-Ed.

GERSTEN, R., & WOODWARD, J. (1993). *Lost opportunities: Observations of the education of language minority students* (Technical Report No. 93-2). Eugene, OR: Eugene Research Institute.

GERSTEN, R., & WOODWARD, J. (in press). The language minority student and special education: Issues, themes and paradoxes. *Exceptional Children.*

GERSTEN, R., WOODWARD, J., & DARCH, C. (1986). Direct instruction: A research-based approach for curriculum design and teaching. *Exceptional Children, 53*(1), 17–36.

GOLDENBERG, C. (1992–1993). Instructional conversations: Promoting comprehension through discussion. *The Reading Teacher, 46*(4), 316–326.

GOODMAN, K. (1988). The reading process. In P. L. Carrell, J. Devine, & D. E. Eskey (Eds.), *Interactive approaches to second language reading* (pp. 11–21). Cambridge: Cambridge University Press.

HAKUTA, K. (1986). *Mirror of language.* New York: Basic Books.

HAKUTA, K., & SNOW, C. (1986). The role of research in policy decisions about bilingual education. *NABE News, 9*(3), 1, 18–21.

JIMÉNEZ, R. T., & GERSTEN, R. (1993). *Culture, community, and classroom: Chicano teachers' knowledge of and instructional strategies for teaching language minority students* (Technical Report No. 93-1). Eugene, OR: Eugene Research Institute.

KRASHEN, S. (1982). *Principles and practice in second language acquisition.* New York: Pergamon.

LAMBERT, W. E., & TUCKER, G. R. (1972). *Bilingual education of children: The St. Lambert experiment*. Rowley, MA: Newbury House.

LEINHARDT, G. (1988). Expertise in instructional lessons: An example from fractions. In D. A. Grouws & T. J. Cooney (Eds.), *Perspectives on research on effective mathematics teaching* (pp. 48–64). Hillsdale, NJ: Lawrence Erlbaum.

LONG, M. H. (1983). Native speaker/non-native speaker conversation in the second language classroom. In M. A. Clarke & J. Handscombe (Eds.), *On TESOL '82: Pacific perspectives on language learning and teaching* (pp. 207–225). Washington, DC: TESOL.

MERCER, J. R., & RUEDA, R. (1991, November). *The impact of changing paradigms of disabilities on assessment for special education*. Paper presented at The Council for Exceptional Children Topical Conference on At-Risk Children and Youth, New Orleans.

MOLL, L. (1992). Bilingual classroom studies and community analysis: Some recent trends. *Educational Researcher, 21*(2), 20–24.

MOLL, L. C., ESTRADA, E., DIAZ, E., & LOPES, L. M. (1980). The organization of bilingual lessons: Implications for schooling. *The Quarterly Newsletter of the Laboratory of Comparative Human Cognition, 2*(3), 53–58.

NORTHCUTT, L., & WATSON, D. (1986). *Sheltered English teaching handbook*. Carlsbad, CA: Northcutt, Watson, Gonzalez.

PALLAS, A., NATRIELLO, G., & McDILL, E. (1989). The changing nature of the disadvantaged population: Current dimensions and future trends. *Educational Researcher, 18*(5), 16–22.

RAMÍREZ, J. D. (1992). Executive summary of volumes I and II of the final report: Longitudinal study of structured English immersion strategy, early-exit and late-exit transitional bilingual education programs for language-minority children. *Bilingual Research Journal, 16*(1), 1–62.

REYES, M. DE LA LUZ (1992). Challenging venerable assumptions: Literacy instruction for linguistically different students. *Harvard Educational Review, 62*(4), 427–446.

REYES, M. DE LA LUZ, & MOLNER, L. A. (1991). Instructional strategies for second-language learners in the content areas. *Journal of Reading, 35*(2), 96–103.

SAVILLE-TROIKE, M. (1982). The development of bilingual and bicultural competence in young children. *Current topics in early childhood education*. Norwood, New Jersey: Alex.

SAVILLE-TROIKE, M. (1984). What really matters in second language learning for academic achievement. *TESOL Quarterly, 18*(2), 199–219.

TIKUNOFF, W. J. (1985). *Applying significant bilingual instructional features in the classroom*. Rosslyn, VA: National Clearinghouse for Bilingual Education.

TROIKE, R. C. (1981). Synthesis of research on bilingual education. *Educational Leadership, 38*(6), 498–504.

WAGGONER, D. (1991). *Undereducation in America: The demography of high school dropouts*. New York: Auburn House.

WILLIAMS, J. D., & SNIPPER, G. C. (1990). *Literacy and bilingualism*. New York: Longman.

WILLIG, A. C. (1985). A meta-analysis of selected studies on the effectiveness of bilingual education. *Review of Educational Research, 55*(3), 269–317.

WONG-FILLMORE, L., & VALADEZ, C. (1986). Teaching bilingual learners. In M. C. Wittrock (Ed.), *Handbook of research on teaching* (pp. 648–685). Upper Saddle River, NJ: Prentice Hall.

YATES, J. R., & ORTIZ, A. A. (1991). Professional development needs of teachers who serve exceptional language minorities in today's schools. *Teacher Education and Special Education, 14*(1), 11–18.

AUTHOR NOTE

Preparation of this chapter manuscript was supported in part by The National Center to Improve the Tools of Educators (H180M10006), funded by the U.S. Department of Education, Office of Special Education Programs.

The research reported in this chapter was supported in part by the Division of Innovation and Development (HO23H00014), U. S. Department of Education, Office of Special Education Programs.

Correspondence concerning this chapter should be addressed to Russell Gersten, Institute for the Development of Educational Achievement, College of Education, University of Oregon, Eugene, OR 97403-1211. Electronic mail may be sent via Internet to Rgersten@oregon.uoregon.edu.

C H A P T E R

9

Contextual Issues and Their Influence on Curricular Change

John P. Woodward
University of Puget Sound

Martin J. Kaufman
University of Oregon

CURRICULUM IS AN elusive term. It can range from "what's on the books" (e.g., courses in your college catalog) to highly specific interactions and learning events in the classroom (Jackson, 1992). The introductory chapter of this text presents a conception of curriculum that includes teaching techniques as well as print or electronic media such as worksheets, textbooks, or technology-based instruction. Explicit strategies, for example, can be presented by a teacher during class (e.g., the teacher models how to sound out a word, or how to revise a paper with an emphasis on strong verbs), or they can be embedded in print materials in the form of carefully sequenced examples and specific suggestions or scripted lesson plans. The central concern in most of the chapters of this book, however, is on the latter: curricular change through well designed printed or electronic instructional materials.

The importance of a detailed analysis and revision of curricula to the many authors of this text cannot be overstated. Their commitment to higher quality instructional materials that convey unambiguous messages is reminiscent of Jeremy Campbell's (1982) characterization of information theory. Campbell argues that at the heart of an information theory is a search for rules or algorithms which govern behavior.

> In information theory, it is the message source which is of primary importance. The source chooses a message out of a set of possible messages and codes it for transmission, sending it to a receiver, which is a sort of transmitter in reverse. In the process, some noise will add itself to the message, distorting and garbling it. Only if the message has been properly encoded at the source will it overcome the muddling effects of the noise, so that when the message is decoded at its destination, it retains its original, intended structure and form. (p. 159)

Big ideas, scaffolding, and explicit and integrated strategies are all ways to "properly encode" information so that it can be transmitted to the learner. By doing so, ambiguity is reduced and learning becomes more efficient (Carnine, 1991). Yet, in the day-to-day world of classrooms, transmission is far from perfect. Thus, continued scaffolding, attention to students' limited background knowledge, and judicious review provide a redundancy and error-checking which insure that the message is adequately received. Careful selection of curricula, then, is a paramount concern for anyone charged with teaching a diverse range of students.

But how does the wider educational context influence adoption and implementation of carefully designed materials? The purpose of this chapter is to explore how the educational context—the district, the school, the classroom, and the individual teacher—affects and constrains an implementation of a new curriculum designed to meet the needs of diverse learners. Much of the discussion revolves around a single case: a teacher who is participating in a current research project being conducted by the senior author of this chapter. This teacher, described in Figure 9–1, is a recent graduate of a teacher training program, and in that regard, may be only two or three years ahead of you in her professional development.

Allison has been hired to teach seventh and eighth grade mathematics. She has recently completed a teacher training program, and her undergraduate emphasis in mathematics as well as a business background made her a good fit for a recent vacancy at Monroe Middle School. While generally enthusiastic about her new job, she has realized that her low-ability, "remedial track" classes will be a challenge.

Half of the students in Math Applications, the lowest math track at Monroe, are mainstreamed special education students. The special education teacher doesn't assist in the instruction, but monitors each student's progress several times throughout the year. Instead, special education services provide Allison with a full-time aide.

The other half of the students in "Math Apps" are in the class for a variety of reasons. Some need just a little extra review before they enter the middle track, pre-algebra classes. Others seem apathetic about math and are taking the class because it is still a required subject. Still others have had a hard time with math since elementary school, but they just don't score low enough to qualify for special education services. As Allison quickly noted, "It really wouldn't make any difference. At this school, they'd still be in my class regardless of whether or not they qualified for special ed."

Allison started her Math Apps class using the district-recommended textbook, a widely marketed commercial basal that begins with a review of basic operations and quickly moves to its main concepts: fractions, decimals and percentages, geometry, and negative numbers. In the beginning of the year, Allison thought she'd supplement the text with some daily living applications like learning how to balance a checkbook.

By the second week, however, Allison was overwhelmed. The range of academic abilities were too great, and the textbook material moved too quickly. Students were frustrated and bored with the introductory review chapter, and most seemed lost when fractions appeared in chapter two of the book. When Allison consulted the special education teacher, she offered her a highly sequenced set of skills worksheets. They were generally computational problems, from simple multiplication and division through decimals.

When Allison tried the worksheets with the majority of the class at the beginning of the third week, most students complained that the work was babyish and that "they'd seen this stuff before and they knew it already." Neither the prescribed textbook for the class nor a common remedial sequence seemed to be the answer. The text was too demanding cognitively, and the worksheets left students unmotivated and indifferent to mathematics.

Clearly, little in Allison's prior training had prepared her to teach these kinds of students. Most importantly, there seemed to be few, if any, resources in the school that could help her adjust the curriculum so that it would adequately meet the needs of her students. When she talked to more experienced faculty about the class, they shared her frustrations and were generally cynical about what could be accomplished with these students. Most felt that students in Math Apps would continue working at the sixth-grade level (at least as measured by district learning objectives) until they graduated from middle school. Allison found the thought of teaching many of these students for three years in a row too depressing.

FIGURE 9–1
Allison's Remedial Track Math Class

For Allison, having complete control over a classroom—and the detailed instructional decisions required to make it run smoothly—is a challenge. And, as the many authors in this book can attest, Allison's experience isn't unique. Her "confrontation" with academic diversity comes in many forms throughout K–12 education.

Kindergarten teachers lament the range of abilities in their classrooms. Some students are ready for reading, reflecting the hundreds if not thousands of hours their parents spent reading to them since birth. Other 5-year-olds show little or no signs of having been exposed to books. Still others, even children who come from "high literacy" environments, have a hard time learning how to decode words (Adams, 1990). Distress over the range of academic abilities of students in regular and remedial classrooms is echoed by teachers at every level of elementary and secondary education.

CONTEXTUAL VARIABLES

Presented in Figure 9–2 is a list of internal and external contextual variables which can affect the adoption of high-quality instructional materials. The list is in no way exhaustive, as the potential number of contextual variables is virtually unlimited: Teachers may go on strike. School levies may not pass, resulting in fewer curricular materials. State legislatures may reallocate significant monies to target populations. School districts may embrace educational fads and disciplinary movements such as whole language.

It should be noted, however, that the contextual variables are not just external to the teacher. Internal contextual variables also mediate the adoption of new materials. Some educators (e.g., Kennedy, 1991) argue that these variables are critical to effective instructional interventions for at-risk learners. Shulman (1987) and others have cited the importance of these elements in contemporary undergraduate education (i.e., a disciplinary major) and teacher preparation programs.

Consider, for example, the teacher described in Figure 9–1. Through an undergraduate major in business and mathematics and a fifth year-teacher training program, Allison is prepared in all three areas listed on the left in Figure 9–2. Her "credentialed" knowledge of mathematics comes from extensive undergraduate course work. No doubt it is an important foundation for detecting and developing "big ideas." Yet, as Ball (1990) has demonstrated, this knowledge alone is inadequate if mathematics instruction is to be conceptual and not a series of algorithms learned by rote practice. Later, we return to the impact of the teacher's subject matter knowledge on curriculum.

Allison's teaching or pedagogical techniques, as well as her knowledge of curriculum, came from her educational methods courses. Unfortunately, Allison's teacher preparation program only offered broad teaching techniques, ones intended for learners with average and above-average abilities. Allison's experience with curriculum analysis was generally limited to reviewing text-

FIGURE 9–2
*Contextual Variables Which
Can Affect the Adoption of
High-Quality Instructional
Materials*

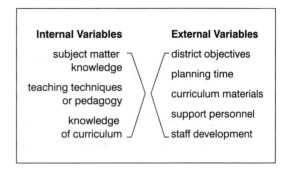

books in the curriculum library. Naturally, she had a more in-depth experience with one commercial textbook during her student teaching.

The external variables which affect Allison's application of her knowledge are listed on the right side of Figure 9–2. While the variables may suggest a range of services and opportunities, they are, in fact, quite limited. Over the last five years, the district has focused on innovative approaches to mathematics, incorporating them into their district math objectives or "essential learnings." Test scores and student performance have risen sharply, and many students take algebra by the second year of middle school. Clearly, this isn't the case for the students in Allison's Math Apps class.

Allison has no more planning time than any of the other teachers in the building. She doesn't begin to get enough done in her 50-minute preparation period. Like the more experienced teachers in the building, she takes student papers home every night to grade and spends a portion of her evening planning the next day's lessons.

Allison finds the curriculum materials (i.e., the textbook) to be of enormous help in determining what she will do over the course of the year, as a guide to major instructional units, and as a way of planning for the week. This reliance on the textbook is not uncommon for beginning teachers (Kaggan & Tippins, 1992). Moreover, research on teacher planning (Brown, 1989) suggests that the text is an important intermediary between a teacher's unit plans, which may span several weeks, and the day-to-day adjustments that need to be made because of interruptions, variations in student performance, and so forth. It is this element of the school context that is the most pertinent to the various chapters in this book. Well designed print or electronic curricula could dramatically assist Allison with her Math Apps class. However, as the vignette indicates, Allison's curricular options at the beginning of the year are Spartan at best.

The special educator's role as a itinerant consultant to teachers (i.e., as support personnel) throughout the building is directly related to an inclusive philosophy followed by many districts in the state. Teachers like Allison, who have a lot of mainstreamed special education students, are provided with at least one instructional aide for a class like Math Apps. Allison's aide tends to work with students in one-on-one tutoring and to assist with behavior management.

Although Allison has yet to attend any district inservices, she has already heard a great deal about the "one shot" fixes that occur for one or two half-days at different times in the winter and spring. Most teachers are skeptical, but they occasionally find something of interest. It is unlikely that anything in this year's planned inservices will help Allison with her Math Apps students.

REVISING CURRICULA FOR A MORE DIVERSE STUDENT POPULATION

Allison's first task was to replace or dramatically reorganize the original text selected for the Math Apps class with one that was more suitable to the needs of her academically low-achieving students. Lack of time and expertise precluded her reorganizing the text. Instead, her participation in our research project made the search for new materials easier. Research staff assisted Allison in finding appropriate, innovative mathematics curricula, ones which had been demonstrated to be successful with educationally disadvantaged and special education students. The curricular materials stressed a much more visual approach to many of the concepts than the commercial text originally selected for the class. The new curriculum also encouraged a higher level of teacher-student interaction in the form of dialogues and conceptual explanations.

Figure 9–3 indicates how the revised curriculum concentrated on more "big ideas" rather than the dense array of concepts, most of which were presented briefly and with little systematic review, that characterized the original curriculum. The revised curriculum allowed Allison to spend more time on proportions, a key idea that permeated the district's essential learnings for the Math Apps class and, more generally, sixth-grade math outcomes. Through the new curriculum, Allison helped students visualize the concept of a fractional parts. In the previous curriculum, only token attempts were made at displaying fractions visually, and while Allison's success in mathematics had trained her to see the subject matter "only abstractly," she quickly appreciated the difference a consistent, visual treatment of fractions made for her students. The revised curriculum also enabled her to use calculators as a daily tool for problem solving. Far less time was spent drilling students on traditional fractional algorithms (e.g., adding fractions with unlike denominators), and more time was devoted to applying the math concepts in everyday contexts. Allison was still able to use portions of her original textbook for the highest ability students in her Math Apps class.

Figure 9–3 also suggests how the new curriculum was affected by an array of other contextual variables, as mentioned earlier. The district's emphasis on innovative mathematics, as expressed through objectives or essential learnings, constrained Allison's search for new materials. While the school's curriculum library had a number of remedial curricula, most taught math in a rigid and highly traditional manner. For example, students were shown how to perform the operations for adding fractions with unlike denominators, and

FIGURE 9–3
The Impact of Contextual Variables on a New Curriculum

Old Curriculum

1. Addition/subtraction of whole numbers
2. Addition/subtraction of decimals
3. Multiplication/division of whole numbers
4. Multiplication of decimals
5. Division of decimals
6. Geometry
7. Number theory and equations
8. Addition/subtraction of fractions
9. Multiplication/division of fractions
10. Measurement: Metric Units
11. Ratio and proportion
12. Percent
13. Circles and cylinders
14. Probability, statistics, and graphs
15. Integers
16. Measurement: Customary Units

New Curriculum

1. Proportions
   Representing common fractions
   Transforming fractions
   Understanding decimals
   Percents
   Ratios

2. Common measurements
   Using fractions
   Metrics

3. Geometry

4. Charting numbers and modeling data

District objectives (the "essential learnings")

teaching techniques or pedagogy knowledge of curriculum

Enhanced through participation in the research project

planning time
curriculum materials
support personel
staff development

Facilitated by the staff of the research project

how to divide .27 into .054, but they weren't taught a conceptual foundation for these operations.

Allison also found these texts objectionable: "I saw teachers use these materials when I was student teaching. Students were bored and seemed to be doing the same thing year after year. I would have had a hard time using them on a regular basis. Also, they don't teach the math these kids need." In effect, Allison's subject matter knowledge affected her curricular decision as much as the district's objectives.

Undoubtedly the greatest influence on Allison's shift to a new curriculum was the assistance from the research staff. They presented her with curricular options, developed explicit strategies for teaching new concepts, revised some lessons by creating "smaller steps" for the lowest-performing students, and showed Allison how to carefully distribute practice over time and review previously taught material in a cumulative manner. In this respect, the staff acted as critical support personnel and as a day-to-day form of staff development. To be sure, the research staff significantly reduced the amount of planning time Allison needed for her Math Apps class. The impact of this kind of assistance is explored in the next section.

THE PROBLEMS OF CONTEXT AND CURRICULAR CHANGE

Allison's case epitomizes the complex nature of curricular change. Rarely do teachers just adopt a new textbook "out of the box." As the variables listed in Figure 9–2 suggest, a new curriculum is mediated by a number of factors. And while it would be natural to weigh each variable equally, two factors seemed to be most pronounced for Allison.

Allison's foremost problem, one that does not have a ready answer, is that she did not have sufficient planning time. She did not have the time (nor the expertise) to reorganize the text originally selected for the class, nor the time to learn the new curriculum and how to modify it in ways which met the needs of the lowest-ability students in her class. The new curriculum became a second curriculum for the class, albeit the predominant one.

A second, related problem was staff development. Without the assistance of staff from the research project, Allison would never have been able to adequately implement the new curriculum. Project staff modified the new curriculum for the lowest-performing mainstreamed special education students and offered feedback and consultation on Allison's day-to-day effectiveness.

Allison's case is instructive in that it shows how much of a difference planning time and staff development can make to innovation. Unfortunately, this kind of support is rare in public schools. For all the merits of technical assistance and coaching discussed in the professional literature (Gersten, Morvant, & Brengelman, 1995; Showers, Joyce, & Bennett, 1987), this kind of mentoring is seldom provided. Financial constraints, along with a number of the interpersonal and political issues surrounding intensive staff development efforts, make the support given to Allison entirely atypical. Even collaborative teaching relationships, while widely advocated in the literature, hardly ever occur (Huberman, 1993; Rosenholtz, 1989).

Allison's case also has a direct bearing on the kinds of curriculum changes suggested in the various chapters of this text. As should now be apparent to the reader, carefully designed instruction takes time and extensive planning. In many instances, materials must be fully prepared and revised well in advance of the day's lesson. A comprehensive, well organized curriculum may involve large instructional units, if not the entire year. Do contextual variables, then, allow teachers to modify curricula effectively to meet the needs of a wide range of student abilities? Answers, at least as measured by the content of different chapters in this book, seem to vary.

Even though 100 years of debate over the role of phonics in beginning reading has led to little in the way of a resolution at an academic level, systematic phonics would still appear to be something that elementary teachers could incorporate into daily practice. This practice, and others described in the chapter on reading, can be obtained within what is typically allotted to teachers in the way of planning time and staff development. While beginning teachers like Allison struggle to "keep their heads above water," more experienced teachers should have the capacity to incorporate a fundamental component of reading like phonics. Similar arguments could be made for the mix of skill and process techniques described in the chapter on writing instruction. If anything, the greatest challenge to introducing a curricular change like phonics would appear to come from district policies or from teachers whose pedagogical beliefs or subject matter knowledge leave them strongly opposed to the practice.

Revising social studies, mathematics, and science instruction in the manner described in this text, however, appears to be an effort of an entirely different order of magnitude. As with Allison, most teachers simply lack the time and expertise to complete such tasks. Equally important is the fact that one teacher's "big ideas" could vary considerably from the kind of detailed, systematic design described in these three chapters. What the chapters on social studies, mathematics, and science tend to present are "finished products" more than step-by-step techniques for curriculum revision in a content area. They reflect lengthy analyses that have been conducted away from the classroom by individuals following a consistent set of curriculum design principles.

These chapters reveal what has been called a "technological perspective" of curriculum development and classroom instruction (House, 1981; Woodward, 1993). From this perspective, one could argue that classroom practice is best improved when teachers adopt new, research-based methods and materials. Designing innovative instruction around the needs of diverse learners becomes a matter of finding logically developed and empirically validated materials. Time constraints on today's teachers and other context issues do not permit teachers this kind of curriculum revision at the classroom level. Instead, the implication is that curriculum materials which meet the needs of diverse learners are best developed by outsiders. This allows for high-quality, *transportable* curricula—that is, instructional programs which can be used in the greatest number of settings with the highest fidelity of implementation.

This notion has appeal in light of the growing number of reports that roundly criticize the content and organization of the texts commonly used in our public schools today. The drift toward the encyclopedic in commercial texts is discussed in the chapters on science and social studies.

The main problem with the technological perspective, however, is its possible clash with a teacher's internal contextual variables: subject matter knowledge, teaching techniques, knowledge of the curriculum, and so forth. The potential for this conflict is acute at the secondary level, because teachers at this level generally have stronger subject matter preparation than elementary teachers. An example of a possible conflict can be found with the approach described in the social studies chapter.

The problem-solution-effect structure is undoubtedly an important big idea in social studies. As with many of the other chapters, we see countless examples of how muddled presentations in commonly used texts can be translated into more comprehensible materials. In Armbruster's (1984) words, they can become "considerate." Understanding why groups succeed through motivation, leadership, resources, and capability comprises another set of big ideas for social studies analysis.

Yet social studies educators (e.g., Banks, 1991; Brophy, 1990; Wilson, 1991) would argue that transforming poorly organized facts and concepts into a more coherent form—one that avails itself to higher-order thinking—is only one part of a discipline's knowledge base and method of teaching. Missing in this analysis, for example, is a place for values clarification. The intricate issues of multicultural education (e.g., examining the same historical phenomena from multiple perspectives) also seem to be absent. This is not an incidental issue for diverse students, many of whom are minorities (see McElroy-Johnson, 1993).

Rather than compressing historical information into a text structural form like problem-solution-effect, there may be many important aspects of historical records which, though incomplete or lost, are nonetheless important. Banks (1991) provides an example: "We have rich accounts of the Lewis and Clark expeditions from their diaries, but only sketchy information about York, the African-American who accompanied them. . . . " (p. 121). Narrative accounts may be crucial to the kind of multicultural education which profiles key figures of a certain racial group, thus motivating diverse learners and enhancing their self-esteem. Weaving themes that arise from actual historical events (e.g., power and liberty as they relate to the development of the U. S. Constitution) and presenting stimulating narratives are also exceedingly effective techniques for the social studies teacher (Leinhardt, 1990; Wilson, 1991). These approaches embody a different orientation than big ideas and are built around different assumptions as to how a secondary social studies teacher might use his or her subject matter knowledge and pedagogy to revise a curriculum for diverse learners.

CONCLUDING REMARKS

Over a decade ago, Gerber and Semmel (1985) noted that education must incur significant costs if it is to meet the needs of diverse learners. These costs take the form of more powerful "technologies." This use of the term includes personnel, staff development, microcomputers, or, as this text suggests throughout, better curricular materials. The various chapters in this text make a compelling case for improved curricula as an essential step toward more effective classrooms.

Yet even after technologies such as clearer, more considerate texts are incorporated into classroom instruction, many challenges remain. Allison, for example, still moves from her new set of curricular materials to the originally selected text in an effort to meet the needs of both her most able students and those who have the greatest difficulties. Investing so much effort in those students who are hardest to teach has its costs, as was evident in the recently conducted research described below:

In the late 1980s, the senior author of this chapter participated in a staff development project in a large Southern California school district (Woodward, 1991). The intent of the project was to assist teachers in meeting the needs of the lowest-achieving students in their elementary school classrooms. The teachers attended special inservices and listened politely to the suggestions offered by project staff. Most were indifferent to the extra assistance offered over the course of three years. At the end of the project, few teachers substantively changed their classroom practices, and the project was unsuccessful.

However, one sixth-grade teacher took a great interest in the assistance, and after four months of collaboration with the research staff the academic performance of the lowest-performing students in her class improved. This included the two students who were certified as learning disabled. Yet, during the end-of-the-year interview in May, the teacher confessed that even though she was very pleased with the change in her students, and with the opportunity to learn new and more effective instructional techniques to use with low-performing students, she found that her work with lowest-performing students to be very demanding. She often was too exhausted to teach in the way that was best for these students, and therefore delegated instructional responsibilities for this group to the paraprofessional aide. Furthermore, when she looked at the rest of her class, she sometimes found herself asking, "How much am I taking away from my higher group?" This teacher's comments are a sober reminder of the immense challenges teachers face in adapting instruction for diverse learners.

REFERENCES

ADAMS, M. (1990). *Beginning to read: Thinking and learning about print.* Cambridge, MA: MIT Press.

ARMBRUSTER, B. B. (1984). The problem of "inconsiderate text." In G. G. Duffy, L. R. Roehler, & J. Masson (Eds.), *Comprehension and instruction* (pp. 202–217). New York: Longman.

BALL, D. (1990). The mathematical understandings that prospective teachers bring to teacher education. *Elementary School Journal, 90*(4), 449–466.

BANKS, J. (1991). Social science knowledge and citizenship education. In M. Kennedy (Ed.), *Teaching academic subjects to diverse learners* (pp. 117–128). New York: Teachers College Press.

BROPHY, J. (1990). Teaching social studies for understanding and higher-order applications. *The Elementary School Journal, 90*(4), 367–417.

BROWN, D. (1989). Twelve middle school teachers' planning. *Elementary School Journal, 89*(1), 69–87.

CAMPBELL, J. (1982). *Grammatical man*. New York: Simon and Schuster.

CARNINE, D. (1991). Curricular interventions for teaching higher order thinking to all students: Introduction to the special series. *Journal of Learning Disabilities, 24*(5), 261–269.

GERBER, M., & SEMMEL, M. (1985). The microeconomics of referral and reintegration: A paradigm for evaluation of special education. *Studies in Educational Evaluation, 11*, 13–19.

GERSTEN, R., MORVANT, M., & BRENGELMAN, S. (1995). Close to the classroom is close to the bone: Coaching as a means to translate research into practice. *Exceptional Children, 62*(1), 52–67.

HOUSE, E. (1981). Three perspectives on innovation: Technological, political, and cultural. In R. Lehming & M. Kane (Eds), *Improving schools: Using what we know*. Beverly Hills, CA: Sage Publications.

HUBERMAN, M. (1993). The model of the independent artisan in teachers' professional relations. In J. Little & M. McLaughlin (Eds.), *Teachers' work: individuals, colleagues, and contexts*. New York: Teachers College Press.

JACKSON, P. (1992). Conceptions of curriculum and curriculum specialists. In P. Jackson (Ed.), *Handbook of research on curriculum*. Upper Saddle River, NJ: Prentice Hall.

KAGGAN, D., & TIPPINS, D. (1992). The evolution of functional lesson plans among twelve elementary and secondary school teachers. *Elementary School Journal, 92*(4), 265–489.

KENNEDY, M. (1991). *Teaching academic subjects to diverse learners*. New York: Teachers College Press.

LEINHARDT, G. (1990). *Towards understanding instructional explanations* (Tech. Rep. No. CLIP 90-03). University of Pittsburgh: Learning Research and Development Center.

McELROY-JOHNSON, B. (1993). Giving voice to the voiceless. *Harvard Educational Review, 63*(1), 85–104.

ROSENHOLTZ, S. J. (1989). Workplace conditions that affect teacher quality and commitment: Implications for teacher induction programs. *Elementary School Journal, 89*(4), 421–439.

SHOWERS, B., JOYCE, B., & BENNETT, B. (1987). Synthesis of research on staff development: A framework for future study and state-of-the-art analysis. *Educational Leadership, 45*(3), 77–87.

SHULMAN, L. (1987). Knowledge and teaching: Foundations of the new reform. *Harvard Educational Review, 57*(1), 1–22.

WILSON, S. (1991). Parades of facts, stories of the past: What do novice history teachers need to know? In M. Kennedy (Ed.) *Teaching academic subjects to diverse learners* (pp. 99–116). New York: Teachers College Press.

WOODWARD, J. (1991). *The school based models project: Six approaches for assisting mildly handicapped students in general education settings*. Paper presented at the annual meeting of the American Educational Research Association, Chicago, Il.

WOODWARD, J. (1993). The technology of technology-based instruction: Comments on the RDD perspective of educational innovation. *Education & Treatment of Children, 16*(4), 345–360.

AUTHOR NOTE

Preparation of this chapter manuscript was supported in part by The National Center to Improve the Tools of Educators (H180M10006), funded by the U. S. Department of Education, Office of Special Education Programs.

Correspondence concerning this chapter should be addressed to John P. Woodward, School of Education, The University of Puget Sound, 1500 North Warner, Tacoma, WA 98416-0220. Electronic mail may be sent to woodward@ups.edu.

Big Ideas:
Beginning Reading
Math
Science
Social Studies

CHAPTER 3: BEGINNING READING

▼ *Big Ideas*

Development: Allocate considerable time/space to teaching the big ideas of phonemic awareness (i.e., ability to perceive spoken words as a sequence of sounds) and alphabetic understanding (i.e., understanding that words are composed of individual letters) and to the development of automaticity with the code (i.e., ability to translate letters-to-sounds-to-words fluently). This is in contrast to giving approximately equal time and resources to a multitude of topics.

Selection: Examine beginning reading tools to determine the extent to which the majority of time/space is allocated to big ideas.

Modification: Identify the most important beginning reading concepts and principles in existing tools and reallocate instructional time so that you may teach those concepts and principles thoroughly. Note that valid and useful assessment should focus on the important beginning reading concepts.

▼ *Conspicuous Strategies*

Development: Provide explicit strategies for learning big ideas. Strategies should not be too narrow because they would likely result in rote learning and the need to learn too many strategies. Neither should they be too broad, like some of the common "strategies" for reading words (e.g., "Think of a word that begins with . . ."). Students may need to be taught more specific strategies with broad potential for transfer of knowledge across letters, sounds, and words (e.g., presenting the parts of words auditorily without printed letters to allow the learner to focus on the sound structure of language).

Selection: Examine tools first to see whether conspicuous strategies exist at all, and if so, whether they generally appear to be "intermediate in generality." Try to imagine yourself as a diverse learner just learning to read an alphabetic language based solely on what the tool you have selected has taught you.

Modification: When students struggle with concepts and principles not directly taught in tools, teachers must develop an explicit strategy for those concepts and principles. When strategies are too narrow, explain the underlying principles that make the strategy work.

▼ *Mediated Scaffolding*

Development: Some scaffolding, such as peer tutoring and instructional feedback, need not be built into instructional tools, but may instead be part of teachers' staff development materials. Scaffolded *tasks,* however, should be built into tools, particularly around the selection of letters and words to include when introducing phonemic awareness, alphabetic understanding, or automaticity with the code. For example, a scaffolded task for teaching students to translate a series of blended sounds into a word would require the teacher to (a) model the individual sounds or words, (b) actually lead students who are having difficulty by responding with them, (c) assess students' ability to blend the sounds independently, and (d) provide students with individual practice opportunities to blend the sounds into a word.

Selection: Examine both "model" or demonstration tasks associated with a strategy and the tasks students will eventually do independently. Ask yourself, "Are there in-between tasks that will help students gradually achieve independence and understanding?"

Modification: Without consuming too much time, teachers can convert independent tasks into scaffolded tasks by providing hints, cues, or prompts for some of the more difficult steps in the strategies associated with those tasks.

▼ Strategic Integration

Development: Develop specific tasks and activities specifically designed to strategically integrate phonemic awareness, alphabetic understanding, and automaticity with the code. Such tasks and activities are particularly useful in relation to those beginning reading skills that predictably cause confusion for many students, such as sound and words that are visually and auditorially similar (e.g., *b/d* and *p/q*; *was* and *saw*). The application of big ideas across beginning reading skills also merits specifically designed tasks and activities regardless of potential "confusability."

Selection: Examine the scope and sequence of instructional tools, specifically looking to see whether some chapters (or units or lessons) are designated as "summary or review" or "integration" or "consolidation." In a well integrated tool, in-program assessments will include tasks representing all topics taught previously, not just those taught immediately before assessment.

Modification: Teachers can improve the effectiveness of tools most notably by identifying common confusions, such as those identified above, and by providing students with additional integrated practice around them. For example, if a tool does not provide practice on a mixture of letter-sound correspondences that have been taught previously for alphabetic understanding, teachers can provide such practice using activities or by making minor modifications of the instructional tool to incorporate critical items.

▼ Primed Background Knowledge

Development: Developers should (1) create assessment tools that determine whether students possess background knowledge for learning the strategies in a program, and (2) provide instruction on essential background knowledge for those who lack essential background knowledge. For diverse learners, it is risky to assume that material taught last year will be fully retained as essential background knowledge for strategies being taught this year.

Selection: A strategy for teaching an important big idea in beginning reading (e.g., phonemic awareness, alphabetic understanding) should be dissected into its component parts. Then, about 15 days worth of instruction *preceding* the introduction of the strategy should be examined to determine whether and how those components are handled. Ideally, components are taught or reviewed a few lessons preceding the introduction of the new strategy. Also, tools should be checked to determine the extent to which assessment tools identify potential problems with background knowledge.

Modification: To some extent, teachers can analyze important strategies in advance of their introduction and provide essential background knowledge based upon that analysis. For example, teachers can review new or difficult words in isolation before reading the same words in a passage context.

▼ Judicious Review

Development: Publishers do a great service to teachers when they provide plentiful review in instructional tools, because it is infinitely easier for teachers to skip review activities than to create additional ones. Programs that include well distributed review are far more efficient than those that do not, and programs with built-in cumulative review promote strategic integration, as described above. Review should also be varied, to promote transfer.

Selection: Locate a particularly difficult skill or activity in beginning reading, such as reading words that end in "ing" or "ed," then trace the review throughout the remainder of the program to determine whether review is plentiful, distributed, cumulative, and appropriately varied.

Modification: Teachers can modify programs to improve the judiciousness of review by (1) taking an extensive set of tasks and distributing them over a period of days, and (2) making review cumulative, as discussed above under "Strategic Integration: Modification." It can be quite time-consuming for teachers to modify programs to vary review appropriately; that is, review that is varied enough to avoid rote practice, but not so varied that it presses students to perform outside of the limits of the strategies they have been taught.

CHAPTER 4: WRITING

▼ *Big Ideas*

Development: Provide intensive instruction on a small number of text structures in each school year. Emphasize stages in the writing process and provide for collaborative work as a means of clarifying the reader-writer relationship. Teach mechanical skills concurrently with composition, focusing upon big ideas such as sentence manipulation to learn usage, or morphology for spelling.

Selection: Evaluate prospective materials to determine the extent to which they focus upon big ideas. More time is allocated to big ideas than to other, less critical content.

Modification: Identify big ideas in existing materials and plan to allocate more time to them, time "borrowed" by de-emphasizing or ignoring less important ideas. Select, for example, just two or three of the most useful text structures presented in materials and teach those thoroughly.

▼ *Conspicuous Strategies*

Development: Most critically, develop explicit strategies. However, strategies should not only be explicit, but should be "medium" in terms of generality as well. Such strategies are not simple to develop, but they are between strategies that are too narrow or too broad. A narrow strategy might be, "Start each paragraph with a topic sentence." A broad writing strategy is, "Plan before writing."

Selection: In reviewing instructional tools, identify which explicit strategies, if any, are associated with important big ideas. The following problems sometimes occur:

1. No explicit strategy can be found.
2. The strategy is explicit, but too narrow or too broad. In general, the strategies used to teach composition tend to be quite broad, and the strategies used to teach writing mechanics tend to be quite narrow.
3. The strategy is explicit and of "medium generality," but some steps are ambiguous or confusing.

Modification: The most difficult modification for teachers or others to make with existing tools is the creation of a strategy where none exists. When strategies are provided, teachers can realistically evaluate them from the point of view of their students and modify those steps that are ambiguous or confusing.

▼ Mediated Scaffolding

Development: After students have studied the text structure of a specific writing genre or something else new, their initial work should be supported temporarily by simplified tasks. For instance, "think sheets" can be provided for each genre and for many mechanics activities. Initially, such aids should lend considerable support to students by virtually "forcing" the appropriate organization of thoughts. Gradually, simplified tasks should be converted into complex, fully self-regulated tasks.

Selection: Examine the activities associated with a major topic to see whether scaffolded tasks are routinely provided. One should be able to imagine students "easing into" full understanding and complete independence as they work from early to later tasks on a given topic. Instructional tools for writing should not, however, go to the extreme of providing scaffolding that is never disassembled. An overzealous dependence upon cooperative work, for example, can effectively prevent many students from achieving individual accountability for their work.

Modification: The independent activities provided in tools can be converted to scaffolded activities in either of two major ways. First, independent writing activities can be converted to group activities, wherein students support one another and teachers provide extensive feedback.

Second, tasks can be temporarily simplified. For example, an instructional tool might provide a task in which students proofread text for errors, such as:

> Rewrite these sentences to make them clearer.
>
> *Many stores make empty promises. We put ours in writing.*

Cues can be added to such tasks to increase the likelihood that students will understand them:

> Did the writer probably mean "our empty promises" or "our promises"? Change the second sentence to show what the writer probably meant.
>
> *We put _____ in writing.*

▼ Strategic Integration

Development: Tools should purposefully highlight knowledge that naturally integrates to promote more complex knowledge structures. Different text structures (explanations, comparisons, arguments) can and should be integrated into more complex, "expert" structures.

Most critically in the arena of writing, composition and writing mechanics should be well integrated.

Selection: The evaluation of tools can focus to a great extent on the degree to which important big ideas are explicitly interrelated. Some tools have emerged in recent years that are excellent in that writing mechanics are not simply "exposed and dropped" but accumulate over time to create more and more realistic writing applications. A straightforward method of evaluating materials for integration is to select an instructional unit that would normally be taught in February or March at a given grade level, and then to examine that unit to determine the extent to which earlier topics are integrated in the selected unit.

Modification: New activities may be created expressly to promote the integration of knowledge. For example, previously taught text structures can be combined into novel assignments as a means of promoting text structures of greater complexity. For instance, if students have mastered a compare-and-contrast text structure as a means of conveying information, and have also mastered a basic argument-and-persuasion text structure, then those two structures can be combined into a more advanced persuasive structure in which comparing and contrasting is used as a principal means for organizing an argument.

▼ *Primed Background Knowledge*

Development: Ideally, instructional tools include placement tools for determining the extent to which students possess relevant background knowledge. Tools should then provide for those students who lack essential background knowledge by presenting the background knowledge relatively close to the introduction of the target knowledge for which it is prerequisite.

For instance, in order for students to write good explanations, they should have some knowledge of words indicating chronology, such as *first, then, next, after,* and *finally.* Such knowledge is likely to be a part of general background knowledge for many students, but not for some diverse learners. If such students spend some time using such words to sequence events prior to the introduction of an explanation text structure, then they will be in a much better position to learn that new structure on a pace with their peers.

Selection: Instructional tools can be examined to determine the extent to which they accommodate prior knowledge requirements. For example, some review of basic paragraph structure a week or two before the introduction of a new text structure can help diminish differences among students. New strategies associated with big ideas, in particular, should be examined from the viewpoint of a diverse learner to determine whether the strategy assumes crucial background knowledge that some students might not possess.

Modification: Existing tools cannot be modified easily to accommodate background knowledge because such modification implies both the development of new instruction and the "resequencing" of existing instruction. Even so, the adage "better late than never" might apply. For example, teachers can diagnose student difficulties to determine whether they arise from a lack of essential background knowledge and provide instruction on such knowledge as needed.

If instruction on particularly crucial background knowledge is not provided in tools, then teachers may need to identify such knowledge and teach it directly.

▼ *Judicious Review*

Development: The kind of deep understanding required for complex problem solving rarely develops in people within a short period of time. Review designed according to solid empirical evidence can help students acquire and maintain deep understanding, as well as the kind of fluency required to successfully complete many complex cognitive tasks (such as most writing tasks).

If less material but more important material is taught thoroughly (big ideas), then there is plenty of "room" in instructional tools for review that is adequate, distributed, and cumulative. Moreover, *thorough* instruction includes many varied opportunities to apply strategies, which in turn result in better transference of knowledge. This is particularly important with respect to writing, where a given text structure can potentially be used for an nearly unlimited array of purposes.

Selection: A "safe" and relatively easy way to evaluate tools for review is, in general, to look for *a lot* of review. Such tools are more likely to be effective and are the most practical for teachers to use, since eliminating review opportunities is much simpler for teachers than adding them.

Modification: Teachers can provide *adequate* review on big ideas by having students write a single text structure, such as an explanation, several times within the same school year. Such basic structures, when learned well initially, are then incorporated into more complex structures, which provides distributed review quite naturally.

For writing, such a practice is principally a matter of scheduling. A teacher can readily modify a tool that covers several text structures in a year by selecting only two or three of the most important ones, then scheduling repeated assignments that involve them.

Developing additional review or finding appropriate review supplements is an option for tools that provide minimal review opportunities, particularly with respect to instruction on the mechanics of writing. For instance, many younger diverse learners require substantial handwriting review opportunities in order to become fluent enough that their handwriting is not a major stumbling block to participation in the processes of writing compositions. For writing mechanics, it is most crucial that review be cumulative, in order to closely replicate authentic writing.

CHAPTER 5: MATH

▼ *Big Ideas*

Development: Allocate considerable time/space to teaching big ideas crucial to understanding mathematics, as opposed to giving approximately equal resources to the exposure of a multitude of topics. Such big ideas would include number families, the identity principle, proportions, volume and area, estimation, and so on.

Selection: Examine mathematics tools to determine the extent to which the majority of time/space is allocated to teaching big ideas.

Modification: Identify the most important mathematics concepts and principles in existing tools and reallocate instructional time so that those concepts and principles can be taught very thoroughly. Note that valid assessment should focus upon the important mathematics concepts selected for thorough instruction.

▼ *Conspicuous Strategies*

Development: Provide explicit strategies for learning big ideas. Strategies should not be too narrow because they would likely result in rote learning. Neither should they be too broad, like some of the common "strategies" for solving verbal problems (draw a picture, etc.). Students can be taught more specific "setups," graphics with broad potential for transference of knowledge across topics:

$$\text{miles}/\text{hour} = \underline{\quad}/\underline{\quad}$$
$$<\text{unit}>/<\text{unit}> = \underline{\quad}/\underline{\quad}$$

Selection: Examine tools first to see whether conspicuous strategies exist at all, and if so, whether they generally appear to be "intermediate in generality." Try to imagine yourself as a diverse learner who has to solve verbal problems presented by the tool based solely on following the taught strategy.

Modification: When students struggle with concepts and principles they are supposed to discover on their own, develop an explicit strategy for those concepts and principles. When strategies are too narrow, such as the "invert and multiply" rule to solve for x in problems of the form $x/a = b/c$, explicitly explain the underlying principles that make such a rule work.

▼ *Mediated Scaffolding*

Development: Some scaffolding, such as peer tutoring or instructional feedback, need not be built into instructional tools, but may instead be part of teachers' inservice training materials. Scaffolded *tasks,* however, should be built into tools. Such tasks are somewhat contrived versions of "outcome" tasks that help students achieve understanding at a reasonable pace. Here is a simple scaffolded task:

$$\tfrac{3}{4} + \tfrac{2}{3} = \quad /_{12} + \quad /_{12} = \quad / \quad +$$

This task guides students through the strategy for converting fractions before adding.

Selection: Examine both "model" or demonstration tasks associated with a strategy and the tasks students eventually do independently. Are there "in-between" tasks that will help students gradually achieve independence and understanding?

Modification: Without consuming too much time, teachers can convert independent tasks into scaffolded tasks by providing hints, cues, or prompts for some of the more difficult steps in the strategies associated with those tasks.

▼ Strategic Integration

Development: Develop strategy tasks and activities that integrate various important mathematics concepts into complex applications, such as the following problem, which incorporates advanced proportions, estimation, data gathering, and probability:

At lunch, each student can choose a carton of white or chocolate milk. Each fifth-grade class is to estimate how many cartons of chocolate and white milk should be ordered for the entire school.

Also develop strategy tasks and activities with widespread potential for interrelating otherwise dissimilar-appearing mathematical concepts, such as a proportion strategy that can be applied variously to verbal problems involving: rate, measurement equivalencies, percentages, probability, the coordinate system, and functions. The principal benefit of integrating conceptual knowledge this way is that it fosters deep understanding of problem solving.

In addition, integrated tasks and activities are useful in relation to those mathematics topics that predictably cause confusion for many students.

Selection: Examine the scope and sequence of instructional tools, looking specifically to see whether some chapters (or units or lessons) are designated as "cumulative review" or "integration" or "consolidation." In a well integrated tool, in-program assessments will include tasks representing all topics taught previously, not just those taught immediately preceding the assessment.

Modification: Teachers can improve the effectiveness of tools notably by identifying common confusions, such as those identified above, and providing students with additional integrated practice centered on them. For instance, if a tool does not provide practice on a mixture of verbal problem types that have been taught previously, teachers can provide it using problems—or minor modifications of problems—from the instructional tool.

▼ *Primed Background Knowledge*

Development: Developers should (1) create assessment tools that determine whether students possess essential background knowledge for learning the strategies taught in a program, and (2) provide instruction on essential background knowledge for students with gaps in such knowledge. For diverse learners, it is risky to assume that material taught last year will be fully retained as essential background knowledge for strategies being taught this year.

Selection: Dissect strategies for teaching important mathematics big ideas into their component parts. Then, examine about 15 days worth of instruction *preceding* the introduction of the strategy to determine whether and how those components are handled. Ideally, components are taught or reviewed a few lessons preceding the introduction of the new strategy. Also, tools should be checked to determine the extent to which assessment tools identify important gaps in background knowledge.

Modification: To some extent, teachers can analyze important strategies in advance of their introduction to students and provide some essential background knowledge based upon that analysis. For example, teachers can review the concept of area and make the connection between area and base before teaching a strategy for understanding volume. Teachers can also examine student errors carefully to determine whether they may be due largely to lack of background knowledge.

▼ *Judicious Review*

Development: Publishers do a great service to teachers when they provide plentiful review with instructional tools, since it is infinitely easier for teachers to simply skip review activities than create additional ones. Programs that include well distributed review are far more efficient than those do not, and programs with built-in cumulative review promote strategic integration, as described above. Review should also be varied, to promote transference.

Selection: Locate a particularly thorny topic in mathematics, such as solving multi-step verbal problems, then "trace" the review throughout the remainder of the program to determine whether review is plentiful, distributed, cumulative, and appropriately varied.

Modification: Teachers can modify programs to improve the judiciousness of review principally by (a) taking a long set of tasks and distributing them over a period of days, and (b) making review cumulative, as discussed above under "Strategic Integration: Modification." It can be quite time-consuming for teachers to modify programs to make review *appropriately* varied—that is, varied enough to avoid rote practice, but not so varied that it presses students to perform outside of the limits of strategies they have been taught.

CHAPTER 6: SCIENCE

▼ *Big Ideas*

Development: Integrate science instruction around only a few very explanative, central scientific ideas. The more phenomena a big idea explains, the less learning is required. Big ideas in science subject matter (a) represent central scientific ideas and organizing principles, (b) have rich explanatory and predictive power, (c) motivate the formulation of significant questions, and (d) are applicable to many situations and contexts common to everyday experiences.

For example, convection is a big idea that explains many of the dynamic phenomena occurring in the solid earth (geology), the atmosphere (meteorology), and the ocean (oceanography). Plate tectonics, earthquakes, volcanoes, and the formation of mountains are all influenced by convection in the mantle.

Science inquiry is another big idea in science. Particularly, the ability to control variables in one's reasoning is central to both informal and formal contexts.

Selection: Evaluate science materials to determine the extent to which science content knowledge is organized into larger scale, cohesive ideas ("big" ideas that have wide application), rather than covering a large number of fragmented and unrelated vocabulary concepts.

Modification: Identify the most important scientific principles and reallocate instructional time so that those concepts and principles are taught more thoroughly.

For example, rather than simply have students memorize all the different types of rock, have them apply their understanding of the rock cycle (convection) to predict the next form the rock would take.

▼ *Conspicuous Strategies*

Development: Teach explicit steps for applying big ideas. Such steps are an approximation of the steps experts follow covertly (and, perhaps, unconsciously) while working toward similar goals. Good strategy instruction starts with teaching a well organized knowledge base of component concepts and their relationships. Strategies for using the big ideas of science should initially be made overt and conspicuous for students through the use of visual maps and models that represent expert knowledge and refute common misconceptions. Wide-ranging application of big ideas facilitates strategy acquisition. Experiential application opportunities should be relevant to better understanding of the instructed big idea and its use.

For example, a strategy for using density could require students to (1) identify equivalent volumes in two substances, (2) compare the masses within those volumes, and (3) predict which substance will sink.

The steps in the strategy for science inquiry are (1) identify the variable to test, (2) create a condition that changes that variable, (3) keep the other variables the same, (4) gather data, and (5) interpret the outcome.

Selection: Look for conspicuous models for using scientific principles (and content) and for conspicuous illustrations of the steps students should use in scientific inquiry. More students become proficient in scientific reasoning (i.e., scientific inquiry) when it is explicitly taught. Many currently popular programs use activity-based instruction to teach the scientific method but do not conspicuously focus instruction on this important strategy.

Modification: To make strategies conspicuous, model each step and verbalize the thinking that accompanies each step.

▼ Component Steps and Concepts

Development: Provide specific instruction in difficult component concepts to achieve an in-depth understanding of the big idea or strategy.

For example, the component concepts of the relationship between mass and volume are particularly important in understanding convection. Other component concepts of convection that also relate to density include the effect of heat on density and dynamic pressure. Instruction in these component concepts and their cause-and-effect relationships is crucial to an in-depth understanding of convection.

Similarly, the component step of controlling variables is crucial to effective use of the scientific method. This difficult step requires specific, explicit instruction and practice in varying only the variable under examination and keeping all the other relevant variables the same.

Selection: Examine whether the key (i.e., fundamental) component concepts underlying the "big ideas" are carefully instructed.

Modification: Teachers can analyze the important big ideas to identify key component concepts. These concepts will answer the question "why?" For example, a thorough understanding of density and its interaction with heat explains in large part "why" convection occurs. Instruction in key concepts requires more than just a teacher explanation. It also requires the other features of instruction described here: mediated scaffolding and judicious review.

▼ Mediated Scaffolding

Development: Scaffolded practice, which should follow the introduction of big ideas, strategies, and component concepts, provides a systematic transition from the initial teacher-directed, modeled, structured, prompted practice within defined problem types to a more naturalistic environment of student-directed, unstructured, unpredictable problems that vary widely across all problem types.

Scaffolding can be provided through the design of the tasks or examples or through teacher talk. For example, initial scaffolded instruction in controlling variables could model the procedures for controlling for one variable, then direct and prompt students as they control for a second variable, reminding them to change only the variable they are testing and keeping all the others the same. Finally students can control variables on their own.

Selection: Examine the initial instruction and the independent application to see if the tool provides "in-between" application tasks that are scaffolded.

Modification: After providing the initial model, teachers can provide prompts and cues borrowed from the model that assist the students in difficult parts of the strategy or concept, gradually removing the prompts and cues until students are able to use the knowledge accurately and without assistance. Such prompting and cueing would be appropriate for any students whose performance on independent tasks indicates that more work is needed before they can successfully perform independently.

▼ Judicious Review

Development: Review should be (1) sufficient, (2) distributed, (3) cumulative, and (4) varied. A program with lots of review is easy to modify: Cut back review for students who need less. This is substantially easier than adding review for diverse learners. Review should be distributed rather than massed. (Ten opportunities over ten days can be more effective than ten opportunities within a single class period.) All that is taught in a program should accumulate within review. That is, review should include not only the most recently learned material, but material from throughout the program. This is particularly true for material that is potentially confusing. Finally, review should include new examples, but new examples of the same type as those used during initial instruction.

Selection: Any or all of the four research-based characteristics of effective review can be used as criteria for selecting educational tools and can be incorporated in existing tools:

1. *Sufficient.* More review than is common is likely to enhance learning, particularly for diverse learners, and with respect to big ideas for all students.
2. *Distributed.* Review can be distributed relatively easily by attending to some sort of distributed review schedule when creating "more review."
3. *Cumulative.* Important older learning should be periodically reviewed with new learning.
4. *Appropriately varied.* Added review should provide safe variation.

Modification: Provide additional review items that have these characteristics:

1. *Sufficient.* Provide continuous opportunities for students to apply a concept until all students are likely to demonstrate mastery of the concept.
2. *Distributed.* Review a concept frequently enough that students will never experience "forgetting" something they have learned.
3. *Cumulative.* If possible, integrate previously learned concepts into a big idea that provides a built-in cumulative review. For example, the introduction of the convection model serves as a cumulative review of all the component concepts that were taught prior to instruction in the basic convection cell. When this is not possible, simply provide review of all previously learned concepts, regardless of whether they were learned in the current "unit" or not.
4. *Varied.* Provide application items that vary across the full range of potential applications of the concept. For example, ask students to apply their knowledge of density to predicting sinking and floating, predicting wind direction, explaining earthquakes, explaining black holes and novas, and so forth.

▼ *Strategic Integration*

Development: All of the above features of effective instruction can be integrated in such a way that their incorporation seems natural in the development of understanding. Organize the topics for instruction into overlapping strands so that the connections of science are more easily communicated, the big ideas are more easily built, and scaffolding can build new learning on top of a foundation of prior learning.

Selection: Many current science materials are organized around units that can be taught in almost any order. While this design allows flexibility in choice of topics, it encourages a fragmented understanding of science content. Curricular materials that use strategic integration to build an integrated understanding around underlying causal principles, such as convection, rather than around more superficial units, such as geology, meteorology, or oceanography, cannot be rearranged so easily.

Modification: Sequence topics so that component concepts are taught first and subsequent material builds on earlier learning. Provide the additional instruction to link the old learning with the new learning for deeper understanding.

CHAPTER 7: SOCIAL STUDIES

▼ *Big Ideas*

Development: Rather than teaching for coverage, one approach for bringing order to social studies content is to organize instructional tools around big ideas. The problem-solution-effect structure is one example of a big idea. When applied to the study of history, it has the potential to help students understand that people and governments tend to encounter problems related to either *economic* or *human rights* issues. Economic problems are associated with the need to acquire or keep things such as food, clothing, and shelter. Human rights problems are associated with the need to achieve religious freedom, freedom of speech, equal protection under the law, equal rights for women, minorities, different social classes, and so forth. Another big idea is that the success of group efforts, such as wars or the establishment of colonies, is frequently associated with four factors: *motivation, leadership, resources,* and *capability.*

Selection: Examine social studies tools to determine whether breadth instead of depth is emphasized. Does the tool strike you as a series of unrelated facts rather than an interrelated network of information?

Modification: Identify several big ideas to incorporate into existing instructional materials, either through supplemental materials or extensive revision of the tool. Select big ideas which (a) have rich explanatory and predictive power, (b) are a point of departure for posing significant questions, and (c) are generalizable to many situations and contexts.

▼ *Conspicuous Strategies*

Development: A strategy is a general framework used to solve problems and analyze content. All students can benefit from learning strategies. One highly generalizable strategy is that group cooperation evolves in four identifiable stages. Knowledge of the four stages can help students relate historical conditions to group behavior.

1. Get together and discuss common problems.
2. Occasional voluntary cooperation
3. Regular voluntary cooperation
4. Legally binding cooperation

If members of a group can agree on solutions to common problems, *then* people will begin to cooperate occasionally. *If* cooperation works for the group and problems continue to occur, *then* people will begin to cooperate regularly. *If* the need for cooperation continues but voluntary cooperation fails, *then* people may agree to legally binding cooperation.

Selection: Examine instructional tools to determine which explicit strategies associated with big ideas are described. If strategies are present, determine whether they: (1) are clearly described, (2) have narrow or broad application, and (3) are an integral part of the tool or just optional. Try to imagine yourself as a diverse learner who must analyze a problem based solely upon a suggested strategy.

Modification: It is difficult for teachers to incorporate strategies into existing tools, especially if a tool is not structured around big ideas. However, if a tool does incorporate strategies, it is realistic to evaluate them from the point of view of students and to modify steps that are unclear or confusing. Ask yourself if a suggested strategy will help students recognize relationships between seemingly different events.

▼ *Mediated Scaffolding*

Development: Instructional programs should provide students with temporary support until their learning becomes self-regulated. Interspersed questions prepared in advance can help reduce the number of irrelevant or obscure questions posed in instructional tools or by a teacher. Such questions should help students identify critical information and relationships needed for conceptual understanding. Another example of scaffolding is for students to read social studies material aloud. Oral reading provides an opportunity for teachers to correct decoding and comprehension errors, prevents students from skipping material, and provides sufficient time for all students to process information.

Selection: Examine tools first to see which forms of scaffolding are present to help students identify critical information and relationships needed for conceptual understanding. Scaffolding is temporary assistance. If scaffolding is provided, it should be gradually withdrawn over time so that students eventually become independent learners.

Modification: Oral reading and interspersed questions can be applied as scaffolding for instructional tools. Teachers can also provide scaffolding with supplemental materials such as graphics, concept maps, study guides, and outlines.

▼ *Primed Background Knowledge*

Development: Students with diverse learning needs often have less background knowledge of social studies content than their normally-achieving peers, so assessment tools are needed to determine what essential background knowledge students already possess and what they must be taught. Provisions are needed for students who are found to lack essential background knowledge.

Selection: Evaluate instructional tools to determine what provisions are made to assess and, if necessary, teach important prerequisite knowledge. If students have gaps in their knowledge, does the tool make provisions to introduce or review important background information *several* lessons prior to introduction of the target knowledge?

Modification: In general, it is difficult for teachers to modify existing tools to accommodate background knowledge. Such modification requires the development of new instruction and affects the sequence of existing instruction. To some extent, teachers can review important big ideas, events, and important prerequisite vocabulary to help students make connections with new information. This requires a thorough analysis of the component skills and concepts needed to understand new knowledge.

▼ Strategic Integration

Development: Tools should emphasize knowledge that can be integrated and applied in multiple contexts. The goal is to promote understanding about when to use specific knowledge by providing students with opportunities to apply several big ideas and strategies to previously introduced topics. For example, students can integrate their knowledge of problem-solution-effect and the stages of group cooperation to analyze historical events such as the Federalists' effort to get the Constitution ratified and the resistance to the new Constitution.

Selection: Examine several big ideas presented in a tool to assess the degree to which they are explicitly interrelated. This evaluation can be achieved by comparing the development of knowledge presented early in a tool with knowledge presented in subsequent sections. If integration is present, determine whether it involves the initial separation of similar ideas to reduce confusion. For example, lower-performing students often become confused when exposed to similar ideas such as the Articles of Confederation, the Constitution, and the Declaration of Independence. However, at some point ideas that are initially separated should be carefully integrated.

Modification: Teachers can develop integration activities in which several important but potentially confusing concepts are included. Such activities should be preceded by instruction which teaches component concepts first, so that the integrated material builds on earlier learning. For example, if students have learned the big idea about the four factors of group success to understand why some colonization efforts failed and others succeeded, they can also apply this big idea to understand changes Britain made during the

French and Indian War which resulted in victory after an initial series of defeats, and the efforts of the Federalists to ratify the Constitution. A more extensive implementation of integration can be achieved through the application of several big ideas to analyze events.

▼ Judicious Review

Development: Social studies content is often sophisticated, so students will benefit from more than one exposure to a big idea. In general, lower-performing students require more review than higher-performing students. Tools with ample review offer a helpful instructional option that teachers can use or skip, depending upon the needs of their students. To avoid rote learning, problems should not be repeatedly reviewed. Effective review promotes transfer of learning by requiring application of content at different times and in different contexts.

Selection: When evaluating a tool for review, "more" is preferable to "less," provided the review is distributed, cumulative, and varied. It is far easier for teachers not to use review when it is provided than to prepare review when it is needed.

Modification: Teachers can prepare review activities before instruction begins. This can be accomplished by evaluating what important information presented in a tool is likely to cause students difficulty. Ask yourself if such information is needed for understanding subsequent material and the extent to which the tool provides sufficient review in anticipated problem areas. Review can also be prepared after instruction takes place and students' knowledge deficiencies become evident. Again, such review should be ample and provide opportunities for practice which can be applied at different times and in different contexts.

INDEX

ℓ